John G Wells, Frank Luzerne

The Lost City!

Drama of the Fire Fiend! or Chicago, as it was, and as it is...

John G Wells, Frank Luzerne

The Lost City!
Drama of the Fire Fiend! or Chicago, as it was, and as it is...

ISBN/EAN: 9783337250072

Printed in Europe, USA, Canada, Australia, Japan

Cover: Foto ©ninafisch / pixelio.de

More available books at **www.hansebooks.com**

MAP SHOWING THE BURNT DISTRICT.

THROUGH THE FLAMES AND BEYOND, OR CHICAGO AS IT WAS AND AS IT IS.

WELLS & CO.

TO THE

GENEROUS AND NOBLE,

WHO PROMPTLY RESPONDED IN THE HOUR
OF NEED, TO THE NECESSITIES
OF THE

Houseless, Homeless, Penniless and Starving,

WHO PASSED

"THROUGH the FLAMES and BEYOND,"

THIS VOLUME

Is Respectfully Dedicated.

THE LOST CITY!

DRAMA OF THE FIRE-FIEND'
—OR—

AS IT WAS, AND AS IT IS!
AND ITS
Glorious Future!

A VIVID AND TRUTHFUL PICTURE OF ALL OF INTEREST CONNECTED WITH THE DESTRUCTION OF CHICAGO AND THE TERRIBLE FIRES OF THE GREAT NORTH-WEST.

STARTLING, THRILLING INCIDENTS,

FRIGHTFUL SCENES, HAIR-BREADTH ESCAPES, INDIVIDUAL HEROISM, SELF-SACRIFICES, PERSONAL ANECDOTES, &c., TOGETHER WITH A HISTORY OF CHICAGO FROM ITS ORIGIN, STATISTICS OF THE GREAT FIRES OF THE WORLD, &c.

BY FRANK LUZERNE,
A RESIDENT OF CHICAGO FOR TWENTY-FIVE YEARS, AND AN EYE WITNESS OF THE TERRIBLE CONFLAGRATION.

EDITED BY JOHN G. WELLS,
AUTHOR OF WELLS' EVERY MAN HIS OWN LAWYER; WELLS' ILLUSTRATED NATIONAL HAND-BOOK; AND OTHER POPULAR WORKS.

PROFUSELY ILLUSTRATED WITH MAPS AND ENGRAVINGS FROM PHOTOGRAPHS TAKEN ON THE SPOT.

New York:
WELLS & COMPANY, 432 BROOME STREET.
M. A. PARKER & CO., 152 SOUTH MORGAN ST., CHICAGO, ILLS.
B. R. STURGES, 81 WASHINGTON ST., BOSTON, MASS.
A. L. BANCROFT & CO., SAN FRANCISCO, CALIFORNIA.
1872.

Entered, according to Act of Congress in the year 1872, by WELLS & Co., in the office of the Librarian of Congress at Washington, D. C.

List of Illustrations.

	PAGE.
CHICAGO IN 1820.	27
A DAY SCENE IN GRACE CHURCH—THE PASTOR AND ASSISTANTS SERVING OUT RATIONS FOR THE DESTITUTE.	243
A NIGHT SCENE IN GRACE CHURCH—CITIZENS PREPARING FOR REST.	247
THE YOUNG LADIES OF CHICAGO MAKING AND DISTRIBUTING SANDWICHES TO THE HUNGRY.	9
CHILDREN THROWN OUT FROM WINDOWS IN BEDS.	129
PANIC STRICKEN CITIZENS CARRYING THE AGED, SICK AND HELPLESS AND ENDEAVORING TO SAVE FAMILY TREASURES.	97
RESCUE OF LADIES FROM A BUILDING IN FLAMES.	309
WEDDING AMID THE RUINS—A ROMANTIC INCIDENT.	165
RUSH FOR LIFE—CROSSING RANDOLPH STREET BRIDGE.	215
HOMELESS CITIZENS IN CAMP ON THE SHORE OF LAKE MICHIGAN.	15
A FIRE SCENE ON THE PRAIRIES.	263
REFUGEES FROM WHITE ROCK, HURON CO., MICH., SEEKING SAFETY IN THE WATER.	295
HON. R. B. MASON, MAYOR OF CHICAGO.	53
THE DESPERATE ATTEMPT OF A FATHER TO SAVE HIS CHILDREN.	147
SWIFT JUSTICE—ILLUSTRATING THE FATE OF THE THIEVES AND INCENDIARIES.	187
INTERIOR VIEW OF THE CINCINNATI SOUP-HOUSE ON PEORIA STREET.	221
ERIE RAILWAY DEPOT, NEW YORK CITY, ON THE STARTING OF THE LIGHTNING TRAIN WITH RELIEF FOR CHICAGO.	201
VIEW OF THE BURNT DISTRICT—SHOWING PROMINENT BUILDINGS DESTROYED AND THOSE PRESERVED.	59
AN EXPRESS TRAIN RUNNING THE GAUNTLET IN THE BLAZING WOODS OF THE PRAIRIES.	13
BURNING OF THE CENTRAL GRAIN ELEVATORS AT THE MOUTH OF THE CHICAGO RIVER.	255
GETTING WATER FROM THE ARTESIAN WELL.	235
THE REV. MR. COLLYER PREACHING ON THE SITE OF HIS CHURCH.	251
GENERAL DEPOT OF SUPPLIES FOR THE SUFFERERS.	205
KERFOOT'S BLOCK AFTER THE FIRE.	229

LIST OF ILLUSTRATIONS—(Continued).

	PAGE.
LAYING THE CORNER STONE OF THE FIRST BUILDING AFTER THE FIRE.	297
INTERIOR VIEW OF THE DEPOT FOR SUPPLIES IN THE WEST SIDE SKATING RINK.	257
THE BURNING OF PESHTIGO.	265
IMPROVISED SHANTIES ON THE NORTH SIDE.	305
SCENE ON THE ROOF OF CAPTAIN'S BUILDING WHERE THE JANITOR AND HIS FAMILY PERISH.	71
SCENE IN THE GERMAN CEMETERY—THE LIVING SEEKING SAFETY IN THE CITY OF THE DEAD.	197
LADIES DISTRIBUTING CLOTHING TO THE SUFFERERS OF BOTH SEXES.	233
WORKMEN HAULING SAFES FROM THE RUINS.	175
OPENING BANK VAULTS, CORNER LAKE AND DEARBORN STREETS.	183
A LADY BETWEEN TWO FEATHER BEDS ABLAZE.	187
RECOVERING VALUABLES FROM THE RUINS.	25
THE COURT HOUSE BELL, AFTER IT HAD FELL.	151
BOOKSELLERS ROW, STATE STREET.	227
VIEW FROM THE COURT HOUSE LOOKING SOUTH-EAST.	103
VIEW FROM THE COURT HOUSE LOOKING SOUTH.	213
CLARK STREET, SOUTH FROM WASHINGTON STREET.	39
COMMENCEMENT OF THE REBUILDING OF CHICAGO.	169
FURNISHING COFFINS TO BURY THE DEAD.	275
DEPOT FOR SUPPLIES AT THE SKATING RINK.	
THE NEW PACIFIC HOTEL.	37
SCENE IN DEARBORN STREET WHEN THE FLAMES REACHED THE TREMONT HOUSE.	81
GRAIN ELEVATORS ON FIRE.	105
BURNING OF THE CROSBY OPERA HOUSE.	87
MAP, SHOWING THE BURNT DISTRICT.	2
THE FLAMES COMMUNICATING WITH THE SHIPPING, AND DESTROYING THE GRAIN ELEVATORS.	5
SCENE IN THE PUBLIC SQUARE—THE COURT HOUSE IN FLAMES	75
AN ENTERPRISING YOUTH DISPOSING OF RELICS.	17
SCENE ON THE PRAIRIES.	271
IN CAMP ON THE SHORE OF LAKE MICHIGAN.	115
EXTERIOR VIEW OF THE CINCINNATI SOUP HOUSE.	220
TRYING TO SAVE A FAVORITE DOG AND CANARY BIRDS.	307

AN EXPRESS TRAIN RUNNING THE GAUNTLET IN THE BLAZING WOODS.

AN ENTERPRIZING YOUTH DISPOSING OF RELICS.

INTRODUCTION.

It is impossible for any mind to grasp and comprehend in one view, the stupendous events narrated in the succeeding chapters of this book. It seems impossible for the ordinary intellect to appreciate that these chapters comprise the details of the most tragic and heart-rending calamity that ever befel a people since the beginning of history. It is not yet adequately understood—perhaps will not be in our generation—that the Conflagration of Chicago, will, in the records of future ages, figure as the crowning disaster of the Nineteenth Century,—a disaster not like that which over-took Herculaneum and Pompeii, for they still lie buried beneath the ruins of their grandeur,—but as the holocaust of that wonderful City which sprang into existence at the behest of the very Aladdin of enterprise, and exhaled before a cloud of flame like the unsubstantial fabric of a vision, that like the Phœnix, has already arisen from her ashes, and is pluming herself for still grander achievements than those which so eminently distinguished her in the past. Her ashes are not yet cold, but they are already surmounted by edifices whose substantial construction would seem to be the result of long and patient toil, and the hum of business is again heard in those streets that but a few days ago were so completely devastated by the Demon of Flame. The new wonder will prove more wonderful than the old, for the fire has operated like the sowing of dragons' teeth, in raising up men equal to the great emergency, who will promptly master the situation and command it.

We have more to do with the old Chicago than the new, with stern facts than prediction, with history that is more romantic than the veriest fiction that ever found its germ in the human intellect. The true record of the Chicago Fire, its facts, figures, incidents, hair breadth escapes, miraculous rescues, individual daring, and the noble charities of the world that flowed in upon its victims with a spontaneity as unprecedented as they were grateful and humane, serve as foundation and superstructure of "CHICAGO AS IT WAS AND IS"; but dealing, as it does, with realities alone, it is almost impossible for the compiler to divest his mind of the impression that he is recording a horrid phantasmagorical vision, rather than the facts of real life. Away from the ruins, and with all the consequences of the disaster removed from view, it is impossible to realize that in the short space of twenty-four hours the wealth of our North-western metropolis was discounted in the sum of near $200,000,000; that, worse than the mere pecuniary loss, treasures of art, and accumulations of the lore of ages, that no amount of wealth can replace, were devoured by the flames; and immeasurably worse yet, that hundreds of precious lives were swept away in the irresistable whirlwind of fire, which respected neither young nor old, beauty nor innocence, the strong nor the helpless, but, more implacable than the demons of the Herodian massacre, pursued them to the death, without regard to age, sex or condition. It is a chapter of horrors that can only be written as it was, with a pen of fire; but our task is to clothe in words an approximate idea of its realities, and a true version of the facts, that are destined to occupy a prominent page in history.

We undertake this task in the belief that an eye-witness of many of the scenes and incidents herein detailed and a personal acquaintance of most of the actors in and sufferers by the overwhelming calamity, is best prepared to give a reliable version of its remarkable phenomena, adventures and contingencies; of its wonderful escapes, fearful tragedies and indescribable results —but it is necessary for the reader to understand, that very few intelligent observers witnessed the scenes and incidents described from the same points of observation; that many were overcome by fear, personal bereavements or great anxiety; that before the bewildered gaze of every onlooker, the appalling panorama of flame passed with the speed of the whirlwind, licking up, with its thousand-forked tongue, great blocks of brick and stone buildings as readily as if they had been mere toy houses of lath; and that intelligible description is necessarily hampered by these and a hundred other influences that encumber the minds of those who are now seeking to make a reliable history of these astounding occurences. The reader that did not witness these scenes never can picture them to his imagination. The readiest writer that saw and mingled in them will never present the picture as he saw it, to the mind of his reader : for neither pen nor pencil can do it justice. However heart-rending the details, the rent hearts of thousands of bereaved ones will declare them far, very far, short of the truth.

The liveliest imagination cannot picture the unutterable sadness of such a reality, but to bring the facts right home to the business and bosom of readers everywhere, let them suppose some of the leading incidents and results of the succeeding history to occur in their own towns and cities. To-day they are prosperous, progressive, happy: in the silent watches of the night the angel of destruction comes with his flaming sword and devastates all their substance ; brings death to their loved ones, poverty to their millionaires, dire want to all their people. The rich man of to-day is to-morrow a beggar; the happy wife and mother, widowed, childless, insane; husbands bereft, and lovers separated by the pathless ocean of death. Everything gone at one fell stroke, even before the fact of the destruction can be realized, and nothing left but the evidences of utter ruin ! The vilest crusts have now become sweet morsels to the pampered children of luxury; and the fop of yesterday, who criticised his tailor without mercy for the slightest wrinkle in his fashionable habiliments, accepts in charity a soiled and thread-bare coat as a priceless boon. Dives and Lazarus are equally solicitous of crumbs. The fashionable belle forgets the length of her trail and the style of her chignon in the merciless gnawings of hunger, and joins the eleemosynary throng in a chintz wrapper, and without a care for the opinion of "society," anxious to satisfy the demands of nature at any sacrifice of pride. In this slight recapitulation of actual occurrences there is something of the grotesque mingled with the tragic, but it is all sufficiently woeful, and unutterably sad.

It seems impossible to give too much emphasis to the noble humanity of people in all parts of the world, when the cry for help was flashed over the wires from Chicago. It was the cry that made all mankind kin on the instant, and the strife immediately began as to who should be first in making an adequate response. Those who were most conveniently located, geographically, were of course first on the ground, but supplies were at once started from all points of the compass, and from every locality where the emergency was understood. No city can honestly claim the credit of having been first in the work, for action was *simultaneous* throughout the land, and in a few hours after receipt of the news, great trains of supplies were on the way from New

York, Philadelphia, Pittsburgh, Cincinnati, St. Louis, Louisville and all the cities of importance. It may appear invidious to particularize, but it is well known, that Col. FISK and the officers of the Erie Road were especially active in measures for the immediate relief of the sufferers. A special train was loaded with the miscellaneous contributions of the people of New York—including clothing, provisions, blankets, mattresses; a great collection of substantial goods,—the road cleared for the occasion, and all arrangements complete under the personal supervision of Col. FISK. The ponderous engine is attached and the colonel stands with watch in hand to give the last directions.

"All ready, Sam?"

"Ready, Colonel."

"What is the quickest time ever made between New York and Buffalo, Sam?"

"12.20, Colonel."

"Make it to-day in 11.20."

"Open her, Sam."

And Sam Walker, a tall, grey eyed, nervy man—just the man for the place, and honestly proud of his position, with compressed lips, drew back the lever, and the train swept away, forty, fifty miles an hour, with help for the houseless, starving hosts of the burned city.

A similar incident in St. Louis:

"What time shall I make, Mr. Johnson?"

"The best your machine can show."

"What stops?"

"Only for wood and water."

"How's the track?"

"All clear. Everything is side-tracked for this special."

An entire railroad line given up to the work of instant relief!

MILES GREENWOOD, one of the oldest and most respected citizens of Cincinnati, came in charge of the detachment of the fire department of that city. He was for several years chief engineer of the department.

"Where is your Engineer?" was his first question.

"Gone home, sir, completely exhausted."

"Who has charge, then?"

"I am in charge," said a young man, stepping to the front.

"Well, the Cincinnati boys are here with their machines. What do you want us to play on?"

"You may play on that elevator over yonder."

"Is it on fire?"

"No, sir."

"Then we shan't play on it. We came here to put out fire. What is that fire over there?" pointing in another direction.

"That is a Coal Yard."

"We'll go and put it out."

At it they went and were as good as their word. Then they extinguished the fire in other coal yards and saved near two millions bushels of coal. These Cincinnati boys did not tire as long as there was anything to do, and accomplished a vast amount of good under the leadership of Mr. Greenwood,—and when their work was done they returned, orderly and in perfect discipline to their honored city, proud of having accomplished something in the work of humanity.

The relief committees who came to us with the bountiful offerings of noble hearts everywhere, were generally the representative men of their communities, but they proved to be workingmen in the great emergency, and took hold of matters with a will that commanded success, and resulted in just what was sought— relief. Their works, their offerings, and kindly sympathy, proved the kinship of humanity beyond a doubt. The skeptic can now find the evidence written in letters of love all over the ashes and ruins of the once proud city. Wherever the story of the conflagration was told, the hearts of mankind responded to the impulse of universal brotherhood. All seemed to act in the spirit of the noble sentiment of Sir Walter Scott: "The race of mankind would perish, did they cease to aid each other. From the time the mother binds the child's head, till the moment that same kind assistant wipes the death-damps from the brow of the dying, we cannot exist without mutual help. All, therefore, that needs aid, have a right to ask it from their fellow mortals; no one who holds the power of granting, can refuse it without guilt." True humanity consists in a disposition of heart to relieve misery. It appertains rather to the mind than the nerves, and prompts men to use real and active endeavors to execute the actions it suggests. Men, women, and even children, throughout the land, responded nobly to this sentiment: and great corporations, that are said to have no souls, felt the thrill of benevolence and responded to its promptings. Bankers opened their hearts and their strong boxes; beggars pawned their all to give to those whose needs were so exigent. A man in St. Louis gave all he had; a poor woman gave her cow; a little negro contributed his only dime; a poor student sold all his books and donated the proceeds; a farmer in Northern Indiana auctioned off his hops for the benefit of the sufferers and handed over the entire proceeds to the Relief Committee; a boot-black announced that the receipts of one day's work would go to the needy of Chicago, and was enabled to make a donation of twenty-five dollars as the result; an Irish laborer gave his wages for an entire week; the theatres gave benefits, that proved benefits indeed; the churches made noble contributions; even inmates of our prisons were enabled to do something in the way of relief. Those who did not give are the unenviable few that have no conception of generous impulses—those who cannot appreciate the blessed principle that no amount of giving can ever impoverish true benevolence. Verily it is "better to give than to receive."

We may be expected to say a word regarding the reconstruction of Chicago, but the following extract from an editorial article in the London *News* is so perfect a reflex of the thoughts and acts of our people, and so admirably expressed, we give place to it instead of similar ideas in our own language:

"This is the consolation which already the pride and energy of Chicago offer to the people. There seems to us something admirable and characteristic in the elasticity and courage which thus leap up the moment the storm of devastation has done its uttermost, and cry out, "We are not wholly conquered after all; let us go to work at once and retrieve what we can." Nay, there are even men in Chicago, who having lost the fortunes of many years accumulations, are heard already to say that the fire has taught a useful lesson; that all the obliterated part of the city was built on a bad plan, and that it must be better done this time. The vastness of this calamity is fully recognized, indeed it is written in letters of blood and flame, which defy any misinterpretation. It is told by the living and the dead; by the houseless wanderers as well as by the cart-loads of corpses. It is proclaimed by what remains as well as by what has fallen. It is simply a story of sudden destruction which stands alone in history. But the one fact remains—Chicago still lives; and the courage which springs up at once from the ground to proclaim that fact is the grandest evidence that the ruins will yet be repaired. Certainly, if any people on earth ever deserved help, these people do, who are thus so ready and resolute to help themselves. The claim to the sympathy and succor of the English nation which were given to Chicago in her unparalleled misfortune, can only be strengthened and increased by her indomitable courage."

Near 5.000 building permits have already been issued, and there will be no interruption in the work of rebuilding until the new Chicago arises from the ashes of the old, in more substantial grandeur, rehabilitated, immeasurably improved, and all the better for her thorough purification. These are bold words, but their verification is near at hand.

This book would be incomplete and unsatisfactory without some general reference to the great fires of history, and especially to those which devasted large tracts of the Northwest, almost contemporaneously with the Chicago holocaust. The leading facts and incidents of these fires are given in their proper place and will be found of no less absorbing interest than the principa event upon which the narrative hinges. In the integrity and completeness of the work the public may place the fullest reliance.

RECOVERING VALUABLES FROM THE RUINS.

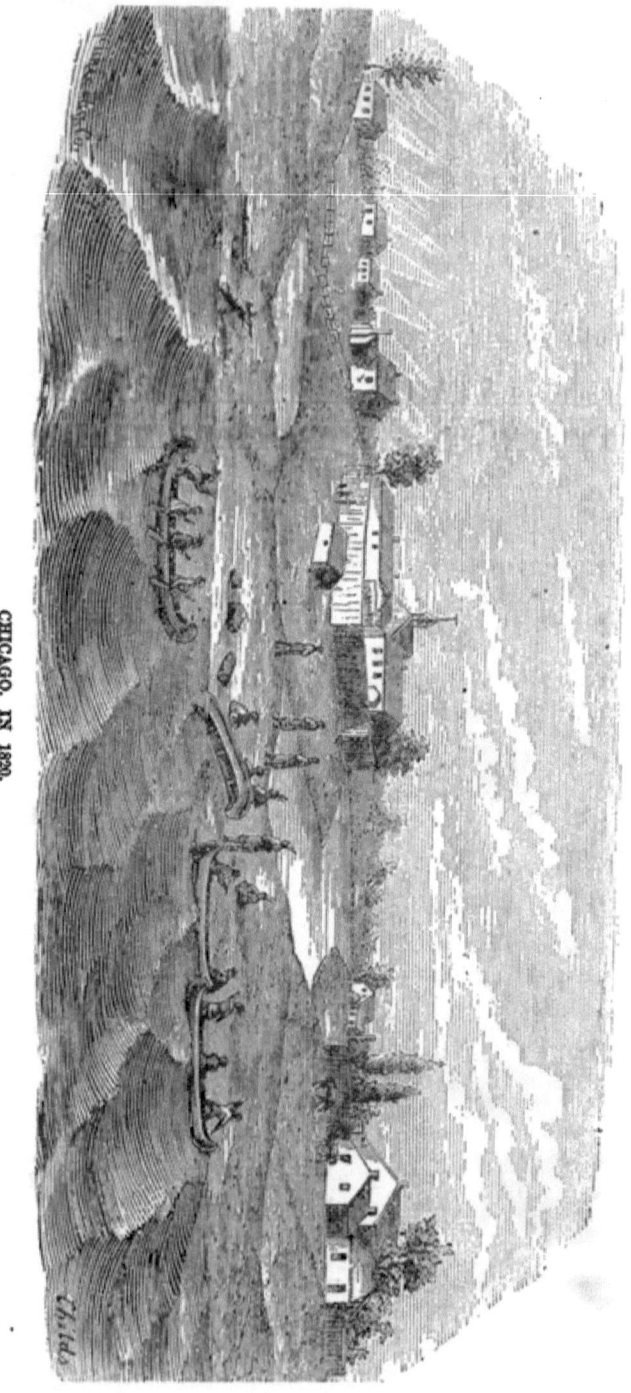

CHICAGO, IN 1820.

PIONEER HISTORY.

CHICAGO AS IT WAS IN THE EARLIER DAYS.

FACTS AND INCIDENTS FROM VARIOUS SOURCES OF AUTHENTIC INFORMATION.

In his masterly essay on History, Dr. Willmott says that the biography of a nation embraces all its works. No trifle is to be neglected. A mouldering medal is a letter of twenty centuries. Antiquities which have been beautifully called history defaced, composed its fullest commentary. In these wrecks of many storms, which time washes to the shore, the scholar looks patiently for treasures. The painting around a vase, the scribble on a wall, the wrath of a demagogue, the drollery of a farce, the point of an epigram—each possesses its own interest and value. A fossil court of law is dug out of an orator; and the Pompeii of Greece is discovered in the Comedies of Aristophanes. Nothing is unimportant that legitimately belongs to the history of a nation or a great city.

That we are permitted to go back more than two hundred years, to 1669, for notes of our sketch of the history of Chicago, will appear novel to a majority of even the more intelligent of our readers, for the impression is very popular, and has obtained wide currency, that not more than half a century ago the spot where the city now stands was worse than a howling wilderness and a *terra incognita*, supposed to be inhabited only by Indians, outlaws and beasts of prey. In some respects this view is not entirely foreign to the truth; but at the time to which we refer it was a trading post of no little importance. Let us go back, however, to the beginning of its existence as a depot for commodities, and find what all its greatness and importance sprang from.

The best authenticated records inform us that the first white men who landed here were the French Jesuit missionaries and fur traders, under lead of the celebrated guide, Nicholas Perrot. They were in search of profitable ventures in the way of an exchange of trinkets and rum for furs, with a little moral teaching thrown in by the missionaries to sanctify the transactions and guarantee the quality of the liquor. This initial visit occurred late in the year 1669, when the territory was the property of the Miami tribe of Indians. Subsequently the Pottowattamies conquered the Miamis, and wrested from them their hunting grounds and all their possessions. Then there was a better supply of furs and a larger demand for beads and "fire water," for the Pottowattamies were excellent hunters and terrible drunkards,—rather anomalous characters, but remarkably well balanced in this tribe of the noble red men.

The records of the succeeding century, referring to this post, offer little of value to the reader of to-day, and certainly do not indicate any noteworthy progress toward its material or moral improvement. Trade with the Indians increased in importance and consequently in profit, and to the few adventurous spirits that were ready to brave its personal risks, this far away frontier settlement proved a modern Djinnestan. In 1795 the Pottowattamies concluded a treaty with General Wayne, by which "a tract of land six miles square, at the mouth of *Chicago* river," was ceded to the United States; and this was the original extinction of Indian title to the site upon which the great city was subsequently erected. Previous to this cession, several of the French Jesuits had taken up their residence here, and had made certain improvements that seemed to give them some shadow of title to the soil, but the Indians ignored their claims and remorselessly sold them out, although the French authority was nominally in the ascendant for ten or twelve years previous to the treaty. They made the improvements, built a rude fort near the mouth of the river, erected comfortable lodges, and cultivated a few acres of the soil after a method that yielded them a fair return. Calumet is supposed to have been the head-quarters, or seat of supreme authority, of this strangely mixed population, and their villages were scattered up and down the lake, for several miles, and on the Des Plaines; and the ranging grounds of the Pottowattamies, from the head-waters of the Illinois to the Chicago river, was the common channel of transportation for goods and furs between the Indians and the traders; but the head-quarters of all this primitive commerce, its shipping point and grand depot, was the port of Chicago, by common consent.

Dating back to this period, there are a hundred traditions of wild adventure, bloody tragedy, savage love, jealousy and hate, to engage the pen of the historian of romantic incidents, wherein he would be enabled to depict a modern Busiris in one of the chiefs of the Pottowattamies, who ruthlessly murdered every stranger that, landing on his territory, failed to bring him a peace offering of five gallons of rum, or an equivalent in trinkets; a prototype of Al Sirat, the bridge over hell no wider than the edge of a sword, across which, according to Mahomedan theology, every one who enters heaven must pass—in the terrible gauntlet appointed to stragglers and unaccredited visitors from other tribes, in which delightful ceremony the young Indians were provided with sharp tomahawks and spears and drawn up in two rows, facing each other, when the delinquent was forced to run between them, while every Indian in the lines dealt him, in passing, as severe a blow as he could muster strength and agility to inflict, killing him at last, unless, as was occasionally the case, he was enabled, by wonderful address, to avoid the death-blow—scalping, flaying alive, burning at the stake, treachery, stratagem,—and all manner of cheats, with only occasionally an instance of faith truly kept. The few white men who were here did not venture for the purpose of settlement, their business was simply to trade with the Indians; overreach them if possible, and away. The gain from this traffic seemed to overbalance all considerations of peril attached to it, and to those well versed in the trade, the profit was very great. Respectable fortunes, for that age, were acquired by the successful operators in two or three seasons; and there is a tradition that an English adventurer, by a single trip among these children of nature, obtained, in exchange for 50 blankets and twelve barrels of rum, a quantity of fine furs that brought him $160.000 in glittering gold, on his return to the mother land. If the Indian was crafty in a trade, the white man was more than a match for him in that experienced bargaining that is the ruling element in every civilized community, and it is pretty certain that the pale-faced trader rarely failed to make the "dicker" to his own advantage.

In the year 1804, the United States government built a fort here, and made it the centre of military operations in the northwest. It was called Fort Dearborn, and remained until 1812, when the Indians destroyed it, at the time of the great massacre, which has associated with the name of Chicago a chapter of romance so closely allied to history, it is very difficult to separate fact from fiction, relative to that most bloody episode in our history. The location of the fort was upon a slight elevated point, or the south side of the river, near the lake shore, and is well known to all intelligent residents of the city. From its ramparts a good view could be had of the lake, **the** prairie extending to **the south, the** fringe of timber along **the** north and south branches, and the glistening white sand hills to the north and south, which drifted about very much like the snows of winter; the sport of the winds from lake and prairie alike. Slowly and laboriously the infant colony gathered around the nucleus **of** civilization, established by the garrison of the fort, but, as the aid to progress, in such a location, the garrison was very weak and inefficient. It was the object of frequent attacks by the Indians, and in danger of surprise at any hour of day **or night.** A few old traders and perhaps a dozen families of French Canadians and half-breeds, none of whom possessed more than the most ordinary degree of intelligence, erected their household shrines in the neighborhood of the fort, and were content, for the most part, with the profits arising to them as "middle-men" in the increasing traffic with the Indians, which now constituted the entire business of the settlement, and invested the Chicago of **that day with** all its importance.

We are told that none **of** the hardy pioneers around the walls of old Fort Dearborn have descendants to claim the honors of so distinguished a paternity, except the Kinzie family, which exhibits the only link in the worn and rusted chain of civilization that admits of positive identity. **The founder of** this family, John Kinzie, came to Chicago in 1804, the year in which the fort was built, and was the first permanent white resident of the settlement. From 1804 to 1812, the lake trade which centered at the port of Chicago was carried on by one small sail vessel, coming in the fall and spring, bringing the season's supply of goods and stores for the fort, and taking away the furs and peltries which had accumulated during the winter months. **Thus began the** commerce of the port, and this was nearly its extent for a period of more than sixteen years. Kinsie pursued the business of fur trading until the breaking out of hostilities with the Indians, which resulted in the massacre of 1812. The friendly feeling which had been assiduously cultivated between him and the redmen preserved himself and family from the fate which befel his neighbors of the fort. They came out unharmed through the scenes of the bloody and relentless slaughter. Returning to Chicago in 1816, he remained here until the date of his death, in 1828, a successful merchant, a good citizen, and a prominent mover in every enterprise calculated to result in the material benefit of the place. Although at the time of his death the settlement contained a population numbering less than one hundred souls, he was very positive in asserting the superior advantages of the site, and predicted that the time would arrive when its residents would be numbered by thousands! Most of his neighbors thought him crazy on this subject, but some of them lived to see the anticipation fully realized, and his immediate decendants are to rejoice with us over a population of 300 000 souls.

Cook County, of which Chicago is the capitol, was organized in March, 1831, and at that time embraced all the territory now comprised in the counties of Cook, McHenry, Lake, Will, DuPage and Iroquois. This is an immense area, reaching down to near the east and west dividing line of the State, and including portions now thickly dotted by enterprising towns and villages, and beautiful farms, and intersected by several lines of prosperous railroads. In 1831, all the buildings in Chicago were log cabins, the more pretentious, including two business houses and a hotel, of hewed logs, which were viewed as an aristocratic pretense by the more humble denizens. Two of the new cabins were store-houses for goods, including calicoes, rum, sugar, coffee and tobacco, which at that date were among the leading necessaries of life; and two were "hotels," that of Elijah Wentworth, on the north side of the river, near the fork, and Mark Beaubiens, on the east side of the river, just south of the fork. These were the hostelries within whose gates the strangers who came to the settlement were entertained, and for many years they amply sufficed to furnish food, drink, fire and shelter for all comers, and their reputation for generous entertainment was well known throughout all the land. Two celebrated Indian traders, Robert A. Kinzie, located near Wentworth's tavern, and M. Bourisso, just south of Beaubiens, monopolized the business of the place. They were both rich, and either was pecuniarily able, had he been so disposed, to purchase all the land thereafter occupied in building the great city; and this without detracting from the capital of his occupation; but everybody would have regarded such an investment as fool-hardy at that time.

On the 15th July, 1831, arrived at the port of Chicago the schooner "Telegraph," from Ashtabula, Ohio, bringing a number of families that did not however settle here; but among the passengers was Mr. P. F. W. Peck, of New York, who accompanied quite a shipment of assorted goods, for which he was desirous of finding a profitable market. He was well satisfied with the appearance of things in and about Chicago, and at once decided to remain here and dispose of his merchandize, provided he could make satisfactory arrangements for a warehouse. There were no buildings for rent, as there had been no renters, up to this time, but Peck conceived the idea of occupying a cabin as joint tenant with a family already located, until his goods were sold. With this idea in his mind he approached Mr. J. B. Beaubien, whose residence was upon the site afterwards occupied by the splendid depot of the Illinois Central Railroad Company, and made him a proposition for the occupancy of the principal room in his humble dwelling. Beaubien was of a speculative turn, and of course always open to a trade, but was in favor of making the proposition himself. No;—he had no room to spare just then, but he would build a cabin for Mr. Peck on fair terms, or he would sell his residence and give possession in three days. He would inquire, just for his own information, as to the value of Mr. Peck's stock.

"About $4.000."

"How would it suit Mr. Peck to trade a half interest in the goods for his cabin and a large lot adjoining?"

Mr. Peck did not care to invest in wild lands.

"Oh!" says Beaubien; "it all lies right here inside of the town. There is about twenty acres with the cabin, but I'll put in a hundred acres on the other side of the river [North Side;] and then the cabin itself is one of the best here—all for a half interest in the goods."

"No," said Peck, "not if it were twice as much."

So he went to work and built a cabin for his stock, and traded it for furs and peltries at good round figures, and was well satisfied; but the property he rejected for $2.000 worth of rum and calicoes, is to-day worth not less than $50.000.000; and Peck remained in Chicago and witnessed all this stupendous advance, and, we are told profited by the lesson in many future transactions. Mr. Peck brought an enterprising spirit and good business judgment to the young settlement, established himself permanently here, and was active in all improvements that promised to benefit the place.

Late in the summer of 1831, western emigration set in largely, and during the fall months the population was more than doubled by emigrant families seeking homes and fortunes in the wilds of the new territory. These pioneers were hardy representatives of the "bone and sinew of the land," generally intelligent, and prepared to endure the hardships and privations of life on the frontier. They were enterprising and far-seeing in their movements, and it was not difficult for the more thoughtful to foresee something of the future of a port location like that of Chicago, commanding, as it must, all the commerce of the immense territory lying to the northwest. Investments in lands—there were as yet no surveys of city lots—now began to be somewhat active, and property advanced in price nearly four fold within the next twelve-months. Some of the more conservative among the inhabitants declared that prices were inflated, but the "inflation" continued, and kept on increasing in volume from year to year, regardless of financial panics elsewhere, up to the very hour of the conflagation.

We learn that in November, 1831, the schooner "Marengo" arrived from Detroit, bringing a consignment of goods of great value for the emigrant population that had taken up their residence in the fort. For a time there were great fears entertained of the loss of the schooner, as during her passage a heavy gale prevailed, but she at length arrived safely, much to the relief of the people, for there were not less than four hundred in the fort who depended on these supplies for subsistance during the winter. These people were not generally counted as residents of the settlement, as many of them expected to, and did remove into the interior of the territory early in the spring, but their places were rapidly taken by actual settlers during the succeeding year, whose history was marked by many substantial improvements for that early time—among which may be mentioned, as a fitting close for this sketch, the erection of the first frame building in the settlement of Chicago!

THE NEW PACIFIC HOTEL BUILDING DESTROYED BY THE FIRE.

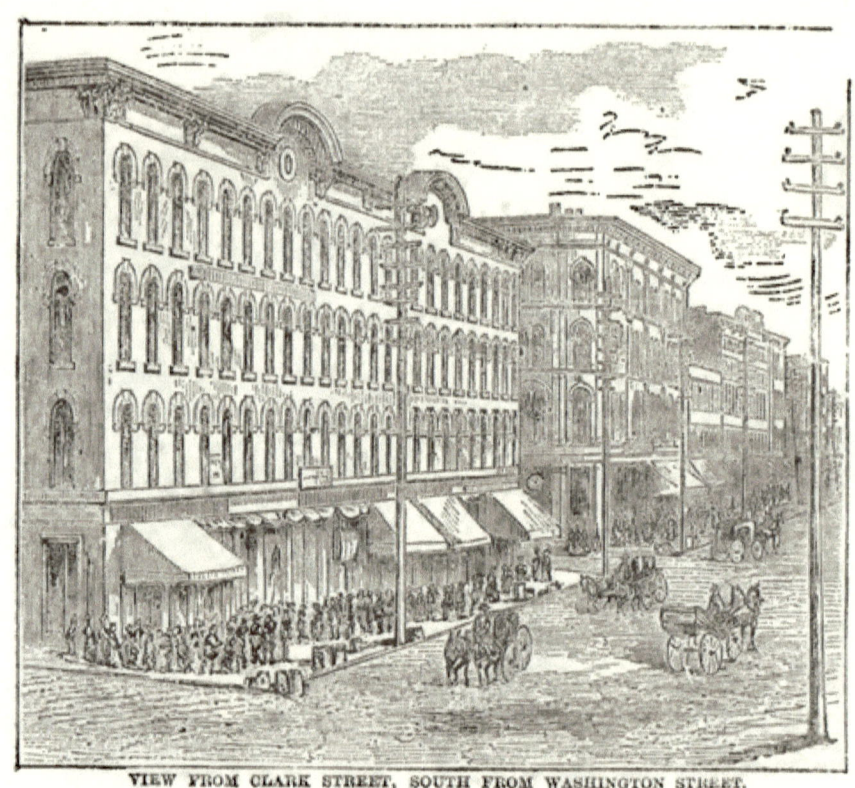

VIEW FROM CLARK STREET, SOUTH FROM WASHINGTON STREET.

GENERAL HISTORY.

IMPROVEMENTS—TOWN AND CITY ORGANIZATIONS—PRICE OF REAL ESTATE—INSTANCES OF SUDDEN FORTUNES, ETC.

It was not untill 1833 that Chicago began to excite general attention throughout the United States as a desirable point for residence and investment. Notices in the newspapers were instrumental in calling public notice to some of its advantages, and the commerce of the country began to show anxiety for a harbor here;—therefore means were taken to bring the subject before Congress in such shape as would be most likely to induce favorable legislation. The legislation was reached after long discussions in both houses, and a large amount of editorial comments in the leading journals, which served to call a great deal of attention to the place, and a bill passed appropriating $30,000 for the improvement of Chicago harbor. This was, in more senses than one, the key note to our prosperity. People were convinced that the place was of some consequence, else this large amount —much larger in those days than now—would not have been granted for its advantage, and the tide of immigration set in earnestly. The work of harbor improvement was commenced in the summer of 1833, and pushed with energy till the cold weather caused its suspension for the season. In the following spring there was a great freshet, which effected more than the labor of man had been able to accomplish, for the land between the piers was entirely washed out and carried away, and the harbor efficiently opened to the commerce of the lake by the hand of nature herself. This was the beginning of that magnificent commerce which now spreads its white wings over all our inland seas, and attracts to our busy warves the traffic of a world. Its history is practically the history of Chicago's prosperity and fame.

The vitality imparted to the business of the place by this improvement is not easy to appreciate now, at a date when a resident of Chicago is accounted to possess the vitality of a Salamander, and the concentrated view and push of at least a dozen ordinary human bipeds; but it seemed to be sufficient to warrant the people in believing themselves and their "burgh" of sufficient importance to risk the organization of a town. As the nucleus of a town organization they already possessed an estray pen and a jail, supplemented by a newly appointed coroner, whose office had been improvised to serve one of those sudden emergencies to which frontier settlements were at that time subject. July 22nd, 1834, a meeting of qualified voters was held, at which it was voted, by twelve good men and true, that it would be a rightful and proper thing, and eminently expedient, to incorporate the town of Chicago. Only one man cast a negative ballot. There were at this time twenty-eight legally qualified voters in the settlement, but all did not see fit to exercise their right. The election for Trustees of the new town was held on the 10th of August following, and five were chosen, who met for the first time on August 12th, at the office of the town clerk, and organized according to the provisions of law. The territory embraced in the corporate limits comprised only about one mile square of the prairie, and coincided very nearly with the area at present bounded by Jackson, Jefferson and Ohio streets, and Lake Michigan, recently the center of trade and wealth, and, most emphatically, the fiery furnace of the great conflagration. Nature pointed it out as the "business center" of the great city, and those far-seeing pioneers were apt at discovering its advantages and profiting by them; and we need scarcely predict an event that is even now in process of transpiring, to wit: That after the rehabilitation of Chicago, this original mile square will remain the centre of trade and wealth of our inland metropolis. A prominent citizen has given publicity to the declaration that "the center of trade may be removed to any point where five thoroughly, wide-awake men, with plenty of capital, desire to establish it;" but we doubt this statement, provided ten "thoroughly wide-awake and enterprising men, with plenty of capital," are equally desirous of establishing it in a different locality; and, in this instance, the majority of business men and capitalists in favor of the old established center is more than ten to one.

CESSION TO THE UNITED STATES OF NORTHERN ILLINOIS AND WISCONSIN BY THE POTTAWATAMIE TRIBE OF INDIANS.

After the act of incorporation had been legally completed, the town began, in the estimation of its citizens, to become invested with additional importance, and to desire the respect of its contemporaries. Its denizens, in casting about for their real estate, found that the Indians, still dominant hereabout, were disposed to resent the spirit of aggrandizement exhibited by the white man; and it was resolved that the requirements of civilization demanded of our dusky brethern that they find new hunting grounds, to the end that the pale face might be permitted to till the soil, navigate the waters, and pursue all the arts of peace for his own special behoof and emolument. This movement was vigorously opposed by a few of the old Indian traders; but the influence of leading men throughout the West was brought to bear in its favor, and after many proposals, much caucusing and plenty of "fire-water," the question was settled by the cession to the United States of all the territory in northern Illinois and Wisconsin, belonging to the Pottowattamie tribe of Indians, at that time numbering more than seven thousand souls. Messrs J. B. Owens, G. B. Porter, and Wm. Weatherford, commissioners on the part of the United States, displayed remarkable tact and ability in concluding this important and perplexing treaty, which extinguished the title of the treacherous, aggressive and thieving tribe, in an immense tract of the most valuable land in all the Northwest, and threw it open to the settlement and improvement of an industrious and worthy class of emigrants. The conditions of the treaty were that the Indians should receive an annuity of $30,000, and that they should be conveyed, at the expense of the government to the territory beyond the Mississippi which had been allotted to their use and occupancy. On the 25th of September the treaty was duly executed, and on the 1st of October following, so prompt was the government in despatching its plans, the train of teams conveying more than fifteen hundred squaws and papooses, started for the destination of the tribe, and consumed forty days in reaching it. This stupendous exodus of the red men and their families is described by those who witnessed it as a spectacle of inconceivable sadness. They were bidding an everlasting farewell to their homes and their birthright; to the land where they had tracked the wild beast and conquered him; to the waters on which they were accustomed to glide in their birchen canoes, in pursuit of the finny game; to the scenes of their boyhood sports and battle triumphs; to the grounds where the ashes of their kindred reposed; the soil sanctified to their hearts by the blood of a long line of heroic ancestors, whose history was recorded in its forests, prairies and streams;—and it is scarcely strange that heart-pangs were plainly shadowed in the lines of those tawney faces as they turned toward the setting sun to undertake their weary march. Where they were going they knew not, except it was a **far-off** locality, where they would be out of the way of the white man, and **removed from** the temptation of killing him as a trespasser. The Indian of history is depicted as a stoic. He must be a stoic indeed to endure, unmoved, the sundering of the dearest ties of the human heart; and these Pottowattamie braves were none the less objects of commisseration because they suffered and made no sign. Although such agony cannot be "winked out of sight," they knew—"how sublime a thing it is to suffer and be strong."

COMMENCEMENT OF PROGRESS.

With the Indians away, the great fear of emigrants was removed, and people from the eastern States flocked **rapidly to** the Northwest, not a few taking up their abode in Chicago. Among the business men who were prominent at this date may be mentioned, **John** H. Kinsie, P. F. W. Peck, G. W. Dole, S. B. Cobb, John S. Wright, Philip Carpenter, Walter Kimball, R. M. Sweet, John Bates, A. Clybourne, Star Foote, E. S. Kimberly, S. D. Peirce, R. J. Hamilton and B. Jones, several of whom are still among us, and **all are** well remembered by our leading citizens of the present.

Real estate, in the form of both "in" and "out" lots, advanced rapidly in price under the fresh demand, and business generally took a new departure. The great increase in the packing of beef and pork was remarkable—Mr. Clybourne alone packing three thousand hogs and six hundred beeves in the winter of 1834-5. This is a small aggregate from our present standpoint, of course, but taking our population and resources at that time into the account, it is wonderful. The valley of the Wabash supplied most of the cattle and hogs that were packed here for several years, and still remains a great source of supply for our porkers.

From this date the business of the town was very brisk, and during the winter it seemed difficult, for several years, to find help enough to transact it satisfactorily. Beef, pork and grain, from all the new settlements, came here for a market; and the furs and peltries, from the far-off hunting grounds, that came, in exchange for all kinds of products, the lumber and other articles, constantly increasing in number and extent, threatened to overwhelm the force employed to take care of them. Emigration from the over crowded states of the east and from foreign countries, was strongly urged, but the demand for labor was in excess of the supply for many years, as business continued to expand even beyond the expectations of those who were most hopeful of the prospects of the town.

GRANTING OF THE CITY CHARTER.

On the 4th of March, 1837, the city charter was granted, an event that was hailed by great rejoicings of the people, as investing them with power to inaugurate and execute certain improvements that could not be encompassed under the town organization. The first municipal election was held on the first Tuesday in May of the same year, at which Hon. Wm. B. Ogden was chosen mayor. The first census taken in the following July, gave a population of 3,989 white persons, 513 of whom were under five years of age; 77 colored; and 194 sailors belonging to the port of Chicago. There were about eight hundred voters, but the poll books indicated that only 707 voted at the municipal election. This census also proved that there were 398 dwellings, 29 dry goods stores, 21 grocery and provision stores, 5 hardware stores, 3 drug stores, 10 hotels, 17 lawyers offices, and 5 churches. Most of this population was the result of three years emigration, and a large majority of the improvements the product of three years of laborious industry. The year 1837 was an eventful one for our people. It was this year that Congress made an appropriation of $40,000 for the enlargement and improvement of the harbor, and this year that the first cargo of wheat was shipped from the port. These events were big with future promise, and have more than fulfilled the just expectations of those who inaugurated them.

RAPID ADVANCES IN VALUATION OF PROPERTY.

The advance in real estate, that commenced to attract attention throughout the country as early as 1833, lies at the foundation of most of the wealth of Chicago capitalists, as well as of many capitalists elsewhere. This advance made many rich quite unexpectedly, and even contrary to their anticipations. The veteran John S. Wright says, in a note to his " CHICAGO;

Past, Present, and Future:" "Although famous for the sagacity of its citizens, Chicago is not without those who have made fortunes in spite of themselves; because they have not been addicted to wasteful benevolence, and have happened to own real estate which has been closely held from natural habit, and not from any appreciation of the future. One of these millionaires, when efforts were making to start the Galena Railroad, argued against it, because railroads would stop the advent of the 'prairie schooners,' 500 to 1,500 teams then daily arriving, and with their stoppage 'grass would grow in the streets,' was his sagacious declaration. Another one thought my distribution of petitions for the grant of lands for the Illinois Central Railroad was impolitic. Said he.

"'Why, don't you see that the railroad will enable farmers to run off their produce to Cairo, while the river and canal are frozen, which, if kept till spring, would have to come to Chicago?'

"I replied, 'Don't *you* see that that gives the farmers of central Illinois the advantage over others in the choice of markets? Whatever the course of the carrying trade, you may risk the prosperity of Chicago upon the prosperity of the farmers.'

"This, however, is the very place for such men to make fortunes. If they will only invest their money, berate the tax gatherer, and never give anything—which is not dangerous—they will surely become rich if they live a few years, however unwise their purchases."

Mr. Wright's reminiscences are peculiarly valuable in this connection, for several reasons. 1. He was one of the early settlers of Chicago, having emigrated here in 1832. 2. He invested largely in property from the first, and had a peculiar interest in watching the fluctuations of prices. 3. He subsequently invested largely for the account of others, and enabled them to become rich on the results of his excellent judgment. 4. He has spent the best years of his life investigating the philosophy of real estate advances in Chicago, and, therefore, "speaks as one with authority." We find his work,* above referred to, more authoritative on the subject under consideration, and more exhaustive, than any publication extant. The extent to which we have used many of its facts and figures is acknowledged in the proper place; but we cannot resist the temptation to make use of the exhibit

* Chicago; Past, Present, Future. By John S. Wright.

following, as detailing the experience of a shrewd but thoroughly concientious "operator," and we take the liberty of extracting it from Mr. Wright's book in such detatched form as seems to us to bear most directly on the main question. He says:

"In 1832, at the age of 17, my father took me to Chicago, with a stock of merchandise. The town then contained 150 people, exclusive of the garrison; two frame stores, and no dwellings except those built of logs. After remaining a few weeks, examining the country south and west, and satisfying himself that he had made the right location, he left me to shift for myself. In 1834 he removed his family to Chicago and lived till 1840, having his first convictions strengthened year by year that it was rapidly to become one of the largest cities of the country and of the world.

"Though a mere boy, I, too, became impressed with the advantages of the point which was the western extremity of the great lake navigation, with a certainty of its connection, by canal, with the Illinois and Mississippi rivers, and which was the natural commercial center of a country so fertile, so easily tilled, and so vast in extent. In the winter of 1833-4 I induced a wealthy uncle to take some purchases which I had made, expecting to share in the profits. He took them, and has made out of those and other operations, through me, several hundred thousand dollars, but all the benefit to me, directly or indirectly, has been $100. He came to Chicago in the spring of 1835, and, the next day after his arrival, said if I would sell his lot—one of those which I had bought about fifteen months previously for $3,500—for $15,000, he would give me *one hundred dollars*. I sold the lot that day for cash, and the $100 was reckoned into my credit in our final settlement in 1838.

* * * * * *

"No one could have then anticipated the power of railroads to build up great commercial points, and their wonderful multiplication, especially from Chicago. These have not only expedited the development of the West, but concentrated and bound to its great commercial center with iron bands the business and traffic which at great cost otherwise would still have come here. They have served to fix, beyond all peradventure, what some might then have regarded as problematical: that is, which city in the west is to have the supremacy.

"In 1834, I began to operate in real estate on my own account, and in February, 1835, went to New York to buy merchandise, and sold for $10,000, a forty acre tract which had cost $4,000, the profits of which more than paid for all my other purchases. Thereafter increasing my operations I sold in the spring of 1836, to various parties in New York, real estate for over $50,000, receiving about two-thirds of the pay cash in hand, and giving my individual obligations to make the conveyance when I became of age, the July following. My father would have been my heir, in the event of my death, and they knew he would fulfil my contracts.

"I had then, in 1836, acquired a property of over $200,000, without any assistance, even from my father, never having used his money for any operations, the store being his, and for conducting it only my expenses were paid. My uncle was the only relative who could have aided me, and he never would, even temporarily. So far from it, he was in my debt continuously from 1834 to our final settlement in 1838.

"But 1837 brought ruin to me, as it did to nearly all who owed anything; though it was not so much speculation in real estate, as engaging in mercantile business, that involved me. At that age it seemed desirable every way to have regular occupation to promote good habits, and in accordance with my father's wishes, I purchased, in 1836, a warehouse and dock lots, to engage in the shipping business, which cost $23,500. My whole indebtedness was about $25,000. I had nearly $20,000 due me, which was supposed to be well secured, it being chiefly the final payments on property of which over half the cost had been paid. To provide ample means for business, I sold in the autumn of 1836 a tract adjoining the city for $50.000, quick pay. This trade was unfortunately broken up by the merest accident, and thereafter I had no opportunity to sell at what was deemed a fair price. I came in possession of the warehouse 1st of May, 1837; and though having small cash resources, I thought best to commence business, hoping there would soon be a favorable turn. But all went down, down, and I was soon inextricably involved. The money used to buy these lots for business, not speculation, would have carried me through.

"In 1840, my property had all gone; one piece that had been worth $100,000, went for $6,000; another that had been worth $12,000, went for $900, and so on."

* * * * * * * *

"I resolved in some way to get a larger interest in property here, and, in the autumn of 1845, went to New York to try and obtain funds. Having leisure, I wrote a series of fifteen or twenty articles for the *Commercial Advertiser* and the *Evening Post*, about the various agricultural products of the West, their profits, etc., the minerals, manufacturing advantages, the canals, railroads, that would be built, etc., but not till the subject of the state debt was reached, was the rapidity of progress realized? Illinois bonds were then only worth 25 to 30 cents on the dollar, and three years of accrued interest not reckoned, so prevalent was the impression that we could never pay the state debt; and such a fearful load was it considered that immigration here was considerably affected. But it was shown fairly and conclusively, that by 1858 or '59, our state would pay her full interest without any increase in the then rate of taxation; and for two years [written in 1860] we have done this, and our bonds are above par.

"No prediction gives more satisfaction than this. Little as the public were influenced by these views, improbable as all then regarded them, to look back upon, they now appear plain common sense, just such as any business man who would study the subject ought to have arrived at.

"Though no one could see the future of the West and of Chicago as I did, my own confidence had never been so strong. The examination incident to the preparation of these newspaper articles brought more clearly to view than ever before the abundant resources and great natural advantages of the immense territory tributary to Chicago, and my determination was strengthened to buy property here.

"By examination, I found Frederick Bronson, Esq., would sell a block on long credit for $30,000, with only $1,000 paid down. It was upon the river, near the heart of the city, and somewhat improved. I made prudent estimates of its present and prospective rental, and found it could be made to pay for itself with a small outlay. But I could make no one so see it. There was not the least confidence in Chicago, it having been for ten years a synonym for all that was wild and visionary. Mr. Dyer, of Chicago, also had commenced prior negotiations with Mr. Bronson, and not wishing to interfere with him, my endeavors were postponed till their negotiations should be closed.

"I had no means of my own to buy with—could get no one in New York to think favorably of my projects—knew not where else to apply, and, after months of vain attempts, returned home, having purchased nothing. In April, 1846, Mr. Bronson sold this block to Mr. Dyer for the $30,000. A few months after I bought it of him for $37,500, having ninety days in which to secure the $7,500 advance, and the $1,000 he had paid. By much solicitation my brothers were prevailed upon to give this security, and the Bronson contract was assigned to me.

"I clung to this block, prefering to pay this large advance, rather than buy other property, because, having no capital, or means of raising any, it was necessary to get such as, by its income, would pay for itself. I knew this would do it, and it was the only piece of the sort, in any considerable amount, to be found. This was large enough, 320 by 600 feet, to be an object, particularly as I was confident that by the time it was paid for in ten years it would be worth $200,000 and over. It was actually worth in 1856 over $450,000.

* * * * * * *

"In 1846 the best lot on the north side, 80 feet on the river and North Water street, and 180 feet on Clark, a bridge street, was offered for $6,000, and for years I urged friends to buy it. The owner kept advancing his price, till in January, 1850, I induced a couple of Virginia friends to take it at $9,000. In 1856 that lot was worth $110,000, and is now (1860) worth $700,000, and has all the time yielded a good ground rent.

"But these purchases, though apparently so judicious and profitable, were a heavy load to me and my brothers for years. I could not make capitalists see through my spectacles, and none would lend me the aid of their money. The widening of the river cut off rents largely for two years, and the excavations, building of docks, warehouses, etc., had run me into debt, at two to five per cent. a month, and a brother was an endorser, greatly against his will, for $15,000 to $20,000. In the spring of 1850 he insisted upon relief, and having our affairs disentangled, and learning the Galena Railroad would buy all of the blocks for a depot, he urged its sale. He had acted generously towards me—few brothers would have done as much—and his request was reasonable, notwithstanding it involved such a sacrifice of my expectations. The block first bought for $37,500, was sold to the company for $60,000.

* * * * * * * *

* * * "In the investigations incident to the writing of several articles for New York and Boston papers, in 1848-9, about western railroads, laying down five or six roads that must be built, I was forcibly struck with the congruity of interest between Chicago and the cities of New York and Boston, in bringing business to the lakes, to make it tributary to those cities and to the intermediate routes. I endeavored to demonstrate the importance of extending to Chicago the eastern lines of railroads, and thence argued that when once they reached here, competition would insure the construction of all paying roads. Has not the result justified these predictions? True it is, the competition and railroad mania have done for us much more than was anticipated, but was it not a natural result of interest that eastern capital should build roads from here as from no other point? That it has been done is a fact, and I see nothing visionary in the predictions."

All the above extracts were included in a circular issued by Mr. Wright in 1860, and reproduced in his excellent book published in 1868. The entire circular, and, in fact, every sentence of the book, is of more interest to the people of Chicago, and to those who own property here, than any other equal amount of printed matter we have any knowledge of, and will be sought after by those who are inclined to be guided by judgment that is tempered by a long, varied and instructive experience. It is also reproduced as a part of the early history of Chicago, as reflected in the business life of one of its representative men, and therefore furnishing a demonstration of the persistence and energy that worked so long and faithfully to encompass the pre-eminence of the great metropolis of the northwest, through the exertions of all who actively participated in the work.

To the general advance in real estate, during the years therein referred to, above extracts are scarcely a fair index, and to the advance in special localities, they give nothing like an adequate idea; but their chief value lies in their truthfulness, as applied to the general subject, and their conservatism from a purely business stand-point. Regarding instances of unprecedented advance and quick fortunes, there were several somewhat like the following:

In the fall of 1866, a friend of the writer, an attorney of large practice, received a letter from an eastern correspondent inquiring as to the location and value of a certain eighty acre lot adjoining the city, and requesting him, provided that in his opinion it was worth $20,000 as an investment, to examine the recorded title and report its condition. The attorney reported the title clear, and, to give emphasis to his opinion of its value, added that he would give $20,000 for a half interest in it as a matter of speculation, provided it was purchased by his correspondent. It had remained the property of a family in New England about twenty-seven years, and their only idea of its value was probably gathered from what it was rated at for taxation; and when they offered it for $20,000, it was doubtless with a slight idea that it would bring this sum. It did, however, but not with the attorney as a party in interest. In a few weeks the purchaser came to look at his property, and had been in the city but one day when he was offered $100,000 cash for it. This was a surprise, but next day $25,000 was added to the inducement. He concluded to "go slow," and therefore made an investigation of values of property correspondingly located. The result was astounding to all his preconceived notions of unproductive real estate, and he found he had bought a fortune for a very small sum. After remaining in Chicago about fifteen days, he closed an agreement by which he received, then and thereafter, $278,000 for his lot—a profit of more than a quarter of a million of dollars on a sixty day's investment of twenty thousand! Instances like this are not common, even in the annals of Chicago.

HON. R. B. MASON, MAYOR OF CHICAGO.

PRESENT HISTORY.

A BRIEF GLANCE AT SOME SALIENT POINTS OF CHICAGO'S PRE-EMINENCE.

The previous pages are designed as a glance at the Chicago of the past, and do not treat of the miraculous advance she made in the last decade in population, wealth, manufactures and trade. A retrospect of the last ten years of her history, properly detailed, would furnish matter for a ponderous volume, and we must therefore remain content with a very brief reference to the most salient points of her eminence. At the head of the immense artery of lake and river navigation of the country, with her web of railways that penetrates the whole land, even now binding the Atlantic and the far away Pacific in its iron bands, her facilities and opportunities, in spite of her recent disaster, seem positively unrivalled. It is abundantly demonstrated that the far off western prairie, even among the remotest of the territories, sends its products here, and comes here for its supplies, as well as the vast forests of Michigan, Wisconsin and Minnesota; that the copper and iron interests of the lake Superior country, the lead mines of the northwest, the coal fields of Illinois, and, to a considerable extent, the iron ores of Missouri, all find here their best and most natural center. Most of the millions of cattle and hogs that annually fatten in the great West, find their way to the slaughter pens of this city, and thence are shipped to the markets of the world. A greater share of all the mineral and agricultural wealth of the great West turns toward Chicago with the faithfulness of the needle to the magnet. Our railway system is the most perfect and far-reaching in the world, and the invincible bulwark of our prosperity. Its great heart lives and pulsates here, and its iron arteries are sentient with the intelligent and sleepless energy of ten millions of producers, and with hundreds of millions of consumers, all keeping pace in the triumphal march of progress, and paying willing tribute to the ability that conceived and the energy that has erected our great mart of commerce. It is this admirable railway system that will do more toward rebuilding

Chicago than all other agencies combined, for it represents a capital in its possessions and dependencies, the loss of which would be sufficient to bankrupt a nation, and that would remain practically dead without the business furnished by the traffic of this city; therefore Chicago must be restored without delay, and rebuilt so thoroughly that a recurrence of the great disaster is rendered impossible. It is out of the question for any railroad system to succeed without commercial interests to feed it, and where these interests are small, railroads cannot be made to pay. It is an invariable rule, however, that as facilities are increased, business will enlarge. Increasing commercial prosperity always demands an increase of railroads, and as railroads are multiplied, commerce naturally increases. The means of increasing our commerce are incomputable by the ordinary intellect. All the vast regions of uncultivated lands in Illinois, Iowa, Wisconsin, Minnesota, and most of the immense undeveloped tracts lying west of the Mississippi, are sources upon which Chicago will eventually depend to accelerate her commercial growth and raise her to empire as the metropolis of the richest domain the sun shines upon. Neither our grain nor packing interests will be materially impeded by the accidents of the fire, and general business has already resumed its accustomed channels and is prosperous—with population and business so alert in the rebound from a fall that would have proven an overwhelming disaster to at least nineteen of every twenty cities of the world, and with vital interests that demand the utmost energy in the rehabitation of the city to save them, it is not an astounding prediction that at the end of the next decade, Chicago will have doubled in business, population and wealth. It will disappoint her best friends if she does not.

Some fears are expressed that real estate will deteriorate now, and that lots in the burnt district will be less valuable than before the fire, for a year or two to come. Those who are badly involved, and therefore obliged to sell, will not realize as much for their property as under more favorable conditions, but prices generally will not recede, and the demand will soon bring about a material advance in really desirable property; for strangers are even now coming here to invest capital and engage in trade, and this influx will increase more rapidly than ever before in our history when the world is convinced, as they soon will be, of our ability and determination to recover from the reverses of the conflagration. And the world will discover then when we have surmounted the temporary inconveniences occasioned by lack of warehouses, elevators, shops and hotels to accommodate our trade, our business will continue to increase in the same or even a larger ratio than that which made us famous and universally envied previous to the events of 8th and 9th of October, 1871, of which the succeeding pages are a faithful and unbiased record.

PROMINENT BUILDINGS DESTROYED AND THOSE PRESERVED WITHIN THE BURNT DISTRICT.

SEE MAP ON OPPOSITE PAGE.

1. Sherman House.
2. Briggs' House.
3. Metropolitan Hotel.
4. Chamber of Commerce.
5. Republican Office.
6. Meller's Jewelry Store, and Baker & Co.'s Engraving Rooms.
7. Matteson House.
8. Asdus' Express Office.
9. A. M. U. Express Office.
10. U. S. Express Office.
11. Tremont House.
12. Opera House, St. James' Hotel.
13. Field & Leiter's Store.
14. First National Bank Building.
15. Chicago Times.
16. Booksellers' Row.
17. Drake & Farwell Block.
18. Tribune Building.
19. Custom House and Post Office.
20. Evening Post and Staats Zeitung.
21. Farwell Hall.
22. Bigelow Hotel.
23. Academy of Fine Arts.
24. Palmer House.
25. Ogden Hotel.
26. Jones' School.
27. Michigan Southern & Chicago, Rock Island & Pacific Railroad Depot.
28. Ill. Central R. R. Land Department.
29. Ill. Cen. R. R. Depot & Freight House.
30. Galena Depot. Chicago & N. W. R. R.
31. Historical Society.
32. Turner Hall.
33. M. Ogdens' House. *Not Burned.*
34. Water-Works and Water Tower. *Not Burned.*
35. Lynn Block. *Not Burned.*
36. P. F. W. & C. R. R. Depot. *Not Burned.*
37. Milwaukee R. R. Depot, Chicago & North Western R. R. *Not Burned.*
38. C. & N. W. R. R. Depot. *Not Burned.*
39. Adams' House.
40. Massasoit House.
41. City Hotel.
42. McVicker's Theatre.
43. Armory Police Court.
44. Gas-Works.
45. Elevator A.
A. Methodist Church, (Wabash Avenue.) *Not Burned.*
B. Elevator. *Not Burned.*
X. Bridges Burned.
 Tunnels under the River at Lasalle St., connecting N. & S. sides at Washington St., also connecting S. & W. sides.

VIEW OF THE BURNT DISTRICT.

FOR LOCATION OF PROMINENT BUILDINGS, DESTROYED AND THOSE PRESERVED WITHIN THE BURNT DISTRICT, SEE OPPOSITE PAGE.

A GENERAL ACCOUNT

OF WHAT THE AUTHOR SAW AND HEARD, INCLUDING HIS PERSONAL VIEW OF THE FIRE, AND MANY THRILLING INCIDENTS.

All intelligent persons that witnessed the burning of Chicago are prepared to testify that nothing is more indescribable than a great conflagration. Nothing is more bewildering, exciting, electrifying, astounding and weirdly stupendous. It is a spectacle that forces into activity all the emotions of the heart, but benumbs judgement and disconcerts action. Its waves and barbed tongues, rolling and darting hither and thither, spangled with phosporic tints, and gleaming against the sky like a surging sea of flame, lashing the shores of the world, and seeking to overwhelm them; or, again, roaring, dancing, and frolicking through block after block of elegant structures, warehouses, residences and factories, sweeping everything in its torrid pathway with the rapidity of thought,

"As though the lightnings there had spent their shafts,
And left the fragments glittering on the field;"

are sights that petrify the intellect and strangle reflection. Another aspect of the freaks of the insatiable fire-fiend was calculated to impress the beholder with the idea that all the magicians, sorcerers and performers of "devil tricks" in Glubdubdrib had found their way to this devoted city, and, inspired by its native spirit of excelling in everything it undertakes, were playing pranks to shame the very imps of Hades. And so the panorama of that most dreadful night of Sunday was ever changing, ever stunning with some new and unexpected catastrophe, melting with its tales of woe and benumbing with its horrors.

Of all the thousands of incidents that are indelibly impressed upon the recollection of the writer, to remain there while life lasts, and probably through the countless ages of eternity, there is one whose details are painted with a distinctness far beyond artist's cunning, and that stands out in the wide waste of misery like the wreck of a noble ship on a desert shore. Still, it would now seem "like the baseless fabric of a vision," were it not that the evidences of its reality are only too tangible, and constantly before the eyes of every denizen of the city that is disposed to see them.

It was near day-light on Monday morning, the 9th of October, that passing along Lake street, we discovered an aged citizen, whose reputation for wealth, integrity and remarkable business capacity is well known throughout the land, hatless, coatless, his teeth chattering and his snowy locks tossed by the wind, gazing with tear-bedimmed eyes at his large warehouse immediately opposite the place where he stood, but which the flames had not attacked.

"Do you think the fire will reach my place?" he asked, as we took him by the hand.

The flames were raging within a block of his place, and, by taking a careful view of the probabilities, it appeared that we would not have long to wait for the wreck of this apparently substantial monument to his affluence.

We expressed a hope, scarcely felt, that it would not, and made a movement to hurry along, when he said, imploringly.

"Stay with me a little while. I have had some bad luck. My house and everything it contained is destroyed, and I must try to save the store."

"Have you saved your books and papers?" we asked.

"They are in the vault, and could not be safer anywhere. Do you think there will be occasion to remove any of the goods?"

"Where could you put them?"

"On the pavement here. There is no other place."

"It would not save them. They would be stolen or burned. Let us hope the fire will not reach you."

We knew it was utterly vain to hope, but what could be said or done under the circumstances? It was equally certain that we could render no assistance by remaining there, but it seemed cruel to leave our old friend in his helplessness. We talked to him very much as one would address a child standing in fear of some threatening injury to its toys, and he seemed to appreciate the attention. The fire was speeding in our direction, roaring, surging and leaping in very madness, bearing down everything before it in crash after crash of ruin, from which each reverberation was like commingling of wails and groans for the loss of homes, and lives, and wealth, and the violent rupture of a great city's throbbing heart! The shrieks and moans of the hurricane were terrific, and doubly so from their weird and unearthly prolongation, until they forced an echo from some point miles away across the foaming waters of the lake, that came back to us like the exultant laugh of ten thousand fiends. The monarchs of Storm and Flame were holding their highest revels in concert, and no human agency could bar their advance.

It appeared from our position that the flames were still more than half a square away, when suddenly a bright shaft, like lava at a white heat, shot skyward from the buildings on the opposite side, and in less time than it takes to write it, our old friend's business house and merchandise were seething in the superheated cauldron of the great conflagration. It was a miracle, and little wonder, that he stood motionless, with both hands raised aloft, his tearless eyes almost bursting from their sockets, and the contortions of his features indicating a degree of agony that words can never paint. It seemed as inexplicable as a thunderbolt from a cloudless summer sky, and was certainly quite as startling. The terrible heat and the flaming embers drifting down upon us rendered our position extremely critical; but the old gentleman refused to move. The loss of his substance was the crowning misery, and the last terror of the calamity for him had passed. As entreaty availed nothing, he was at last borne away by gentle force to a place of refuge.

There was a strange commotion in his brain, and the light in his eyes appeared of more than earthly brightness, painful to look upon, and giving him a strange aspect to even his most intimate acquaintances. He was left in charge of a brotherhood whose charities are indiscriminate as the dew and illimitable as the globe we inhabit; and he could not have had kinder care nor more assiduous attention from those of his own blood. Two days thereafter we saw him again. Twenty-five years of toil could not have added more to the infirmity of his appearance than was wrought in those forty-eight hours. At the first greeting his mind recurred to the scenes of Monday morning, and he commanded, in a piping voice.

"Save the store at all hazards. Blow up every building for ten squares on all sides, and do it thoroughly. The store *must* be saved. Hah! there's the fire now. Where did it come from? Why didn't you blow up those buildings? Then he commenced lamenting: "All gone—the labor of a life-time ends in smoke. It is a hard fate, for nothing can be more certain than that I and my family are beggars——d——d beggars! We must go to the poor house or starve."

We tried to console him, but in vain. He soon became sullenly uncommunicative, and in a few moments sprang to his feet with a sudden start, and strode up and down the room at so rapid a pace that ere long he was covered with perspiration, and breathing like one almost exhausted. No entreaty could prevail upon him to desist from this violent exercise; but finally he commenced biting his lips, and soon large drops of blood and froth were falling from his white beard to the floor. He was suddenly bereft of articulation; tried to speak, but could not. Then his gestures and the contortions of his countenance were hideous to behold, and it appeared that death must end his sufferings in a short space, unless means of relief were devised. He continued to stride up and down the room, but with a reeling gait, and sudden, momentary stops, striking his forehead with clenched fist, beating his breast, and clawing the air like a blind man in a desert.

"He must be quieted," remarked good Dr. H——, who had been untiring in his attentions on the stricken man. "How to do it is beyond my comprehension, but we must manage it in some way, or put him in a straight jacket."

"Is the case so bad as to require such a measure?" we asked.

"One of the worst I ever saw."

At this juncture the old bookkeeper of our aged friend entered the room and gleefully exclaimed.

"Our insurance is all right. We will get every dollar of it."

The old merchant turned and stared at him for a moment, then a smile of recognition passed over his features, and to our utter surprise, he inquired.

"Eh, J——,? what's wanted now? Anything the matter?"

"I came to tell you the insurance is all good. It will all be paid,"

"We had $40,000 on the stock," mused our friend.

"It was $50,000," said J——. "Don't you remember telling me to take out an additional policy for $10,000, more than a month ago, when the new stock commenced arriving?"

"Yes."

"Then there's $45,000 on the building."

"Yes."

"And $27,500 on your house and furniture."

"Making ——, how much does it all make, J——? I'm not apt at figures to-day."

"The whole amount is $122,500,"

"Just so. And that is all we have left. It will scarcely cover what we owe."

"We don't owe the half of it, sir; and then we have three times as much due us as we owe altogether, and every dollar of it good."

"But the notes and books are gone."

"Oh, no; they are all safe. We have opened the vault and found everything sufficiently preserved to answer the purpose of settlement; and, unless I greatly miscalculate, we have at least a quarter million left to resume business on."

"Is this all true?"

"Every word of it, sir."

Such information was medicine to the diseased intellect, and the merchant looked around into the faces of attendants and visitors as though just awaking from a terrible nightmare. He had forgotten insurance, debtors, everything but the fact that the material evidence of his wealth had vanished, and therefore his mind had followed it away into the strange oblivion that swallows up so much of the wealth, happiness and intellect of this strangely chequered life; but the information that he was not pecuniarily ruined, reanimated that wandering mind, when it was shut and barred to all other intelligence, and the estimable old gentleman recovered his health and much of his former appearance within the next ten days, and has now resumed business in as good credit as ever. This incident was almost a tragedy, and very tragic up to the turning point. Its most valuable lesson points to those precautions against utter loss that every thorough business man avails himself of, and which, in times of disaster, are always sure to save him something as a foundation for a fresh start in his trade or profession. There is still another lesson, which inculcates the rule, that, at the worst, affairs are never as bad as they seem, and that a calm review will always demonstrate the truth of this principle. The account is less sad than a different termination would have rendered it, but no other result could have impressed it more indelibly upon the mind of the writer.

The detailed history of the Chicago fire will never be written, because there is an almost inconceivable mass of details that can never be gathered—many that can never be known, because their principal actors fell before the advance of the enemy they were striving to repulse—and even if all could be readily obtained, their voluminousness would prevent publication in any but a book of the most extraordinary size. It is well understood that the first fire, on Saturday evening, the 7th of October, 1871, would have become historical as "the great Chicago fire," had the calamity stopped with its extinction; for it burned over more than twenty acres of a densely settled portion of the city, including many warehouses, residences and factories; and its losses were summed up in an aggregate quite appalling to the insurance companies throughout the country. The fire of the following night was the Jormungundar that encompassed almost three quarters (in money value) of the city, and crushed it in its incandescent embrace. And it was the calamity that to-day stands out on the historic page as the severest that ever befell a people through the ravages of the fiery element—therefore the point upon which this narration inevitably challenges the attention of the reader.

It was about ten o'clock of Sunday night, October 8, 1871, that an ominous alarm rang out upon the devoted city from the great bell of the Court-House, booming far above the shrill whistle of the angry gale, now fast increasing to a hurricane, and admonishing our citizens of more than ordinary danger, in the doubly destructive combination of wind and flame. The bell continued, at short intervals, to toll the deep-toned notes of danger, which, borne afar upon the angry blast, struck consternation to every heart that realized the peril of a fire under the conditions of the city at that date, urged on by blustering Libycus. Hundreds with whom the writer has since conversed felt strange premonitions of disaster—mysterious feelings, creepings of the flesh and a great change in the vital circulation—as the notes of alarm continued; and it is probable that many other hundreds were similarly affected. It was really the portent of doom to many brave hearts, of a sort, akin, to that which is described in the following lines of Dryden:

> "A kind of weight hangs heavy at my heart;
> My flagging soul flies under her own pitch,
> Like fowl in air, too damp, and lugs along,
> As if she wore a body in a body,
> And not a mounting substance made of fire.
> My senses too are dull and stupified,
> Their edge rebated; sure some ill approaches,
> And some kind spirit knocks softly at my soul,
> To tell me fate's at hand."

When the general alarm sounded, and all the steamers flew through the streets, prolonging the boom of the bell in shrill shrieks, thousands of citizens rushed out to learn the location and progress of the conflagration. Most of the buildings in Dekoven and Taylor streets were already destroyed, and the great tongues of flame were licking up the wooden structures in that part of the city as though they were the merest tinder boxes, leaving no trace of their form or material to mark the place where they stood, but a moment before. The crackling of the fire among the dry lumber resembled the regular discharge of musketry by an army corps in retreat; but there were still worse evidences of panic than are usually displayed by a routed army, in the hundreds of people, men, women and children, already fleeing to a place of safety, and bearing upon their shoulders such articles of household use as seemed to them valuable at the moment. They were utterly demoralized, and mingled screams of agony, shouts of alarm, prayers and imprecations, with occasional blows right and left, in a jangling noise of words unknown, and gabble without meaning. Eyes blind with blood, and features wildly distorted with terror, people unclad, half-clad, some wrapped in bed-clothing, women dressed in the apparel of the opposite sex, and some protected only by their night-wrappers, carrying beds, babies, tables, tubs, carpets, crockery, cradles, almost every conceivable thing of household use, formed the most noticeable features of this terrific route. An aged dame, with a dog under one arm and a large mirror across the opposite shoulder, was apparently impressed with the belief that she had saved the better part of her fortune, and marched forward with a smile of satisfaction illuminating her grim physiognomy. An Irishman attempting to drive a pig of a remarkably piggish disposition, found he had taken a contract too great for his ability, and as the porcine quadruped at length eluded his pursuer, and fled back toward the flames at a tremendous lope, the porcine biped exclaimed with an inadmissable adjective:

"To hell wid ye, ye spalpeen;—ye's poor pruperty onyways."

A man carrying a bed and leading a goat met with even worse luck. A horse-cart, evidently driven by a mad-man, came rattling through the crowd at breakneck speed, and the goat, docile enough before, was panic-struck at the noise and unusual commotion, and braced himself to pull away. The man laid his bed on the ground to have the use of both hands in managing the goat, but he was too slow. One wheel of the horse-cart cut the goat in twain, and the other struck, tore and tossed the bed, and scattered it to the winds in a shower of feathers.

A drunken brute came swaggering along with a delicate, well-dressed little girl in his arms. The child was crying bitterly, and appeared anxious to escape from her custodian, who addressed her with oaths and threats.

"Whose child is that?" inquired a citizen.

"Mine," replied the ruffian, and he attempted to hurry along,

"Not so fast," said his interlocutor, detaining him. "Is this man your father, little girl?"

"No sir; he's a bad man, carrying me away from ma," said the child.

The scoundrel raised her aloft and dashed her from him with such force that she would have been killed instantly had she struck the ground; but fortunately she was caught in the arms of a gentleman who had stopped to learn the cause of the dispute, and who proved to be a friend of her parents and glad to take charge of her as a temporary protector. The kidnapper was summarily sobered by half a dozen blows well administered by a sturdy fist, which was the only means of punishment at hand, but had he ornamented the nearest lamp-post, with a rope about his neck, justice would have been better satisfied.

These incidents are related merely to show the general character of the panic, and the nature of the flight, and not for their intrinsic importance. The picture as a whole, treated by a Hogarthian pencil, or described by a Dante, might be readily accepted as a "Grand march through hell, of the legions of the powers of darkness."

Meanwhile, the flames were keeping even pace with the terrible gale, and spreading fearfully. The efforts of the firemen to stay their progress, although apparently well directed, were futile It was the remark of one of them that they might as well have pumped oil as water upon the burning mass, for the water appeared to burn like some intensely inflamable liquid, and certainly had no effect in extinguishing flame. Another declared that three feet from the nozzle the stream was broken and scattered in spray like a heavy dew, or the foam on the crest of a dividing wave, and of course utterly ineffective to stay the spreading of the fire. So the fearful pyrotechnic wall, seething with the power of an inborn, indescribable calidity, and towering skyward more than a hundred feet, came rumbling down to the banks of the river, near Twelfth street, and, at a single bound crossed over to destroy the heart of Chicago's business life. The firemen were now completely exhausted, and there were none to dispute the advance of the destructive element, that extended its Briarean tongues and arms in every direction. With the people, it was a race for life, and the stampede that now commenced will live in the recollection of those who witnessed it as long as time shall last. The inclemency of the night had increased, and the temperature was of that disagreeable, penetrating sort that searches the very marrow and chills it to torpidity.

Libycus was still in the ascendant, and so the fire struck out, in obedience to his prompting, for the northeast, where its approaches were most to be dreaded. People were now driven from elegant residences, from comfortably furnished rooms on the upper floors of business houses, from hotels, cottages and janitors' lofts, and all at once the streets were swarming with an excited mass of humanity, of all ages, colors and conditions. If the crowd was less motley than the first described, it was quite as varied in nationality, and no less noteworthy on account of the "impediments" with which it burdened itself. Men staggering under large trunks, immense bundles, even bureaus, seemed inextricably mingled with express wagons, carts, wheelbarrows, trucks, drays and buggies, with which the streets were filled, all overloaded with goods and furniture, and making their best speed to escape the approaching destruction. Mothers slightly enrobed, and carrying tender babes, were crying bitterly, while others cherished their young at their panting breasts and were silent in their overpowering agony. Little children, unattended, many in their night-dresses, bare-footed, bare-limbed, heads uncovered, ran about in utter distraction, crying for parents or nurses; and even the poor dogs added their howls and cries to the general dismay, making that night of doom still more hideous and appalling. Still the colossal besom of that holocaust swept down toward them with terrific speed, presenting the appearance of a great wall of glowing brass, and increasing its altitude as it devoured block after block of towering edifices. Many a man and woman sank to the earth in sore affright, many from utter exhaustion, and probably a few from hopelessness of their ability to escape the impending catastrophe. Some were recovered by friends, and others remained and met a fate too ghastly for contemplation.

Away sped the crowd, afar off to the bleak prairie, to the lake shore, to parks, cemetaries, any where remote from combustible material, and out of the way of the blinding storm of sparks, embers and smoke. The streets were constantly filled by reinforcements to the mad chase, and frequently so tightly wedged by the great mass of humanity that the weak were trampled, bruised, and some probably killed outright. Persons conveying valuables were ruthlessly despoiled of them, pockets were picked, and one gentleman reported that his coat was stripped from his back in the very thickest of the crowd, and taken away, as by some invisible hand, before he could discover the perpetrator of the outrage. Even women and children were robbed of shawls, cloaks and trinkets, and outrageously abused by the mob of thieves and roughs that now came, like so many vultures, for their prey.

Well authenticated instances of remarkable hair-breath escapes are sufficiently numerous and interesting to form an attractive book by themselves, full of startling details and semi-tragic catastrophes; but real tragedies are scarcely less plentiful, and probably deserve precedence in the record, but we must be permitted to intermingle them to some extent, for the purpose of avoiding monotomy.

At the intersection of Randolph and Market streets stood a large building, rented in separate rooms and suits for offices. On the fourth floor lived the janitor with his wife and four children, and an orphan niece, Marie. When the flames reached the building the family rushed out upon the roof, but all escape was cut off. The mother sank down, with the babe in her arms, smothered by a blinding cloud of smoke and flame, and expired. The father stood up strong and resolute, lifted the little boy of

four years to his shoulder, placed a protecting arm about his two little daughters, and strove to find his way to an neighboring roof, from which a stairway descended. His efforts were vain. The little girls ran back and fell beside the mother. Then a great cry of anguish went up from the father's heart, and even above the roar of gale and flame his voice was heard by the people below, and piteous, helpless hands reached out in futile sympathy, as if to help him. Then through the smoke and flame, to the very edge of the building, the poor man rushed, and for a moment lifting eyes and hands toward heaven as if in silent prayer, he sprang out from the burning roof and came downward. The awe-struck people gazed upon a shapeless mass on the pavement, which for a moment appeared very still and lifeless, and then a bright little head showed itself, and a child's voice cried out.

"You hurt my w'ist, papa. Lif' you head up—dat a'dood papa."

The father was dead, but the child only slightly bruised, and is now well and well cared for.

At the corner of Clark and Washington streets, in a window of a third floor room, a man stood serenely watching the general devastation, while the roof over his head was on fire. People shouted themselves hoarse to call his attention to the impending danger, but he merely smiled without moving. "He's crazy," said one; "drunk," said another; but he appeared both sane and sober, and was probably inclined to tempt fate a little, and save himself at the last moment. He waited too long. The heavy roof came crashing down through the floors, and he was inextricably buried in a heap of burning timber that landed in the basement, a perfect mass of glowing embers, within three minutes from the time the the roof gave way.

In one of the larger buildings on Randolph street, a portion of the upper floors of which were used for lodging rooms, men were seen dodging about from window to window, the untold agony depicted on their features, after the basement and first floor had became like "a furnace seven times heated." Two were rescued at great risk before the walls began to totter, but just as it began to seem possible to those outside that all might be saved, the huge walls swayed to and fro, and came down so heavily that they smothered the flames they had fed but a moment before, and buried several lives in the smouldering debris.

A young man named George Armstrong, a fireman, **had been hard at work** through many weary hours down town, when somehow word came to him that the fire was sweeping along Randolph street at a rapid rate. His home was on that great thoroughfare. His pretty wife had held up their wee baby to kiss him for the first time that morning. He sprang away like a deer, spite of his weariness, for he must know at once that his loved ones were safe. Reaching the spot, he saw his wife, Jennie, at the window with the babe in her arms. The fire had reached the lower part of the building and cut off all hope of her escape. He screamed frantically for a ladder, and, when it was brought, threw it against the window and sprang up the rungs. The flames caught it at the bottom, and a longer one was raised, reaching the roof. George swung himself lightly from one to the other, and soon touched the eaves. Quick as light he ran along the already hot slating, opened the sky-light and called " Jennie, darling, come up quickly. You will be safe here." She had fainted when she heard the ladder go crashing down, for she imagined her brave young husband had fallen a victim to the sea of fire below; and now, hearing his voice calling her far up in the dim space, she thought him in heaven, and that she and baby would soon join him there. But some blind instinct led her to clamber up as fast and far as possible, and soon the fresh air kissed her hot, blind eyes, and she found herself in her husband's arms. As he took the babe from her, she whispered, "We can die together, George. Thank God for that!" Just then a stream of water from a well-directed hose fell full upon them, and through the drenching torrent a brother fireman came and guided them down the slender, swaying ladder, down past windows where the glass was crackling and the flames playing in and out like the forked tongues of ten thousand devils, in safety to the firm pavement. And though they had nothing left but each other, no happier people are living to-day than George Armstrong and his sweet little wife, in their humble shanty on the lake shore.

And now the fire-fiend ruled the city like a tyrant, and man was powerless. Dismay took possession of the bravest hearts. Some wildly declared this to be the beginning of the destruction of all things earthly, and railed at those who strove to save life **or property.** Others, both **men and women,** besotted themselves

SCENE IN THE PUBLIC SQUARE. THE COURT HOUSE IN FLAMES.

with whisky, and indulged in orgies more gross and unseemly than those of the licentious Bacchanals of the old legends.

Many of the drunken were roasted alive, and others died in the streets from exposure, or were trampled to death. With those who kept their heads, it became necessary to make quick decisions on all questions concerning life, property and a temporary retreat, and especially on means to remove themselves and families beyond the reach of the flames. When the fire attacked the Smith and Nixon block, at the southwest corner of Clark and Washington streets, the panic was at its height; but some wise acres declared it could not reach the court house, although the block above named was known to be a colossal tinder-box, as it proved. The court house was in a blaze before the spectators were aware that fire had been communicated to it in any manner, although the shower of sparks with which it was enveloped should have taught them that its tar roof must go and after that its utter destruction was inevitable. The great bell was still thundering forth the note of alarm when the flames caught its frail tenement in the windings of their hot embrace, wrestled and surged for a moment, and then the deep-mouthed brass went tumbling and ominously clanging to the earth. The people had become so accustomed to its—boom—boom—that for a moment after it fell they were startled into silence; but it was only the silence that preceeded the louder peal, and soon the uproar redoubled with Babel sounds and Bedlam outcries. The Sherman House and all the towering blocks in that vincinity were soon ablaze, and the wild retreat of guests and lodgers, in hacks, express wagons, carts, and all manner of vehicles, gave an additional impetus to the motions of those already occupying the thronged thoroughfares thereabout, hustling, maiming, crushing the old and feeble and the poor, trebly excited and exhausted watchers of, and participators in the terrible events of five hours of continued, everchanging, but bloody and remorseless tradgedy. It was here, amid these scenes of terrible affright, and wild hallo, "confusion worse confounded," that the panic took a new departure, and divided the column of the retreating rabble into two sections, one of which dashed madly up Washington street to escape by the tunnel, and the other rushed in indescribable confusion for Randolph street bridge. Both of these points were reached amid the clatter of heavy wagons and steel shod hoofs, the cracking of whips, oaths of the drivers, curses of staid citizens, and wild screams of women and children. The crush at the tunnel is said to have been unutterably terrific. The occasion had made every point where safety could be sought common ground to all classes and conditions of people, and so there rushed into the dark, cavern-like tunnel, bankers and thieves, merchants and gamblers, artizans and loafers, clergymen and burglars, matrons and rag-pickers, maidens and prostitutes—representatives of virtue and vice, industry and improvidence, in every grade, and strangely commingling all the diverse elements of a mixed community, animated by one purpose and seeking a common object. Here the Graces and Gorgons met, Euphrosyne, Aglaia and Thalia, hand in hand with Stheno, Euryale and Medusa, seeking the poor boon of life at the utter sacrifice of all those weak conventialisms, that only a few short hours ago were thought to be the sole object and aim of existence. Here Pudicitia mingled her tears with the Lady Godivas and Cyprian nymphs; and here Mercurius joined Œdipus in supplicating the triple throne of Clotho, Lachesis and Atropos. There were bruises and groans, blows and piercing shrieks, prayers, imprecations, pocket-picking, and indignities unmentionable: but, strange to contemplate, no loss of life, nor fatal hurt. And so this motley crowd, finding ingress and egress reasonably free, under all the circumstances, and the prospect beyond promising of chances for life, continued to pass through the Cimmerian cavern, with their little savings and pilferings, their treasures and trinkets and babies, in tolerable order.

But the lord of misrule was indubitably the reigning genius at the bridge. The stampede here continued to increase in wildness and disorder until cursing became the only mode of expression, and blows were soon as free as curses. Every imaginable variety of vehicle had been called in requisition to convey the trunks and merchandise of fleeing citizens to a place of safety, and many of the drivers were clerks and mere boys, whose skill at the business was born of the occasion, and awkwardly demonstrated. Wagons, carts, and trucks were constantly colliding, and the shouting of men, the whistling of the steam tugs, the roar of the conflagration, the terrified snorting of horses, and barking of dogs, together with the prolonged shrieks of the tempestuous wind, made a discord as harsh, weird and uncouth, as if

> * * * "all the imps that fell,
> Had raised the banner-cry of hell."

Many persons were sadly abused and terribly hurt in the struggle for precedence, and many valuable articles destroyed in the shameful contention. To gratify a momentary spite goods were seized and thrown into the river, and a case is reported where the entire effects of a family, including the vehicle, a light handcart, were dumped into the water in return for an insolent word. Gunpowder had now been called into requisition to stay the further progress of the devouring element, and on every side the heavy detonation indicated the demolition of proud structures that other proud' structures might be spared. The great warehouses in Lake street were going down before the fiery wall as though they were mere bundles of piece shavings, and among the ruins and impending catastrophes of this mart of commerce is where the present chapter was introduced to the reader.

It seems appropriate to present, just here, a strictly historical narration of the fire; and thereafter its main incidents are detailed by "a cloud of witnesses," as embodied in their personal experience.

SCENE IN DEARBORN STREET WHEN THE FIRE REACHED THE TREMONT HOUSE.

The Great Conflagration

HISTORICALLY TREATED.

THE FIRST FIRE.

Saturday night, October 7th, witnessed one of the fiercest conflagrations that had ever previously occurred, not excepting the conflagration of 1857, in the Garden City. At about two o'clock the alarm sounded from Box 248, and ere the quivering boom of the great bell had ceased to vibrate over the empty streets, the sky grew fiercely red in the direction of Canal and Van Buren streets, and soon long bright flames leaped through the glow, and lit up the whole neighborhood with wonderous brilliancy before the fire department could arrive at the scene of destruction. Late as the hour was, the glare of the fiery illumination soon attracted vast crowds to the neighborhood of the fire from all quarters of the city, who thronged and choked up all the streets in the neighborhood. The wind rose as the flames gained in strength, blowing strongly from the South-west, so strongly, indeed, that blazing fragments of wood of no inconsiderable size shot along on the gale like rockets, to the distance of many hundred yards. Indeed, as lookers on beheld the meteor shower of white and crimson charcoal sparks raining all over the space enclosed between the river, the South branch, Wells street and Jackson street, and even flying over the river to the North-side, they began to fear, with reason, that the conflagration might spread beyond control of the fire department.

The fire had been raging for some time before discovered, and owing to the nature of the substance feeding it, soon converted the building into a furnace. It originated from some unknown cause in Lull & Holmes planing-mill on Canal street near Van Buren, the wind then blowing due North, and the flames consequently spread in a Northward direction. But soon after the wind veered to the North-east, and the flames commenced to rush that way. The fire had already spread to the right and left, and burnt a distance of two blocks from Clinton to the river; but when the wind changed everything combustible from the East line of Clinton to the river, midway between Jackson and

Van Buren streets, was swept away by the flames. Unfortunately frame buildings—lumberyards, and substances inflammable as tinder almost, covered and surrounded the space which the fire was threatening, and the fire department was powerless to quench such a hell of flame as roared over several squares within a very short time. Then the bright waves of fire swept to the North of Jackson street, and seemed as though they would spread in the very heart of the city. Jackson street, between Clinton and Canal, was composed in great part of wooden buildings, lumberyards, carpenters' shops, frame dwelling houses, and saloons, and in little more than a quarter of an hour, the whole of this space was enveloped in roaring flame. Between the railroad tracks and the East side of Canal street, bounded by Jackson and Adams streets, were several coal and lumber offices, to the rear of which lay vast piles of anthracite coal to the amount of many hundreds of tons. The slight office buildings were licked up by the flames within the space of a few minutes, and the coal-mounds actually set on fire. And then the fire ran under and over the Adams street Viaduct, licked up the railings and sidewalks of the iron bridge, and devoured the timber freight depot of the United States and Adams Express Companies at the North-east corner of Adams and Canal. But a comparatively small quantity of the contents could be removed in time, the greater part of the goods being consumed.

To the east of the long shed, then blazing, stood a number of passenger cars belonging to the Pittsburg and Fort Wayne Railroad. To save the cars it was necessary to tear down the shed, which was effected in time to prevent the cars catching fire, in which case the flames must have communicated with the Pittsburg and Fort Wayne depot, and thence burned as far as Madison street bridge. The citizens, however, worked desperately here, for they recognized the possible danger of the fire spreading still further to the East and North-east, and the fire department was unable to operate with any chance of success in this locality. Here the fight with the flames was successful, and the citizens conquered, in spite of a hail of crimson cinders and clouds of acrid dun-colored smoke, so thick, that it might almost have been cut with a knife.

Meanwhile the firemen were battling with desperate energy against the progressing flames on the South line of Adams street,

West of Canal, and stretching nearly to Clinton street. The buildings were nearly all frame residences, and should the flame make good its position here, or cross to the North line of wooden structures, the consequences would be terrible. The firemen could, as it was, being but twelve hose-nozzles to play upon the leaping battalion of fire that was marching grandly over the roofs. The heat was so terrible that the crowd, several hundred feet away, shrank further back before the angry glare—yet the heroic firemen would stand within a few yards of the blaze itself, only retiring to take breath. Of course so hot a wood fire must burn itself out to a certain extent, there was no possibility of absolutely extinguishing it, but they subdued the fiery ardor of the flames and prevented them from spreading to the houses on the other side of the street.

The crowd that stood upon Madison street bridge, and thronged the thoroughfare itself, were appalled by the spectacle before them. The sight was almost sublime, the heavens were speckled and spangled with flying cinders and vivid sparks, and the flames of the burning coal-heaps and lumberyards threw a vast Rembrandtesque light far down the streets on the North side, upon the rigging of the tall-masted vessels in the river, and upon the sea of awe-struck faces that gazed into the crimson sky and the tossing sea of flame.

Many were obliged to flee for their lives, mostly poor laborers who lived in the consumed frame buildings with their families, or in the cheap boarding houses in the burnt quarter. But happily no lives were lost as far as is known. One old woman was only awakened from her sleep by the entrance of the flames into her bedroom on Jackson street, and was only saved by the heroism of a printer, Robert Campsie by name, who, at the risk of his own life, brought her out of the burning building. Both rescuer and rescued were severely, but not dangerously burnt. Her daughter-in-law, a young woman of the name of Margaret Headley, was left behind, and has not been heard of; it is, however, probable, that she succeeded in making her escape.

One accident of a rather serious nature occurred during this conflagration. A large shed stood at the corner of Clinton and Jackson streets, whose roof afforded a splendid view of the fire, and was moreover easy of access. The crowd continued to gather upon it, until it suddenly gave way beneath the weight of about 150 persons, and the whole structure caved in. A considerable number of the victims of this disaster were severely injured, none we believe fatally.

Many of the saloon-keepers in the burning district, distributed their stock gratis to the crowd, when they perceived their property was doomed.

The "Chicago" steam fire-engine was working away at the northwest corner of Canal and Jackson streets, when the side of a burning edifice close by suddenly fell in, giving vent to a whirlwind of flames which enveloped the steamer in an instant. The engineer and firemen were compelled to desert her as they valued their lives, but shortly the fury of the flames spent themselves in that quarter, and they rushed in and pulled her out of the reach of the fire. The engine was considerably damaged, but was able to continue operations during the latter part of the fire.

The heat destroyed the western wires of the Western Union Telegraph Company, as well as several of the fire alarm telegraph wires. In one of the lumber yards a party of eight men found themselves overwhelmed by fire on all sides, and only saved themselves by throwing a quantity of lumber into the river, and paddling across. The only effective method of saving about thirty wagons and trucks belonging to the coal-yard, was by sinking them in the river.

Altogether the fire of Saturday night, October 7th, covered about twenty acres of ground and destroyed in the neighborhood of $700,000 worth of property. The insurance cannot cover more than a third of the loss, according to the Chicago Tribune. The following extract from the same paper gives perhaps the most accurate summary of the extent of the conflagration.

"The boundaries of the fire may be briefly summarized as follows:

Between Clinton and Canal streets, about three-fourths of the area south toward Van Buren street.

Between Canal street and the river, about nine-tenths of the area, south toward Van Buren street.

Between Canal street and the river, and Adams and Jackson streets, the entire area.

Between Canal and Clinton streets, and Adams and Jackson streets about seven-eights of the entire area, the only remaining buildings being the frontage of about 80 feet on Adams and 128 feet on Clinton street.

On the east side of Canal, north of Adams, about 100 feet in frontage, consuming the Express Company freight sheds."

BURNING OF THE CROSBY OPERA HOUSE.

THE GREAT FIRE

OF THE EIGHTH OF OCTOBER.

Since the day when "tall Troy" crumbled away in flames, no fire has surpassed the Chicago conflagration in its terrible work of destruction. The value of the merchandise alone consumed by the flames was at least double that of the goods destroyed in the great fires of Moscow and London combined. No city ever suffered a greater pecuniary loss by fire, whether Jerusalem smitten by Titus, Rome when sacked by Alaric, or Carthage when given up to fire and sword by her Roman conquerors. The estimate of loss of life, great as it seems, is really astonishingly low when we consider the extent, rapidity and fierceness of the fire whose devastating power was trebled by the furious gale. For two days the city was a rolling ocean of flame, and presented an aspect whose awful grandeur might rival the spectacle of a seething roaring volcano crater. The torrent of fire swept over a space of from five to seven miles in length, averaging a mile in width, and no building, probably in any city of the world could have withstood the typhoon of flame and fire combined. In many instances the action of the fire bore a strange resemblance to that of lightning. Blank walls were pierced in an instant by a vast tongue of flame, as though struck by powerful artillery—indeed a sheet of fire would frequently leap from the roof of a blazing edifice over a space of several hundred feet, and dash through the blank wall of a loftier edifice opposite, at one flaming bound.

It must of course puzzle the reader to imagine how the fire could make such appalling and rapid progress, licking up marble edifices like wax-work, and sweeping over a space of hundreds of square acres, all in a few hours from its commencement. To understand this appalling fact it must be remembered that in the first place the very finest and most solidly built portion of the city was surrounded and sprinkled with a vast number of frame buildings, and were thus, as it were, encircled by fuel of the driest and most inflammable description. Once the wood, tar and shingles were well lit the more lightly built portion of the city was a terrific furnace, and the buildings of iron and marble were as nothing to withstand the fearful force of the flames. It is pretty generally known that shortly before the fire, an agent of one of the great English Insurance companies visited the city with the intention of establishing a branch office there, but immediately abandoned the design, upon observing the material of which a great part of the city was built, and its exposed situation. He expressed his opinion freely enough that were a conflagration once well started the city must be partially if not entirely consumed'; and scarcely had he returned to England when his predictions were verified. If any one desires to comprehend accurately the effect of the flames upon those massive buildings of iron and stone which we considered impervious to flame—let him build a small model of such a building with the usual materials, and place it in an iron blast furnace. In the furnace-fire of Chicago the *blast* came in the form of a strong wind from the south and west, which fanned what might otherwise have been but a serious conflagration into a Phlegethon of looming, flashing, rolling, rushing, crackling billows of furious fire, which hurled a fiery spray into the red bosom of the incandescent heavens above.

"For nearly fifteen weeks," says the Chicago *Journal of Commerce*, "there had not fallen enough rain to penetrate the earth one full inch. Everything in and around the city was heated, dry and parched. Indeed, all through the West, fires were devastating extensive forests and destroying ripening crops, driving frontier settlers from their cabins and even overwhelming entire villages. For days the prevailing atmosphere of our city seemed ready to kindle into a blaze." With such surroundings and antecedents, with a hard gale blowing over the city from the hot, parched-up prairies, we can hardly be surprised that the fire did its work with such fearful rapidity at the outset, that the efforts of the firemen to master the terrible scourge proved wholly unavailing.

Much has been said on the subject of the demoralization, real or imagined, of the Fire Department on the night of the 8th. It has been hinted that several were intoxicated, and that the brigade, as a body, were utterly inefficient to accomplish their duty properly. These shameful rumors have happily proved to be without foundation. A more gallant struggle against an overwhelming, all-powerful, merciless league of wind and fire, was never sustained by braver men who freely risked, and lost, life and limb in the terribly unequal fight.

The truth is that courage and strength and energy must wither under excessive fatigue consequent on unintermitting labor and want of rest; and at the time of the general alarm, on the evening of the eighth, the whole department was almost worn out with the labor of previous weeks. "During the first week in October," affirms the same able periodical, from which we quote above, "our fire department had been alarmed more than thirty times, and within a few previous weeks there had been several very large and fearful fires. The burning of an immense warehouse, in the rear of Burlington Hall, had involved a loss of three-quarters of a million. When the great calamity came upon us, these ruins had hardly ceased to smoke. * * *

On Tuesday, October 8th, the last day of the Chicago of twenty years, our fire department was 'used up.'" It appears that in addition to the labors of weeks, weary labors of fighting flame, the entire department had worked unceasingly for twelve hours immediately preceding the final summons of the alarm bells. Human strength, whether constitutional or muscular, cannot endure such a strain without yielding to fatigue. Nor is it to be supposed, as many seem to have imagined, that under these circumstances they could compete in vigor and celerity with the firemen of Cincinnati or St. Louis, who rushed to bear aid in the terrible emergency. All such comparisons as those we hint at, are at least cruelly unjust, not to say imbecile.

The origin of the fire is not known, or rather we have no means of ascertaining by what agency the first building was ignited. The story about the old woman who went into her stable to milk her cow by the light of a kerosene lamp, which lamp said cow kicked over, is a pure fabrication. No such woman or cow probably existed, save in the imagination of some manufacturer of *canards*.

The fire first broke out, it is well known, in a small stable to the rear of a frame building on the north side of De Koven street, almost half-way between Jefferson and Clinton streets. The cottage belongs, (for yet it stands isolated in the midst of ruin, a strange fact!) to a laboring man and his family. The famous stable at the rear contained their little stock, a horse and several cows. Perhaps we might more properly call the building a barn. They never milked their cows later than 5 A. M., and 4½ P. M. in order to be in full readiness to dispose of their milk in time for their neighbor's breakfasts and suppers. On the Sunday in question the cows were milked as usual by the wife and daughter, and at an hour when daylight rendered the use of lamp or candle unnecessary. Witnesses prove beyond a doubt that the family were all in bed, without exception, before the fire broke out, when they rushed to the barn only to find it too late either to extinguish the flame or to liberate the animals.

It is, therefore, certain that neither old woman, cow or kerosene lamp had anything to do with the fire whatever. It is also highly incredible that incendiarism on the part of the owners of the frame house on De Koven street should have originated the conflagration. Neither is it at all likely that the fire was anything but wholly accidental, notwithstanding rumors. The *Journal of Commerce* remarks that in a high wind smokers might step aside in the lee of this little edifice to light their pipes and cigars. At least from the situation of the house, they would be more likely to stop there for the purpose of striking a match than at any other part in that neighborhood. A spark alighting on this tinder of hay and shingles, and fanned by the wind, would soon wrap the slight barn in flames.

From this point the fire spread East, West, and North, with incredible swiftness, and when aid arrived the fire had taken so strong a hold upon the slight structures in the neighborhood, that all efforts to check it proved unavailing. All the buildings on De Koven street, from Jefferson to Clinton, were burned level with the pavement, if we except the little dwelling house in the rear of the fatal barn, which stands perfectly uninjured among the charred remains surrounding it.

As the fire extended, it gained in strength and fierceness, spreading faster and faster—and, as is always the case, the flames seemed to increase the power of the wind which gained power and fury in proportion.

The fire department worked bravely and well in this neighborhood. The fire did not extend further West than Jefferson street, and all the buildings on that side were rescued, although several caught fire from the intense heat. About two squares and a half were saved on the other side of the street through the gallant efforts of the firemen. But the furious wind now commenced to catch up burning shingles, showers of charcoal sparks, and firebrands of all kinds, carrying them towards the North-east with terrible effect. From Clinton street to the South branch of the Chicago River, including Canal street, Beech street, and the railway tracks, the whole space was covered with lumber-yards, wooden buildings, quantities of coal, and, in short, everything that would make a good fire. With the exception of a few buildings at the corner of De Koven and Canal, and a few on Canal itself, everything was burned to ashes, the very streets being scorched and blackened. But the remainder of the West side of the city was saved. The fire had reached the portion devastated by the flames in the conflagration of Saturday night. North of Harrison and Van Buren streets was the blank space upon which the fire of the previous evening had spent itself, and the skeleton walls and scorched brick afforded it nothing to feed upon. Were it not for this fact, the south side would have been altogether destroyed as completely as the north had been. As it was the fire ate up more than fifty squares of the West Division, also devouring four or five of the bridges to the south side.

When the fire leaped the south branch of the Chicago river, it revelled among the very same combustible material as it had devoured on the West-side; coal, lumber, planing mills, frame houses, &c. It attacked the Armory and licked up everything in it, surrounded the gas works and exploded the gasometer, and then the situation really became alarming. Iron and stone melted and crumbled in the terrible heat, and the fire brigade had barely obtained a good position, when the flames, rushing along as fast as a man can walk, drove them before it, and it was with difficulty that they could save their engines, so that finally it became extremely dangerous to oppose the fire. "Marble buildings" says a Chicago paper "were burned to quicklime, crumbled, fell and disappeared as though they were mere toys of children. Thus onward rushed the flames, advancing north and east with great rapidity and 'eating,' even against the wind, steadily south."

The fire then leaped the stone-yards and open lots to the north of the Michigan, Southern and Rock Island Railroads, and in an extraordinary short time devoured the famous Pacific Hotel, one of the largest in the world; and the huge depot with its lines of cars soon melted away in the flames. Far north of Van Buren street the fire licked up gigantic squares of marble palaces, and approached the court house. This splendid building occupied the center of a square, and owing to its isolated situation, and its being surrounded by fire-proof buildings, was considered free from danger. But even before the sea of flames surrounded it, the ruthless wind hurled flaming brands and sparks upon the great dome, and the edifice was soon a mass of flames. The watchman started the machinery that tolled the ponderous bell, and fled from the building, the bell boomed forth the news of the terrible catastrophe until the vast dome tottered, reeled, and fell, crashing into the interior with all the weight of its several million pounds. The awful shock shook the burning city, and then the Chief of the Fire Department threw up his arms in despair; for he felt that all hope was gone.

The prisoners were liberated when it became evident that the court house was doomed, and all escaped with the exception of five murderers who were securely handcuffed and marched off by the police. It is said that the liberated thieves commenced their nefarious trade under the very walls of their blazing prison, and cleared a wagon load of clothing that was passing at the time.

The interior of the Post-Office was completely eaten out by the devouring fire, but its walls successfully resisted the raging element, and even checked the flames for a time in a northeasterly direction. Near this were many of the finest buildings Chicago could boast of, including the elegant hotels between Madison and Lake streets; and the splendid office of the Chicago Tribune, McVickers Theatre, and the Palmer House, all stood within a few squares of the glowing walls of the Post-Office. Soon, however, the flame advancing eastwardly seized upon the Palmer House, wrapping it from roof to basement in a shroud of yellow fire, and the flames bursting from the roof, leaped astonishing distances to yet intact edifices. In a very short space of time all the surrounding buildings were blazing as fiercely as the Palmer House, itself, and the Tribune building, as well as McVicker's theatre, crumbled away before the flames which rushed in upon them from the rear.

The North division was untouched until a little after twelve o'clock, on the same night, when the fire leaped the main branch of the Chicago river, and licked up everything combustible with its vast tongues of flame. The people dwelling in the North division—which indeed was composed mostly of dwelling houses—soon found themselves compelled to fly to the lake-shore. Many, however, plunged into the North branch of the river, or sought to cross on anything that would sustain them. This side of the city contained the greater number of the fine churches, palace residences, shade-trees, several depots, and enormous warehouses and manufactories. The North pier extended far into the lake a thousand feet, and close by were great stores of valuable material of all kinds. One of the finest buildings in the West was here consumed—McCormick's Agricultural Implement Works, containing property and stock valued at over $1,000 000. But the chief loss which the city endured was that of the Water Works.

It may as well be known, that although the water works were uninjured at the time when the fire seized the North-side of the river, yet soon after they ceased to supply water. This may prove a good lesson to those who believe that a city can always depend upon an engine-supplied reservoir for its supply of water. Although the Water Works' structure was deemed fire-proof, yet there was a considerable amount of woodwork about it. The *Journal of Commerce* wisely exclaims: "A few thousand dollars additional expense on the water works would have saved many lives and much treasure." The flying brands and sparks set fire to the roof immediately above the engine-room, the furthest point from the sweeping surging ocean of flame, that had already traveled at least three miles in six hours. This was instantly extinguished, but soon after the great breweries close by burst into roaring flames, and tongues of fire were darting over the turreted roof of the Water-Works' building. Within the atmosphere became heated to a degree that rendered it almost impossible for the workmen and engineers to perform their duties through danger of suffocation. At last the fire burst through the roof above their heads, and they were compelled to abandon the building, having first stopped the machinery in order that it might be injured as little as possible, and the safety valves were raised in order that the ponderous boilers might not burst. Then the immense roof crumbled in upon the three mammoth engines, and for ten days and ten nights, three hundred thousand people suffered from the want of pure water, even for cooking purposes, many being obliged to content themselves with the water from the river. Happily the canal had lately been deepened, which caused the cool pure water of the lake to flow towards the Mississippi; and the South branch of the river was sweet and pure compared to what it had been one year ago. Even at this time, however, it was water only to be used in cases of necessity.

Now the fire advanced without enemy to oppose it, and swept on towards the cemetery which bounded Lincoln Park on the South. The fire department had drawn off to the lake-shore, there to oppose the progress of the rushing whirlwind of fire by another mode of attack, while the flames were swallowing all the buildings in the direction of Lincoln Park. One remarkably handsome wooden residence, together with a fine conservatory, were spared, however, by the hungry element which left no other building standing it its destroying path. The ghoulish flames even battened upon the tombs and monuments in the burial ground, cracking and calcining marble monuments, licking up wooden crosses and signs, and even devouring the trees that shadowed, and the grass that grew upon the graves of the dead. It could gain no hold, however, upon the green foliage and shrubbery of Lincoln Park, whereupon it changed its course to the North-west. It licked up everything until it reached the prairie, and then it burned up acres of prairie grass and trees. All the bridges to the West-side soon disappeared, and the La Salle street tunnel, which communicated with the South-side, was so heated by the surrounding flames, that at the entrances on both sides of the river the iron railings were twisted and bent as though warped by the hands of a fiery Vulcan, and the rocks split and shivered as though by lightning. As long as the bridges remained intact, they were covered with fugitives and vehicles of every description. But soon the only means of communication with the North, South, and West sides of the river was cut off, and fugitives could only obtain succor through vessels along the lake-shore, or by a circuitous route to the remoter bridges, which were soon as crowded with fugitives as the others had been. And so the fire rushed on with its appallingly rapid work of destruction, until the prairie about the city was crowded with homeless men, women, and children, without shelter, food or drink.

. As long as liquor could be obtained many men drank freely, and not a few fell in a state of sleepy intoxication upon the

PANIC STRICKEN CITIZENS CARRYING THE AGED, SICK AND HELPLESS AND ENDEAVORING TO SAVE FAMILY TREASURES.

scorching pavement, little heeding the swiftly approaching and their terrible death. Alcohol had deadened their consciousness of all things. Then the roar of the red flames grew louder and louder, and the earth-shaking crash of falling buildings sounded nearer and nearer, till the scorching pavement upon which they lay seemed to rock beneath the terrible weight of the falling walls, but they slept on under the red rain of fire, till they became as the ashes which fell upon them.

The gutters of the sidewalks and roads were frequently filled with blazing whiskey, alcohol, petroleum, or other inflammable fluids, which ran in streams of curling blue fire, or dancing red flames down the pavements. In several places the tar between the seams of the newly-laid wooden pavements caught fire and blazed from end to end; yet with few exceptions the wooden pavements proved a success and still remain in a marvellous state of preservation. The flagged pavements did not escape so well, and the huge stones cracked and splintered in the vast heat. Brick is the material that best endured the terrible ordeal; indeed, the greater part of the brick is still serviceable for building purposes. But marble was burnt to quicklime, freestone and limestone crumbled and splintered, iron melted and trickled like lava among the glowing ruins, and strong iron pillars were twisted and warped into strangely fantastic shapes.

The rails of the street-railways were subjected to such terrible heat, from the blazing buildings on either side of the street, that they were raised in the middle from six to twelve inches and even two feet above the ground, the center bolts being drawn and those at the ends remaining undetached.

Anything combustible would of course be burnt to a cinder by the mere heat of that awful furnace, even though the actual flames had left it untouched. One curious fact with regard to the manner in which the various kinds of pavements endured the heat, which is chronicled by the *Journal of Commerce*, is well worthy of record. "On the north-west corner of the Court-House Square is now to be seen artificial stone flagging, perfect, while the sandstone on both sides of it, and also the curbing, are entirely destroyed." But we are also told that even where the rails were lifted from the center of the streets and bent like a bow, from the terrific heat, the wooden pavements remain materially uninjured.

The panic of that great multitude was truly terrible. With, in some instances, fire on three sides of them, they rushed to the waters of the lakes and dashed the liquid over themselves to keep their garments from being burned by the shower of falling fire or the intense heat of blazing buildings. The cattle rushed blindly about bellowing with terror and trampling upon men, women and children. Rats, cats, pigs, and dogs, rushed among the crowd uttering cries of terror. Flocks of pigeons rose in the red glare and sought safety in flight until scorched by the fearful heat, bewildered and blinded by the terrible rain of fire, and the stifling smoke, they fell back into the blaze. Horses, maddened with terror, shrieked with that horrible shriek which is never forgotten by those who have once heard it, kicked and plunged, and often lay down in their harness under the rain of sparks, foaming at the mouth, and shivering in every limb. Perhaps the roar of the fire was even more appalling than the spectacle.

The thieves had, as the popular phrase goes, "a fine time." Among the struggling, cursing, praying, shrieking crowd, their nimble fingers worked unceasingly, and we have no doubt they reaped a rich harvest. It is tolerably certain, however, that many of them perished in burning houses, where, in their eagerness to obtain booty, they remained until after every chance of escape had been cut off. The police at such a time were almost powerless to act, and crime was, perforce, permitted to revel in well-nigh unrestrained freedom for a while. Under the guise of friendship, sharpers would frequently volunteer to take charge of valuable goods, which, of course, were never again seen by their rightful owners. The hack-drivers were little better than swindlers, charging from fifty to a hundred and fifty dollars fare—even to crippled invalids.

The reports of incendiarism, hanging, shooting, and summary popular vengeance, or mob-law, are probably without foundation, or, at least, may be regarded as imperfectly substantiated. Several very horrible, and numerous romantically dreadful stories, have been circulated, we believe, by the lovers of the sensational. That a mob, under such circumstances, and in such a state of half-mad terror and frantic despair, would not hesitate to execute summary vengeance upon any parties who might be even slightly suspected of incendiarism, is pretty certain. But the accounts of this nature lack evidence and can hardly be credited for want of proper substantiation. With regard to romance, however, there have certainly occurred more hair-breadth escapes and thrilling incidents than would fill a large volume, and these, too, of such a nature as would vie with the wildest fancies of the sensationalist.

Twelve hours after the first alarm on Sunday night, the greater part of Chicago was dust and ashes. The fire soon began to work south against the wind, actually traveling along State street and Wabash avenue with almost as fatal swiftness as where the burning gale helped it along. It is curious, too, that the wind seemed to veer and blow from all points south, east and west as the fire proceeded, but the prevailing point was steadily south. Here, however, Phil. Sheridan led a forlorn hope against the flames, and began to oppose their progress in a new and yet more efficient manner. Powder was brought from the arsenal and buildings blown up all along the line of fire, but it was only by superhuman efforts that the fire was last checked at Harrison street.

The sufferings of the women and children no pen can depict. The terrible shock brought on premature delivery in numerous instances. It is said that between four and five hundred children were born within twenty-four hours after the fire, and many an infant's first cry was heard by the bleak lake shore, or upon the cheerless prairie, on that terrible night. Many of the little sufferers born under a sky of flame, and many a fair and delicate woman, perished before the sun had risen upon the smoking ruins. A great number of children and young women were compelled to fly in their night-clothes, and died from the consequent exposure. In the fire itself, probably nearly two hundred souls perished, and the total loss of life, from all causes connected with the fire, must come to nearly a thousand.

The telegraph operators stuck to their posts with an unshrinking heroism well worthy of record, until the flames had snapped, curled up, and whitened the wires, consumed the poles, and even destroyed the lamp-posts at the corners of the streets.

Before the fire had ceased, except where the coal piles continued to blaze furiously and the shivering thousands returned to look upon the ruins of their homes, the city was placed for a time under martial law. Sheridan brought down troops, the command of the city being given into his hands, and Allan Pinkerton issued orders to shoot all thieves, incendiaries, or malefactors, without mercy. It was a timely order, roughs, thieves, sharpers, swindlers, robbers, burglars, came from all quarters like vultures to prey upon the corpse of Chicago. But after the panic was over, and the authorities were enabled to give their undivided attention to the preservation of law and public order, these rascals found themselves utterly baffled.

When the news of the terrible fire flashed along the glowing wires to St. Louis, Cincinnati, and Louisville, the horror of the announcement lay like a nightmare shadow upon every heart and brain—when even the last means of communicating with the sister cities was cut off, the alarm almost grew into a panic. A whole city on fire in the North-west! Five square miles of splendid buildings roaring to the skies in flames! Five hundred millions worth of property destroyed! Thousands homeless, thousands starving, breadless, dying, millionaires reduced to beggars! The richest city of the west, whose wonderous speedy growth and prosperity was the admiration of the whole land, even of its rivals, turned into a hell of fire! Such was the news which appeared on the bulletin boards of every daily newspaper office, surrounded by awe-struck, sympathizing crowds.

For an instant all was horror, astonishment, and terror. Then the trance was broken by the cry of "give us food, give us shelter, as you are men and brothers. Our beautiful city, of which the world was proud, is gone. Our women and children are dying, without food, shelter, or money. Help us in our terrible affliction." And then the great sympathy of millions awoke, the sister cities forgot all petty rivalries, and nobly set to work to rescue the desolate people. Firemen and engines poured from all quarters to the scene of smoke and flame. Money, food, and clothing, came in plenty, and the mother country, too, poured forth her gold, remembering that the new world had sent succor to the old in the day of need. The Nineteenth century showed it had a heart.

The fire consumed nearly 3,200 acres, or nearly 5 square miles. The great fires of London, Moscow, and Constantinople, all combined, will scarcely equal the Chicago fire in the amount of space burned over. Nearly twenty-five thousand buildings of all discriptions have been leveled with the ground, and the number of human beings rendered homeless is 111,000 at the very lowest calculation, according to the *Journal of Commerce*. No perfectly

VIEW FROM THE COURT HOUSE LOOKING SOUTH-EAST.

SCENE ON THE CHICAGO RIVER. GRAIN ELEVATORS ON FIRE.

reliable estimate of the amount of property destroyed has yet been made, the various reckonings ranging from one hundred to five hundred millions of dollars. Many of the most accurate calculations have unanimously agreed on placing the loss occasioned, by destruction of property, and damage to business, at from three to four hundred millions of dollars, on which there was, according to the "Underwriter," nearly $100,000,000, insurance.

The richest and finest portion of the city has been, as our readers must perceive, utterly swept away, nothing but blackened heaps of brick, stone and iron being visible. The only buildings left standing between the river and the lake, and the river and Madison street, are the Lind block, at the corner of Randolph and Market streets, Hathaway's coal-office and one of the Buckingham elevators on the lake shore. The destruction of five of the great elevators alone involved an enormous loss.

THE ELEVATORS.

Chicago possessed seventeen elevators at the time of the great fire, with a storage capacity for over eleven millions and a half bushels of grain. The fire consumed five of these with their contents, amounting to 1,600,000 bushels, of all kinds of grain—principally corn. The elevators destroyed include the "Hiram Wheeler" with a capacity of 500,000 bushels; "Munger & Armor's Galena—600,000 bushels; "Illinois Central A," 700,000 bushels; and the "Union," 700,000 bushels. The remaining elevators however contain about 5,000,000 bushels which is more than sufficient for all present wants.

PUBLIC BUILDINGS.

The Court-House walls have successfully resisted the fire in the wings, although the central portion must be rebuilt, and the dome, with the famous electric clock, has been completely destroyed. The massive walls of the water works building are almost uninjured. With the exception of the Michigan Avenue Hotel, and a few others, the great hotels of Chicago are reduced to heaps of mortar, calcined marble, bricks and broken iron. The Pacific Hotel had been almost completed at a cost of nearly a million when the huge flames rushed into its fourteen hundred rooms and roared out of its numberless windows. The building occupied an entire square, was eight stories in height, and calculated when furnished to accommodate two thousand guests. It made perhaps the grandest spectacle of the great fire. Besides the Pacific and St. James Hotel, the Sherman, Palmer, Tremont, Briggs, Everett, Clifton, Orient, Oldridge and other houses fell a prey to the flames.

The brewers suffered terribly, nothing being saved of their huge establishments but a portion of the stock in the beer vaults. Moreover, the insurance on the property was generally light.

BREWERIES DESTROYED.

Lill's Brewing Company	$500,000
J. A. Huck	400,000
Sand's Brewing Company	335,000
Bush & Brand	250,000
Buffalo Brewery	150,000
Schmid, Katz & Co	60,000
Metz & Stage	80,000
Doyle Bros. & Co	45,000
Moeller Bros	20,000
K. G. Schmidt	90,000
Schmidt & Bender	25,000
George Hiller	35,000
Mitivet & Puoptel	12,000
John Behringer	15,000
J. Miller	8,000
William Bowman	5,000
John Wagner	5,000
Total	$2,025,000

The above loss includes, of course, the destruction of ice-houses, malt-houses, stables, cooper and blacksmith shops connected with the establishments, which were utterly reduced to ashes.

FIELD, LEITER AND CO'S

Monster store only caught fire at day break. For more than an hour and a half several hundred men did all in their power to save it from the advancing ocean of flame. The building occupied an entire block, and from its isolated position, and its surroundings, being all vast structures of iron and marble, it was hoped that it might be saved. But the buildings on the opposite sides of the square, burst into furious flames, melting the great business blocks as though formed of wax and timber, and the heat became like that of Nebuchadnezzar's furnace. Then the largest dry-goods house in the West had to be left to its fate, and the flames were soon rioting among 2,000,000 dollars' worth of costly winter stock.

BANKS &C.

There is not a single one of these buildings left intact in Chicago. The bank vaults have, however, resisted the flames with success. The principal Telegraph offices were all consumed. All the records of deeds and mortgages—all the real estate titles, have been destroyed. The abstracts of titles in the office of Shortale & Hoard, conveyancers, were luckily saved.

LAWYERS.

There is not a law-office, or law-library, left in Chicago, nor an indictment in existence in the country against anybody, nor a judgment, nor a petition in bankruptcy. Duplicate files of important cases which the lawyers kept in their offices are likewise destroyed.

DISTILLERIES.

But three Distrilleries remain in running order. The establishments owned by Thomas Lynch, Graefft, Roelle & Co., Dickinson, Leech & Co., Keller Distilling Company, Kirchoff and Shufeldt's rectifying works were consumed.

COAL YARDS.

There is no doubt that fuel in Chicago will be dear and scarce during the winter. Every coal yard in the city caught fire, and vast piles laid in for winter were utterly destroyed. The coal stock of Rogers & Co., (lower yard), Robert Law, Dyer & Paynes, Holbrook, W. Johnson, Sydacker, Goit & Curtiss, Sweet & Williams, Richardson & Pratt Bros.—amounting to about 50,000 tons of soft coal, and 10,000 of hard coal, insured—was totally lost. Five considerable winter stores of coal were, however, saved, including Roger & Co.'s upper yards.

NEWSPAPER OFFICES.

The offices of no less than eighty-five newspapers and periodicals were consumed. Several dailies reappeared in very small size soon after the fire, and since that time many of them have attained their former size. The *Tribune, Post, Republican, Staats-Zeitung, Mail, Times* and *Journal* offices were among the finest offices destroyed. The Tribune Building was the last to succumb to the flames by several hours, indeed it was considered one of the most thoroughly fire-proof buildings in Chicago. It was, moreover, one of the chief architectural beauties of the city. Every partition wall in the whole structure was of brick, the ceilings were of corrugated iron beams. It was erected in 1869, at a cost of not less than $225,000, and was seemingly so thoroughly secure that the Tribune Company had taken no insurance. On the first floor was the fire-proof vault, safes, &c., and the basement contained the engines, with two of Hoe's eight cylinder presses, with several folding machines, quantities of paper, &c. The building was completely gutted from roof to basement, and the loss of contents alone cannot have been less than $100,000. The fire-proof vault of the Tribune, however, proved perfectly trustworthy, and everything in it, even, a box of matches, was found intact.

CITY PROPERTY.

The following estimate of losses of city property under the jurisdiction of the Board of Public Works is given by Commissioner Redmond Prindiville, who has devoted considerable attention to the subject. This estimate does not include the school-houses, engine-houses and apparatus, police stations, sidewalks, &c. The item of sidewalks only referring to those in front of city property, together with all street and alley crossings, which are constructed by the Board of Public Works. The item of the City Hall embraces only the west half of the Court-house, the remainder being owned by the county. The list is as follows:

City Hall, including furniture	$470,000
Water Works engines	15,000
Water Works buildings and tools	20,000
Rush street bridge	15,000
State street bridge	15,000
Clark street bridge	13,000
Wells street bridge	15,000
Chicago avenue bridge	26,700
Adams street bridge	37,800
Van Buren street bridge	13,470
Polk street bridge	29,450
Washington street tunnel	2,000
La Salle street tunnel	1,800
Lamp posts	25,000
Fire hydrants	15,000
Street pavements	250,000
Sidewalks and crossings	70,000
Reservoirs	15,000

Docks	10,000
Sewers	10,000
Water service	15.000
Total	$1,085,080

The schooner **Stampede** and the bark Glenbendal, with several other crafts, were burned in the river and in the dry dock, and two steam fire-engines at least, viz., Long John, and A. C. Coventry, were destroyed by the flames on the West-side, being caught among the burning buildings.

The walls of the Custom House, the First National Bank, and the Tribune building, are yet standing, but it is doubtful whether they will be serviceable again. Nearly all the mail matters were secured from the Custom House building. Bank safes were terribly heated, to such an extent, in fact, that in several instances gold was melted into a solid mass, and notes reduced to ashes. Several packages of postage stamps, worth about $100,000, presented a curious appearance upon being taken from one of the safes. The gum-adhesive had become heated and the sheets were soldered together into masses as hard as wooden or composition blocks.

ADDITIONAL LOSSES.

As has been previously mentioned accounts vary as to the destruction of property in Chicago, estimates varying from 150,000,000 to more than double that amount. But certain it is that over sixty miles of streets, and more than 20,000 buildings have been utterly and completely destroyed. Fifty million feet of lumber have been consumed, together with thousands of tons of coal. The stock of leather was reduced about one quarter, $95,000 worth being burnt.

Cyrus McCormick the manufacturer of the "reaper and mower machines," was perhaps the heaviest individual sufferer by the fire, losing, independently of insurance, no less than three millions. William B. Ogden, who also lost considerable property in the great Wisconsin fires, suffered to the amount of two millions. Potter Palmer was said to have lost the incredible amount of ten millions, and really loses at least a fifth part of that amount. John V. Farwell and John Young Scammon lost respectively $1,500,000 and $1,000,000. Several other eminent millionaires lost similar amounts.

The city of Chicago must have lost at least five millions in public buildings, bridges, destruction to fire-engines, &c., none of which property was insured. The loss by damage to street improvements, sidewalks, pavements, &c., falls upon the owners of building property. This is probably about the heaviest loss of all.

Only about 50,000 people have left the city, leaving it still with a population of over 280,000. The shrewdest business men of the West are all confident that in less than five years the commerce and prosperity of Chicago will be even greater than it had been previous to the fire.

The Methodist Episcopal church lost over $295,000 worth of property, insured for about $80,000. Eight school-houses were destroyed, the loss on which aggregates $290,000. The churches burned on the North-side were the North Presbyterian, Westminster Presbyterian, Grace Methodist, Moody's Mission, St. Jame's Cathedral of the Holy Name, St. Joseph's, with the Orphan Asylum, and Convent of the Immaculate Conception, St. Ausgine's, New England, Unity, Fullerton avenue Presbyterian, and one or two other smaller. On the Southern Division the following were consumed: First and Second Presbyterian, St. Paul, Trinity, Swedenborgian, St. Mary's, Wabash avenue Methodist, and First Methodist Churches.

Thousands of valuables, that cannot be replaced, were of course consumed. The original Emancipation Proclamation of Lincoln, and a statue of that President, being the only one for which he ever sat, have been destroyed. The losses involved by the destruction of the Court-house are irreparable, and among them one of the most important is the destruction of all of Pinkerton's Criminal records, &c.

Allan Pinkerton has long been famous as the "champion thief-catcher" of the States, and his reputation was the result of years of patient, succesful toil, and energy. His detective agency was as famous as the Boston Common, and besides the central office at Chicago, there were branches at New York and Philadelphia. This agency was first started in 1852 at Chicago, and two years later the famous records were commenced. The most minute details of every case were carefully recorded, the statement of the applicant seeking for assistance to recover his lost property, the names of the detectives employed, his orders, and reports of his operations—in a word, every detail of the case, even to the testimony given in court, and the sentence of the prisoner. More than $50,000 had been paid for clerical work alone upon this matter, which filled no less than four hundred huge volumes of great value. The greater portion of these were placed in six of Harris' safes, and some of them in wooden cases. They were all burnt.

Pinkerton had been offered $30,000 by the Goverment for fifty-nine large volumes containing complete records of the secret service of the Army of the Potomac. They were the only set in existence, and valued by their owner at $50,000. Negotiations for the transfer of these volumes were still going on when the fire broke out and reduced them all to tinder.

The reports of the night police occupied forty great volumes, of enormous value. There were forty-eight patrolmen whose duty it was to report everything that had happened on their respective beats, as well as the state of the weather and other important particulars. They were frequently consulted in court proceedings for the purpose of obtaining information as regards the weather, the condition of the streets, the presence or absence of the moon, and policemen. Only two of these huge volumes were saved. There were, likewise, 105 volumes of files of all the daily and weekly papers since 1854. Pinkerton had printed instructions pasted all around the walls, ordering the men to remove these valuable articles first of all in case of fire, but before they could be lowered into the wagon the flames compelled the men to flee for their lives. Thus the work of more than twenty years was destroyed in about half an hour.

The *Chicago Tribune* declared, in an editorial after the fire, that there was no necessity for any able-bodied man to leave Chicago. This is certainly true. There was and is plenty of work for hundreds more at present. Quite a number of merchants intend building up their business edifices shortly, and many are already in course of erection.

HOMELESS CITIZENS IN CAMP ON THE SHORE OF LAKE MICHIGAN.

The Burning City.

BY N. S. EMERSON.

Calm and still, in her strength and pride:
The City lay, like a sleeping bride,
The stars turned pale in the Eastern sky,
And slipped out of sight, for the morn was nigh,
When up through the twilight, cool and grey,
Burned a ruddier light than the dawning day,
And a cry rang out on the startled air,
"The City is burning!" "Burning? Where?"
"The City is burning! Burning! There!"
And swift feet hurried forward and fro,
And strong hands fought with the awful foe;
Fought till the golden banners fell,
And flames and embers were smothered well.

All day long had the battle raged,
All day long had the strife been waged,
And the weary fireman slept at night,
Calmly, thinking that all was right.

Nine o'clock! Ten o'clock! Eleven! went by,
And still no cloud stained the clear blue sky;
But scarce had the clang of the midnight bells
Been hushed in softly echoing swells,
When loud their fierce alarm arose,
And banished every eye's repose.

Again the city was on fire.
The red flames sprang like serpents, higher
From roof to tower, from tower to spire,
Great golden surges throbbed and beat,
And rolled and hissed from street to street;
Stern granite walls, we had builded well,
In one wild hour to ashes fell,
And household treasures, cherished long,
Were swallowed by that dragon strong.

In anguish, which we may not speak,
Which dries the tear drop on the cheek,
And makes all words seem vain and weak;
We watched that night of horror through,
Watched till again the dawning grew
To broader light of perfect day,
And then beheld our city lay,
Blackened and shrivelled, ruined, lost,
In that stupendous Holocaust.

We looked into each others eyes,
Too dumbly stricken for surprise,
And said we've but escaped the fire,
"To starve upon our funeral pyre."
But when we saw the young, the fair,
Our helpless loved ones gathered there,
We raised one piteous wailing cry,
"Help us, or we shall surely die!"

From Orient to Occident
The echo of our anguish went,
And Occident and Orient
Made answer as with one intent;
They gave and gave, and still had more
To give from Loves' exhaustless store.

As flowers give perfume sweet and rare,
Unbidden to the evening air,
As clouds give raindrops bounteous,
So did the world give help to us.
From town and city, far and near,
Came deeds of kindness, words of cheer,
And hearts bowed down in sorrow, then,
In sweet surprise grew strong again.

For He who walked of old on earth,
Is with us in this later birth:
We lost Him in our greed for pelf,
But to His higher, purer Self,
He leads us through this golden tide,
And thus our loss is glorified.

Incidents, Accidents, Tragedies, and Wonderful Escapes.

A RECORD OF FACTS STRANGER THAN ANY FICTION.

The inquirer for incidents, unless insatiable, is quickly surfeited. Incidents abound: and they comprise a larger variety than was ever before known to spring from a single disaster. Those of a tragic character unfortunately predominate, in which, "sorrow, like an ocean, deep, dark, rough, and shoreless, roll'd its billows o'er the souls" of ten thousand hapless victims. Some are full of a sad grotesqueness that force an equipoise of tears and smiles, but the great volume of woe is appalling. It has already crushed many a brave heart, and destroyed many a noble intellect. It has written the untimely epitaph of the highest worldly hopes and loftiest ambitions of men of enterprise and worth, in the several departments of human endeavor, in the ashes of their achievements!

SUFFERINGS OF WOMEN.

There is so much material for this chapter of calamity, the question at once arises as to what shall be rejected, that it may be comprised within reasonable limits. At the best, it will require a very stout heart to read, without flinching, what are herein set down as verified facts. The great whirlwind of fire was no respecter of persons, and did not accomodate its course to any of the desires or movements of our people. The sick, the dying and the dead, were all in its path, and consumed by its torrid breath. Many women, in the pains of childbirth, driven from shelter by the flames, were found away out on the prairies, or on the shores of the lake, the bleak winds chilling them and extinquishing the new life just ushered into the world. In scores of instances, both mother and child were dead, without attendance, and unrecognized. With no sympathising friends, no helping hand, no eye save God's, to witness their agony and despair, they passed to "a land of darkness as darkness itself, and of the shadow of death; without any order, and where the light is darkness." It is trebly hard, under such conditions,

"To feel the hand of death arrest one's steps,
Throw a chill blight o'er all one's budding hopes,
And hurl one's soul untimely to the shades,
Lost in the gaping gulf of black oblivion."

The daughter of an eminent clergyman gave birth to a child during the rush and panic of the wild flight of women and children along the lake shore, and in some inexplicable way was separated from her friends, and neither mother nor child have been found.

A well-dressed and apparently intelligent lady, running away from the scorching flames, fell down in Adams street, near State. It was discovered by those near that she was in the pains of labor, and an effort made to convey her to a place of safety. She had been carried scarcely three squares when she expired in great agony.

A lady was carried out of the Sherman House in the arms of her husband, a new born babe clasped to her breast, and both died in the arms of the husband and father before reaching a place of safety. He was last seen marching along the shore of the lake, with the dead woman and child in his arms, shouting, laughing, and blaspheming, in all the delirium of grief. He was unquestionably burned or drowned.

The lake shore was a scene of many a blood-curdling tragedy. A fine-looking woman of commanding presence, and almost regal air, was observed wading in the shallow water, holding twin babes but a few hours old in her arms. At last she sank upon the shore from utter exhaustion, and both mother and children died unrecognized and unattended, and two days after were buried by the city.

A well known matron, whose husband was absent from the city at the time of the fire, personally superintended the packing and securing of most of her valuables, (although in a condition of the utmost delicacy regarding physical health), and sent them to a place of safety. She then engaged an express wagon, at an enormous charge, to convey her to the residence of a friend in the West Division; but, in consequence of her unusual exertions during the night, the excitement, anxiety, and fatigue, she was attacked with labor pains shortly after leaving her residence, and found herself compelled to lie down in the wagon. Just after crossing Randolph street bridge she gave birth to a living child, but before reaching her destination its little life had been extinguished by the chilling blast. The mother, strong and healthy before, is now an invalid.

Among women of the baser sort, who had their dens and haunts in Wells, Clark, and other streets in the burned district, there were tragedies innumerable, and probably more horrible deaths than among people occupying ten times the amount of space in other parts of the city. As the flames attacked their squalid tenements, they were seen issuing forth scantily clad, some almost nude, many in a maudlin stage of intoxication, others rubbing their eyes in drowsy stupidity—dismayed, weeping, laughing, cursing and singing. One, somewhat intoxicated, carried a young child, which she abandoned before walking a single square; and it would have been consumed had not a patrolman rescued it. Another carried a bottle, from which she quaffed frequent and copious draughts, and, despite the urging of her companions, finally lagged behind, and was left to her fate. A young girl in tawdry attire, after emerging from a low Wells street hovel that had just ignited, swore she would sooner lose her life than her gay new hat, and went back in quest of it. She did not return. A painted Jezebel rushed into the glowing street from a burning house, just as the roof commenced falling, with a large feather-bed in her arms. She was clad in nothing but a light wrapper, which the gale swept away from her limbs, and, ere she had proceeded many steps the flames seized upon it. The bed was also in some way ignited, and in an instant the woman was enveloped in a raging bonfire. People hastened to her rescue, but she had inhaled the intense caloric into a stomach already heated with alcohol, and fell dead before one could reach her. A poor depraved creature sat in an attic window of a large building in Clark street, chattering, singing, and laughing, while the flames were raging through every part of the structure, even in the room she occupied. She shouted obscene epithets, and snatches of erotic songs to the people below, hurrahed for the fire and cursed everything else; and, finally, as the huge walls commenced swaying forward and back, she laughed hideously, ending in a shriek like the yell of a hyena, as the immense pile of brick and mortar came thundering to the ground, burying her beneath its tremendous weight. A great number of this class of women were overtaken in the slumber of intoxication, smothered and roasted without consciousness of the calamity; while others, tired of life, made no exertion to save themselves, and perished in various ways.

Who can realize the excruciating anguish of such a moment?

Physicians testify that not less than eight hundred cases of premature birth have already been made known, and most of them involve instances of suffering that no strength of language can adequately describe. The poor women, away from their natural protectors, with no friends at hand, and without even the commonest attention from strangers, so absorbed was every one in the immediate danger to life and property, were left, in all their helplessness, to encounter the most critical period in their lives—rendered a thousand fold more momentous by the appalling character of their surroundings.

A HEART-RENDING MISTAKE.

A family was just rushing from their smoking residence, that the fire had only that moment attacked, when the wife said to her husband.

"You have the baby, Charles?"

"No; I thought you took him."

"Mary has him, then?"

"Oh, no mem; I brought the silver."

The babe is still in the house, and the father rushes back to save him. The half-distracted mother, supported by the faithful servant, awaits his return in an agony of fear. The roof is on fire, and the flames are just bursting from the upper windows, when he appears with the precious bundle.

"I wrapped him closely, so he would not inhale the smoke."

"Is he asleep?"

"Yes; very soundly."

"Let's hurry along to a safer place and unwrap his face or he will smother."

When a little remote from the raging flames and blinding smoke, they undid the carefully guarded parcel, and found within—nothing but a large pillow! The child had been left to the flames. The mother understood her great bereavement on the instant, then her mind darkened, and she is hopelessly a maniac.

AN UNEXAMPLED BEREAVEMENT.

A prominent business man returned from a trip to New York on the second day after the fire. He had been enabled to obtain no particulars regarding his own personal disaster, and the occular demonstration of the ruin of his home and warehouses preceeded all verbal intimation of the facts. Of his elegant residence nothing was left but the smoking stones of the foundation, and a few warped iron pillars marked the spot where he had left a commodious and well-filled business house. He inquired for his family. Nobody could furnish the desired information. His brother had lived in another part of the city, and he concluded they must be there. He went to see, but found only the ruins of the household shrines. A cousin living two miles in another direction must have furnished them refuge, but, on searching that locality, he discovered the fire fiend had not spared him even this hope, and his investigation from that time forth was directed to a general search, and advertisements in the newspapers, but, up to the moment of this writing, without result. No tidings whatever from his wife and children, none from his brother, none from the cousin; and the poor man is now driven to the belief that all were utterly destroyed!

GEORGE HOWARD.

A bright little fellow, only eleven years of age, was the hero of the following incident: His parents moved from New York to Chicago abouts two months before the fire. Here the father started in the merchant tailoring business, and was getting along comfortably. They lived on Randolph street, and when they retired to bed on the second night of the conflagration, there was no fear entertained by the people of that locality that the flames would reach them. The little fellow, who gives his name as George Howard, says he was aroused from his sleep by the heat, and when he opened his eyes found their building on fire, and the windows already in flames. He jumped up, awakened his father, and mother, and told them of the danger. The heat at this time was intense, and George managed to save himself by jumping through one of the burning windows, which was in the second story, down to the pavement below. There he waited, expecting his father and mother would also escape by jumping from the windows; but he waited in vain. In less time almost than it takes to relate it, the building was a crumbling mass, and roof, walls, partitions, and furniture, all went blazing together into the cellars. He states that next morning he made search, and found the bones of his father and mother beneath the ruins.

A STRANGE ERROR.

The great uncertainty regarding the fate of friends, for several days succeeding the fire, and the absence of any thoroughly organized effort to trace those who were missing, occasioned untold anxiety, and in several instances resulted in the most terrible misapprehensions. A young gentlemen telegraphed to relatives in Syracuse as follows:

"I am safe, but father cannot be found. He was probably asleep, and burned to death.   "FRED."

In less than two hours after the receipt of the above, the parties in Syracuse were astounded by this dispatch from the father:

"Everything burned, and FRED is missing. Havn't seen him since the general alarm, and fear the worst.   "R. J. F."

Father and son were at once informed by return messages, of the safety of each other, and were soon reunited.

A HAPPY OCCASION.

There never was a happier re-union of people who had been given up as lost by their friends, than that which occured at one of the relief "headquarters" on Thursday succeeding the calamity. A well known gentleman was relating to sympthising friends that, in his desire to save his cash box, which contained bonds and money for a large sum, he had been neglectful, for the moment, of the safety of his wife and children, that he lost sight of them in the great rush of flying, panic-stricken citizens, and that they were either burned or trampled to death. Pausing a moment in the narration, he overheard the sound of a familiar voice in an adjoining room, and springing to his feet, he rushed through the door:

"My dear wife!"

"O, my husband!"

were the ejaculations that reached the ears of those within hearing. The wife was there accompanied by the children, and was relating to some acquaintances the circumstances attending the loss of her husband and all their property. She was about to apply for the relief of absolute necessities in the way of food and raiment, when she was interrupted by the entrance of her companion alive and well. They were at once clasped in each other's arms, and stood there silent, overcome, in an eloquence of joy that could find no expression in words. The children—there were three—laughed, cried and shouted, and at last the oldest, a fine boy of twelve, gave vent to his feelings in words that have since become historic: "Bully for father! the fire could'nt burn *him!*" An expression, at once so vigorous and original, broke the spell, and everybody returned to the realities of the occasion. The family were all there; they had saved enough to insure comfort; and the benevolent German who gave refuge to the wife and children in his poor cottage during the hour of peril, and divided with them his frugal loaf, now rejoices in the addition of a $1,000 government bond to his worldly possessions.

A SURPRISE.

A Chicago matron, on a visit to some friends in Massachusetts, addressed several telegraphic messages to her husband during the three or four days succeeding the fire, and received no reply. She telegraphed to acquaintances with the same result. Concluding her family had met with disaster, perhaps death, she resolved to return and ascertain the facts. The husband had attempted to send a message to his wife, but could not get it through. There were no mails even, and he therefore took a train, for the purpose of assuring her of the safety of himself and family by his personal presence, on Wednesday of the terrible week of darkness. The wife started a day later. Reaching Albany she was partaking of a lunch in the railroad restaurant when some one tapped her on the shoulder and inquired, "What are you doing here?" She turned and beheld her husband; and her gloomy forebodings gave place to rejoicing. They returned to Chicago with all speed, to assist, relieve and encourage their less fortunate neighbors.

It was the afternoon of that dreadful Monday, that Chicago people can never think of without a shudder. The ladies of our block had sat out on their stone steps since two o'clock of the previous morning, with black faces, uncombed hair, and red, bleared eyes, gazing with hearts of lead at the roaring, rushing fire-fiend that was devouring the homes of our friends on the North Side. There was no water, the Mayor had ordered us to have no fires. One energetic Yankee lady proposed sending six miles to an artesian well to get water to go on with her house cleaning, for, she said, "she would have to pay the woman she had hired any way."

FUEL TO THE FLAME.

Thousands of children were running in every direction, screaming, crying, and beseeching the people they met to find their parents or friends; many were in their night dresses, with bare feet, scratched, burned and bleeding, heads uncovered, and long hair streaming in the wind. A gentleman reports that he saw one little girl whose great wealth of loose golden hair had caught fire, and she was running and screaming in sore affright. As she passed the place where he stood, some thoughtless person threw a glass of whisky upon her, with the evident intention of quenching the flame. It of course had the contrary effect, and flared up at once, covering her from head to foot with a blue blaze. She was burned to death almost on the instant.

HORRORS.

Several people were severely injured, and some killed outright, during their flight through the streets, by the bricks, stones, cornices, etc., from the falling buildings. One man, carrying a child in his arms, and leading another by the hand, was struck on the head by a stone, which crushed his skull, and scattered his brains over the little ones. The horrified mother uttered a heart-rending shriek, gave one look of unutterable anguish at her dead companion, then seized the children and hurried away.

A newspaper reporter writes that he saw a woman kneeling in the street, with a crucifix held up before her, and the skirt of her dress burning while she prayed. She appeared to be utterly absorbed in her devotions, and regardless of danger. While the reporter was looking at her, a run-away team attached to a truck dashed her to the ground, and she was left torn and mangled.

A great many occupants of tenement-houses were burned to death. They are a class of people that are helpless in a panic, and proved to be no exception on that terrible Sunday night. One woman in a tenement-house on Wells street was awakened by the heat and smoke, and ran to a window for air, but either fainted or was smothered, and fell across the window-sill, where she lay, and was burned with the building.

On the battlements of one of the high blocks in Randolph street a man was seen standing and wildly gesticulating, with the terrible flames raging and roaring through all the apartments beneath, and escape entirely cut off. All who saw him knew that he was doomed to a terrible death, for rescue was out of the question. Still he gesticulated, pointed in various directions, and was evidently trying to make the people understand some plan of relief that he thought feasible, but his voice was drowned in the tremendous roar of wind and flame, and no one moved to attempt what everybody knew would prove utterly resultless for good. At length the great walls became unsteady, swerved for a moment in mid air, and then came down with a crash and weight that shook the very ground, and the life of him who a moment before had stood there imploring help was crushed out in the glowing furnace of destruction.

A similar incident is reported of two men on the top of Armour's block, who found themselves completely environed by the flames. They tested the full strength of their lungs in useless shouts, threw up their hands, pointed hither and thither, ran to and fro, and finally seemed intent on plunging headlong to the pavement. It was impossible to reach them, but at length they stood on the parapet at the back part of the building, whence the roof of an adjoining structure, some thirty feet below, seemed to offer means of escape. The flames were eagerly pressing upon them, giving but little time for consideration, and so, hand in hand, they jumped. It was a fearful leap and badly calculated. They came down with a terrible crash, were badly bruised, and lay senseless and bleeding until rescued by their friends.

A gentlemen, rushing past a drug store at the top of his speed, was suddenly overwhelmed by the explosion of some combustible stuff, and deluged with liquid flame. Death was instantaneous.

BEREAVEMENT IN HUMBLE LIFE.

A number of Irish families took refuge beneath the sheds of a brick-yard. They had saved nothing, not even a quilt. Not a cent of money to buy even a roll, even had there been a roll to buy. One poor woman, who, with her young daughter, was sitting disconsolate, their backs against a pile of bricks, alone seemed disposed to communicate her bereavements. The girl's hands were burnt and blackened, and the mother had wrapped them in some dirty rags she picked up in the street, and there the poor creatures sat in drear desolation, although surrounded by fifty persons similarly situated. The mother's eyes were red and swollen from heat and smoke, yet, in the face of all their woe, she answered cheerfully when addressed. Their great calamity was the loss of the husband and father. "Patrick and meself," said she; "beat off the flames as long as we could, and poor Mary here, she worked as hard as any of us; but it was of no use. So true as I tell you, the flames came upon us quicker than a railroad train, and meself and Mary started out Division street, and Patrick, poor man, went into the house to get a few dollars he had saved from working on the docks, and, and—I never saw him any more. Oh, dear, oh, oh!" And as the full measure of their griefs burst with full force upon their hearts, they fell to sobbing and bemoaning their loss.

A MIRACULOUS ESCAPE.

"Clear the way there, below!" shouted a gentlemen from a fourth story window of a large building in State street. The crowd opened right and left, and stood with bated breath awaiting the catastrophe.

"He dare not jump," said one.

"If he does he's a dead man," remarked another.

"I am coming!" shouted the individual aloft.

And then, swift as an arrow, people saw a dark object shoot downwards through the sparks and smoke and flashes of light, down to the earth. The dull thud of the concussion was immediately followed by the exclamation:—

"All right!"

And it was discovered that he had alighted in a large pile of bedding, escaping without a bruise, and scarcely a momentary inconvenience.

THE LAST SCENE.

The coroner's office and morgue were the saddest and most forbidding places in the city, two days after the fire. The roasted bodies of men, women, and children, unrecognized and unknown, were piled one upon the other, awaiting the visits of those who should claim them and perform the rites of Christian sepulchre. There were many visits of those whose relatives were missing, and occasionally an expression of the belief that one of the blackened bodies might be that of a husband, father, wife, brother, sister, or dear friend, but the clues were very faint, generally im-

RESCUE OF CHILDREN BY TYING THEM IN BEDS AND THROWING THEM FROM THE WINDOWS.

probable, and in nearly every case abandoned on closer investigation. More than two hundred of these bodies were unrecognized, and finely buried by the city; and it is estimated that bones and other evidences of human remains, representing at least four hundred and fifty persons, in addition to the two hundred, were found among the ruins. It is probably safe to estimate that not less than twelve hundred people lost their lives in the Chicago calamity, in one way or another, and it is known that the list of the missing over-runs this aggregate. Where, in the whole history of human disaster, can we find a more agonizing record?

THE MORGUE.

At the far end of the room was a partitioned space lighted by dirty cobwebbed windows, and on the floor, arranged in rows, first all around three sides and then down the middle, were the charred remains of seventy human beings.

The first noticeable object in this dreadful company was the form of a Sister of some Roman Catholic Order, completely shrouded in her brown habit with the cross and I. H. S. in white letters stitched on the bosom. The face was thickly veiled and even the feet carefully covered up. "She was smothered, but not burned," observed the grim master of ceremonies.

The next was the body of a young man partially clad in common workingmen's attire. The hair was completely burned off his head and body; the features were blackened and distorted with pain; the swollen lips were wide apart, disclosing the glistening teeth, and imparting a horrid grin, such only as agonizing death can stamp upon the face. The flesh was bloated to an astonishing size. The poor wretch was roasted alive. What is the use now of giving utterance to the passing thought as these two corpses—the only two whose faces could be recognized—met the gaze? Let it pass.

There was one charred form in the attitude of prayer—the form of a woman, but every feature of the face, every graceful line of the body was gone. The head was nothing but a black lump; the body a blackened, hideous shape.

Some bodies of men could be distinguished by the remnants of clothing and boots, but nearly all traces of humanity were gone. Then there were remains of children and young people; but they, with the majority, were nothing more than mere blackened, charred torsos. Those whose limbs or arms remained, exhibited a supplicatory attitude, as if begging mercy of the destroyer.

To this ghastly, hideous, and melancholy spectacle, were admitted in little parties of four or five at a time, those who had friends or relatives missing, but no language can describe the scenes of heart-rendering agony which these grim visits elicited.

A family of little children, led by an elder sister, comes, and after the first sickening shock tries to distinguish her mother. A frantic wife, attended by a friend, comes in search of her unreturning husband. Brothers seek sisters lost, and sisters their brothers gone; but who can tell in that undistinguishable charnel, what home the living being made happy. All personal identification was gone with the obliterating fire, and nothing was left but ashes. But perhaps the bitter disappointment at not finding, or rather recognizing the lost one was worse than if there and then had ended the fearful search. Heart-bursting sobs, hysterical exclamations, and unutterable wailings, rent the air as the disappointed sad ones turned away from the sickening scene.

But besides the bodies burned to a crisp, the impoverished morgue had other horrors to reveal. On the near side of the partitioned space lay half a dozen tenanted coffins—pauper's coffins—of unpainted pine, with the bodies laid in without any preparatory equipment for the grave, not even the common composure of the arms and limbs, the closing of the eyes, and the washing of the features. In one the visitor was shown the corpse of the man shot through the head and hung to the lamp post—a dreadful warning to incendiaries. In another lay the body of a man with a bayonet stab through the body—by whom stabbed no one knew. In another was squeezed the body of a German tailor, well known in the neighborhood, who had lost his all by the fire, and acting upon the cowardly principle sentimentally inculcated by Goethe in "The Sorrows of Werther," committed suicide rather than bravely live out his allotted time. He had first opened a vein in his arm and then cut his throat from ear to ear with a razor. His hands, face and clothes were smeared with gore, and a more ghastly and sickening spectacle than that coffin presented could hardly be found. There, shut it up forever and shut out the sight from our eyes—if we can, and leave the horrid place, never, never, to return.

A RETROSPECT.

Murat Halstead, Esq., the well-known and accomplished editor of the *Cincinnati Commercial*, visited our city in the last days of October, and wrote his impressions of "Chicago three weeks after the fire." As the testimony of a close observer of men, things and ruins, and of one who is wholly disinterested, his letter is of more than ordinary value, and is inserted here that we may avail ourselves of the most convenient opportunity of being seen as others see us:

All speak of the appalling roar of the conflagration, fanned by a hurricane, and the tremendous power of the mass of flame before which the tall business houses withered and collapsed. The heat was so dreadful, and the force of the wind so great, that the serpents of fire pierced walls like lightning. The sky was lurid. The heavens seemed to be filled with fiery billows, and an awful volume of densely black smoke rolled away with frightful rapidity and the majesty of a gigantic thunder cloud. "You have seen a violent hail storm," said one, "imagine the hail to be all fire and you have the shower of sparks." The tempest beat upon the roofs far in advance of the torrent of flame. The air was filled with blazing shingles, and boards several feet in length were whirled aloft and flung in advance, while fragments of composition roofs made infernal fire brands, and hissed with fierce combustion as they flew. Before such a storm as this any city in the world would have perished, and if Chicago had extended forty miles in the direction of the wind it would have been swept throughout.

Every one has some strange experience to relate. The wife of one of the first citizens of Chicago—a man of great wealth, and whose home was famed for a genial hospitality—was separated from her husband, and, with two small children, driven into the edge of the lake, and crouched shivering in the shallow water for hours, when she ventured upon the land again, and walked six miles to the house of a friend. The daughter and only child of a prominent gentleman, who had one of the handsomest residences in Chicago, and was well able to enjoy it, was obliged to take her place, with a basket on her arm, in a line of sufferers seeking food, and there was recognized by a ruffian and thrust out of the line with an oath and exclamation of joy that she was "on the same level with the rest of us now." A resolute business man, believing, for an hour or two before his store was swept away, that the fire was uncontrollable, succeeded in removing a quantity of valuable goods to the lake shore. When the fiery hail descended there, he found a tub, which he placed on his head, and remained brushing the embers from a lot of goods, and wetting them; and, when the danger was over, he had the satisfaction of ascertaining that he had protected, with desperate energy, and at the risk of his life, the property of another. His pile unguarded was consumed. While the black smoke was still ascending, and the streets were yet hot, and the wind swept through the ruins, with the breath and dust of a Sahara sirocco, a business man made his way to the ruins of the Court-house, and there he declared he saw flying across the square a white owl. He is not an imaginative or superstitious person, but most literal and exact in his statements, but he confesses to have been slightly disturbed to see an owl just then. It had an uncanny look, even to a prosaic person. The great bell of the city was in the Court-house, and the noise that it made in falling was heard through all the uproar by almost everybody. As the fire became irresistible the great bell was sounded incessantly to warn all hearers of the peril that beset them. The clamor ceased as the fire took possession of the Court-house, and then the long reverberation of the bell as it tumbled crashing down the tower, and the great, dull, far resounding throb that it gave when it struck the earth, seemed to the maddened fugitives, driven before the flames, something superhuman—a voice calling that all was lost.

There is an exaggerated impression abroad about the annihilation of the buildings in the burnt district. It is not true, as some graphic writers have related, that the bricks were burnt to ashes and blown into the lake. There are millions upon millions of brick that will do very well to go into the walls again. It is stated that where they were exposed to the greatest heat they shrank and lost weight, and that sometimes the corners crumble from them easily. I do not know how that is, as I did not see any of them weighed or crumble. Then there are ruins that are inexpressibly picturesque. Some of the stone-fronts standing blasted and scathed by the flames, have the appearance of extreme antiquity. Bayard Taylor said of one of these scarred fronts, "It looks like the marble of Grecian temples two thousand years old." The stone roasted to lime, and beaten by the rain, had in three weeks acquired an imposing venerableness, and in this, the newest of the great cities, there seemed to appear the august imprint of the ages. The churches, which, with the breweries, are conspicuous by the towering fragments that attest their former safety proportions, present the most startling effects. Many of the Chicago churches were very beautiful, and in ruins several of them are so remarkable that it is a pity not to preserve them, as they are the most impressive memorials of a memorable event. The roofs are utterly gone, the walls broken, the steeples shattered, upholding tottering pinacles; the great arches through which the congregations walked, shivered in part and fallen in massive fragments upon the stately steps, yet spanning grandly the space between double towers. There is one that is a striking suggestion of Melrose Abbey—seen through the dust, or the mist, or in the moonlight—it has a weird look, and it seems that only the associations of centuries would be appropriate. One misses though, the clinging ivy and the groups of tombs of the Knights and Kings of the chivalric ages. Some tall arches cling together, strangely upheld to a great height in the center of the business quarter, and suggest a section of the Colosseum. The completest destruction is where there was the most use made of iron in building. Field & Leiter's immense dry goods house, supported all around on iron columns, is utterly gone into the cellar, where there is a large display of the massive iron-work, in which there was so much confidence before the hour of trial proved its frailty.

The business men burned out have signs on the sights of their old establishments, telling where they are to be seen. There are thousands of these, and they would be more useful if it were not almost impossible for persons not intimately acquainted with the city as it was, to find the old places. There is an astounding bewilderment. A friend told me he had more than once passed the ruins of his own residence without knowing it. On the West Side, and the South, private residences are appropriated for business purposes, and it is a reminder of peculiar times to see bank and real estate and insurance office signs, painted in black on a rough board, and nailed at a parlor window. I noticed the name of C. H. McCormick, the millionaire manufacturer of reapers, on a board, sticking from the second story window of a modest house; and a stake, driven into a pile of bricks near the court-house, supports a sign that tells where he can be found. On Lake Park there are some hundreds of frames already up, and carpenters are within hammering away at rough counters and shelving, and the merchant princes of other days have their firm names already well displayed, by the aid of marking brushes, over their doors. It would look curious to see the names of our most flourishing Fourth and Pearl street merchants, on shanties of fresh boards on the landing, and in Washington and Lincoln Parks, but such instances of observation are common-place in Chicago.

The Chicago men of affairs are full of courage. They meet each other with uplifted faces and talk resolutely of "beginning again;" of their ability to "do it over again and more too;" of their determination to have "fire-proof houses next time" beyond doubt. They are against stone veneering and iron pillars and braces, and have confidence in honest brick work. They will not build so loftily, and will make room for heavy walls. The Chicago of the future will be a city of bricks, and more sober in character, as well as substantial in construction, than the city of the past.

The faces among Chicago men that were known to me were strongly marked with the excitements and fatigues through which they have passed. Amid the ruins, looking at the laborers removing the debris, were sad faces, and some of those who wear brave countenances before the public, and even jest at their own misfortunes, are badly hurt indeed; and resolute as they may be, will **never** " do it again," though they take up the hard, long task, ever so hopefully. The catastrophe represented in the vast sweep of ruins grows as it is understood, and many a brave life will go out in the work of restoration.

While three-fourths of the business houses of the city were destroyed, but one-fourth of the city, estimated by the number of inhabitants on the ground, was burned. In the streets of the West Side, especially, there is a concentration of business that makes an immense stir. Throngs of hurried, anxious men are on the sidewalks, and omnibuses, drays and wagons crowd the streets. The bridges are inadequate. Whenever one of them is swung aside to admit the passage of a vessel, there is a procession formed on each side, of those in hot haste, and the confusion is dire. The tunnels ring with rapid hoofs incessantly. The manifestations of the excellent and unbroken vitality of the city, and of the unquenchable faith of her people in a future that shall be filled with a splendor surpassing the past, are plain on all sides.

TAKEN BY SURPRISE.

A boarder at the Mallory House, on the west side, who had watched through the night of Saturday with a sick friend, and therefore slept soundly, was rudely awakened at about 4 o'clock Monday morning by a heavy rumbling sound, and shaking of the house, that induced apprehensions in his mind of an earthquake. Opening his eyes, he found his room alight with a red glare that startled him from the bed, and he rushed to a window. He was spell-bound by the hideous night-mare of destruction, and gazed upon it as upon the head of Medusa. Another crashing detonation recalled him to the realities of the occasion, and, hastily dressing, he descended to the office, then filled with anxious, unhoused citizens, made his way to the desk and interrogated the clerk. The reply that Chicago was "two-thirds burnt and no hope for the balance," smote him like a blow from a rapier, for the outlook at that moment appeared to confirm the report, and to reproach him with the gross lapse of duty of having slept through all those long, terrible hours, that threatened the existence of the great city. But now—the resolve was strong and instantaneous—he would do everything in his power to atone for the dereliction.

He describes his feelings at the moment as "reckless," involving a total disregard of personal safety, and a full determination to assist in saving life and property, wherever opportunity might present, without regard to consequences to himself. He made his way across Randolph street bridge, to the South Side, just as the flames had reached their sublimest altitude in Wabash and Michigan Avenues, and supposing his services might be made available in that locality, he was soon on the ground. The scene was of the wildest confusion. From stately mansions people were flying with the extremest alarm—from some, goods and furniture were issuing in great parcels, as they were thrown from doors and windows, pell-mell into the streets, where many caught fire almost as soon as landed, and were consumed,—from some, the valuables were loaded into vehicles and driven rapidly away. Our friend ran into a house, apparently deserted and already blazing on one side, in the hope that he might still save a portion of its contents. The smoke within was thick and strangling, but he pushed forward. Entering a sitting room, he was greeted with the sullen growl of a dog, and was about to retreat, when he descried a woman sitting near the grate, from which a slight blaze flickered, fast asleep in her chair. He shouted at the top of his voice,

"Wake up! wake up! Your house is burning, and you must get out quick to save your life."

"Has the fire really turned this way? Where is my husband? Where are the servants?"

"Is your husband in the house?"

"He went to the fire about midnight"—

"And hasn't returned, of course. I will assist you and then look for the servants; but there is not a moment to spare."

To his great surprise she took a young baby from a cradle standing near, and began leisurely to dress it.

"This won't do at all," said he. "Take the child's clothing on your arm, and dress it when you reach a place of safety. You must go now."

The falling timbers and a great puff of black smoke through the carpet beneath their feet, gave emphasis to his words, and the woman seized the child and some articles of apparel and hastened to the street.

He then, accompanied by the dog, who appeared to comprehend the exigencies of the occasion, ran to the upper stories of the house and examined all the rooms, but found no one. Seeing several articles of value, he concluded to save those which he thought the family would prize most, and gathering as many as he could carry, descended the stairs with the flames playing around him from the burning hall.

Just as he reached the pavement once more, a well-dressed gentleman (?) ran up and accosted him:

"What are you doing, sir?"

"Trying to save something from this burning house."

"Trying to steal something, would be nearer the truth. That is my house, sir. Hand me the articles."

"Come with me to your wife, and she will acquit me of any unworthy design. Had I not entered your house, the chances are that she would not be alive at this moment."

"Hum! Well, let me place these things where they will be safe, and then we'll see what madam has to say."

He took them and disappeared around a corner. Our friend waited, ten, fifteen, twenty minutes, and then went to seek the lady. He walked nearly three squares, and found her seated upon a trunk in the street, with a gentleman attending her.

"Your servants had all left the house. I examined every room, and did not find a living soul; but there were some articles of value which I brought away, and, meeting your husband at the door, delivered them into his hands."

"My husband? Why, this is my husband! He has just found me."

And the other was a confidence man, plying his wonderful vocation. The trick was evident enough, but the real husband was too thankful for the safety of wife and child to regret the loss of anything else, and he expressed gratitude in no measured terms.

There was no time for ceremony, certainly, with those who wished to save life or substance, and our friend was encouraged by the success of the first exploit to continue his exertions. It was quite daylight, but the heavy smoke hanging over city and lake filled all the atmosphere with a gloomy haze that proved extremely dispiriting, especially in combination with the desolation everywhere apparent; but he aroused his energies and returned to the burning houses. A building from which the fire issued in great wreaths was attracting the attention of quite a crowd of men, who were gazing upon it as if in momentary expectation of something to which they attached unusual interest. He made inquiries, and learned that a man was seen rushing in at the door but a few moments previous, and they were looking for his return.

"Perhaps he has smothered."

"He's a dead man if he stays two minutes longer."

"Probably dead already."

"Who'll go with me and find him?" asked our hero.

"I will," replied a little fellow, a mere boy, and, as subsequently ascertained, a boot-black.

"Well, take one of these," (suiting the action to the word by seizing two heavy blankets from a pile of "plunder" near by, in one of which he enveloped himself, and told the little fellow to do the same), "and now come on."

The crowd expostulated, but they did not wait for words. Inside the building they found it much worse than anticipated; the first floor burned through in several places, and the smoke thick and blinding, rendering their progress extremely dangerous.

"We must move quickly if we would do any good and escape with life. Follow me and jump;" and our hero, exerting all his strength, made a tremendous leap through the fire, but the distance was miscalculated, for he alighted upon a section of the charred floor, which gave way like so much paper, and he was precipitated to the cellar beneath, and into a large cistern filled with water. Disengaging himself from the blanket, he managed to get out and drag it after him, but only to find that he was environed by fire on every side, as well as overhead! Fire everywhere! His companion either did not follow or had met with better luck in going "through the flames and beyond," for he was alone, and oppressed by the most terrible loneliness he ever experienced. The roar of the flames was terrific, and soon the walls of the building must fall and bury him in the great tomb of the conflagration. He could see no help for it.

He was kept busy in efforts to avoid the falling embers, and retreated before the advancing flames to another cellar, and still to another, when he came to a door that was securely barred on the opposite side. It resisted all his efforts to open it, and he found himself completely hemmed in by the fire behind, which was following him certainly to his death. There is a great rumbling, a crash, and the ground shakes with the concussion of the falling walls. Within ten feet of where he stands, there is a fearful pile of smoking brick, from which the heat is so intense as to scorch his damp clothing, and the atmosphere is impregnated with a gas that chokes his lungs and checks respiration. Another rumbling and a terrific crash right over his head. He looks up for his doom, and finds a strongly vaulted arch overhead, which resists the concussion—but to what purpose for him? Better be crushed at once than suffer the lingering death of slow combustion. The third crash, and the most fearful, follows quickly—the barred door flies from its hinges—and beyond he sees a basement kitchen almost untouched by the flames, and quite open to his egress, for the rear wall has fallen outward. The flames are playing wildly through the back yard, consuming fences and outbuildings, and the prospect is still poor for his escape. He espies two coal scuttles in the room, one nearly filled with ashes. Scarcely knowing what he did, he emptied a portion of the ashes into the other scuttle, and placing an arm through the handles, made his way to the yard. Here the ground was thickly strewn with the glowing bricks and flaming embers, over which he must pass, or perish. Wrapping the still wet blanket closely about him, he placed a foot in each of the scuttles among the ashes, seizing the handles, and thus uniquely shod, commenced his tiresome journey through the ruins.

This journey, as related to us, involves a longer story, in all its details, than we can find space for, although of absorbing interest. He did not readily find his way out of the place of danger, for obstacles intervened on every side in the shape of burning debris. Where he found openings that seemed to promise relief they led to greater dangers beyond, and finally the awkward mode of locomotion, the stooping and constrained position, the terrible heat and previous fatigue and excitement, overcame him so much that he gave up in despair, and determined to await the issue without further effort to save himself. Bringing the scuttles close together in an open space, he managed to recline upon them in a half sitting posture, and was obtaining a little rest in this way when by some means the blanket around him caught fire, and was so far under way when discovered that he was obliged to cast it from him. Then the heat affected him terribly, and he made another effort for release. Walls were falling in every direction, and now, scarcely a hundred feet from his position, he saw one coming to the ground about which there was little indication of heat. Thither he made his way, and, after reconnoitering the situation, concluded to risk a run to the street without the aid of the scuttles. But he repented it bitterly before the street was gained. The bricks were still very hot, and not only burnt his boots to a crisp, but burnt his stockings completely off, and then took the skin as clean from the flesh as it could be done by the most scientific flaying! As he reached the street he fell fainting upon the pavement, but was promptly removed to a hospital, where for several weeks he was tenderly nursed by kind friends, with the plucky little boot-black as a constant attendant. As we conclude the notes of this incident, he stands at our side, leaning upon his crutches, a cripple for life.

ADVENTURE OF A YOUNG ENGLISHMAN AND HIS ROOM-MATE—A TIMELY RESCUE.

[We have made some slight verbal changes in the following narrative, but none to affect the facts therein detailed].

I went to my room early on Sunday evening, for I was very tired and sleepy, having helped the firemen on Saturday night. John Wilson, a Scotchman, had also been at the scene of the previous night's conflagration, and, being room-mates, we retired about the same time to our room on North-Wells street.

About nine o'clock I was aroused by the fire-bells. John leaped out of bed to look at his card, and said that the alarm was from DeKoven and Clinton streets. We both agreed it was too far to go, particularly as we were quite "played out" with fatigue, and we droped asleep very soon; John, indeed, was snoring five minutes later, and there was this peculiarity about John, that when he was once sound asleep, you might fire off a cannon close to his ear without awaking him.

Sometimes when we sleep external sounds affect us but little if we are very tired, and seem to melt into and become a part of our dreams, so that we cannot tell whether noises within or without the bed-chamber are real, or whether they are only dream sounds. I had not been asleep very long when I began to dream about the last night's fire, and I can remember every particular of my dream as distinctly as the terrible reality that followed it. It seemed to me that the fire-bells kept ringing, ringing, unceasingly; but although I fancied the fire was in the same place, the bells did not strike 248, which was the box from which the alarm was sounded on Saturday night. Then I began to reason in a strange drowsy way, as to what the cause might be, and soon "a change came over the spirit of my dream," and I began to think about the old country, and old times, and the vision of fire melted into one of green fields and sunny villages in far off England.

But the bells in my dream were no fancy. The second alarm had rung, and it was not from box 248, yet the fire had swept at least a fifth part of the city before I woke to hear a tremendous clamor and rush as of a great mob in the streets, and to see the flames leaping and roaring a full hundred feet over the fine buildings across the street.

I called John, but he did not stir. I had to dash water in his face before I could arouse him. When he did awake he rushed to the window, looked out upon the awful fire before him, and pulled his clothes on with such haste that he was ready for flight and had thrown our most valuable clothes into a valise, before I was half dressed.

We were in much greater danger than either of us had imagined. The instant we opened the door, the room was filled with a thick choking smoke and we knew that the back part of the house was on fire. There was but little escape in that direction, at least without being seriously burned, and John shut the door again, remarking that as we were only two stories from the ground we could more easily escape by the window.

We seized the bed-clothes, and tore them up into strips, but while we were so occupied the heat became suffocating; the plaster cracked and dropped from the ceiling, and we knew that in five minutes everything in the room would be reduced to ashes—so you may be sure we worked pretty desperately. Just as John had dragged the heavy bed to the window and fastened the end of our blanket rope to it, I heard a crash of broken glass, and looking out perceived that the window immediately beneath us had yielded to the heat and a thick smoke with clouds of sparks was pouring through the broken panes. "You get down first, Jack," said my friend, throwing the rope out, "I can jump better than you if the rope takes fire." I slid down pretty quick, and landed safe upon the flags below, although the rope was at least eight feet too short. John threw out the valise and was beginning to let himself down, when the flames leabed through the window below and the rope was in flames. I was never so frightened, perhaps, as at that minute, but John saw what had happened, and let go the burning blanket strips at once. He had to drop more than twenty feet, but he fell upon his feet on the pavement without other injury than a few bruises. But the shock made him stagger and fall over the edge of the curbing.

This was all the work of about seven or eight minutes, but in that short space, the fire had made terrible progress. There were great arches of fire stretching across the street beyond Michigan street, only a square and a half from us, and near Water street. At that distance, however, one could only catch a glimpse of a building at intervals, so wholly enveloped were they in sheets of fire. It was nevertheless a spectacles so grandly, awfully beautiful, that could one but look upon it in safety, he could gaze for weeks at the sight. The whole street where we stood was lighted up with a bright glow, which faded into a deep red, almost blood-red, towards Chestnut street, where the flying crowds stood look back upon the fire, and the sea of human faces looked to gastly in that colored glare. Towards the river the glow brightened into white heat, like that of iron in a furnace and when the veil of flame parted; for an instant the walls beyond looked like the brightest gold. Red cinders were flying like red-hot shot carried by a fierce wind, hot with the breath of the fire that almost carried us off our legs upon turning a corner, and which even blew several trees down.

Neilson and I made our way to Chicago Avenue, and turned down to Lasalle street. The flames had spread almost as far and as fast as we had walked. The crowd surged about, pushing, shoving, cursing, shouting, shrieking. John's valise gave him no end of trouble, and taught me to pity those who were carrying larger bundles. At last, completely tired out, he laid it on a doorstep and paused to wipe the sweat from his forehead. At that instant a hand crept round from behind, and the valise disappeared amid the crowd "in less than no time." John rushed frantically into the struggling mob shouting, "stop thief!" and swearing "Lowland" oaths without number, but neither of us ever beheld the valise again, nor did we ever know who had absconded with it.

We were suddenly startled by a piercing cry for help. In a window of the upper story of a lofty building which the flames were rapidly devouring, the figure of a girl appeared, extending her arms to the crowd for aid. Several of us stood beneath the window in a moment. One man in his excitement shouted to her to jump, and a fireman struck him on the mouth. "Do you want her to kill herself, you wild fool? Clear out and keep your infernal mouth shut. Hold on, my girl," he cried, "we'll have a ladder here in a moment," and he dashed through the crowd to fetch one.

But the heat grew terrible around us, like that of an iron furnace, and we felt that before the ladder could be procured the upper story must fall in. One of the men shouted: "Have you got a blanket up there? Throw it down." She seemed stupefied with fear at first, but after a few seconds in answer to our shout of "a blanket, a blanket, a quilt! a carpet! anything!" Throw it down—we'll catch you!"—she disappeared in the interior of the room, as if to fetch it. Clouds of thick smoke commenced to pour from the window, first black, then mingled with sparks, then tinged with a glow of red, which told us that the fire had burst into the chamber. For a minute we thought all was over with the unfortunate girl, but she reappeared with a large bundle of something dark, and threw it to us. It proved to be a heavy carpet, the tacks still clinging to its binding, proving she must have just torn it from the floor. A dozen strong pair of arms extended it immediately, but the cinders and sparks were falling so thickly that it began to smoulder and burn in our very hands. "Jump, my lassie, jump at once," shouted Neilson, "Don't be afraid, we'll catch you." She caught hold of the window-frame and had got one foot upon the window-sill when a piece of the stone caping above, split by the terrible heat, fell and struck her upon the forehead before she could spring, about the same moment the ceiling of the room fell in, and the fire rushed in solid sheets from the window. Luckily, upon being stunned by the blow, she fell forward instead of backward, for in the latter case, nothing could have saved her. We were well braced to receive the shock, and she fell into the carpet. Had we been better prepared, we should have counteracted the whole force of the shock by giving the carpet a strong pull at the proper moment, as we used to do in our school-days, when we amused ourselves with the rough game of blanket-tossing. As it was, however, the shock of a body falling between forty and fifty feet, staggered most of us, and those nearest the sidewalk fell pell-mell one over the other, under the hail of fire. We who stood nearest the wall held the young woman up, however, and John, who was as brawny a Scot as any in the Queen's heavy cavalry, raised her in his arms like a child and insisted on carrying her to a place of safety, although several others volunteered their services for the same purpose. Just then the fireman returned breathless, with two of his associates, carrying a ladder.

"By Jove (he used a stronger phrase, however,) they have her there. Did she jump? Damn it, they had carried the ladder two or three blocks down Pearson street before I could get it. What! Not dead after such a jump as that! Oh, I see, the carpet! eh? Well, I feel better now, for by—"

"Fall back for your lives! Look out!" cried one of the men, whose keen eye had observed that the walls of the tall building were swaying and trembling. In a moment we had rushed to the opposite side, and the upper portion of the great wall tottered and fell in a heap of glowing timbers and stone, which vomited a storm of sparks, hot dust, and crimson cinders as it struck the Nicolson. "Come on! run boys! we're in for it now," shouted John, as he led the way with his precious burden. He stumbled once or twice over fallen timbers, broken furniture, and other debris, but held up bravely, and we were soon at Huron street. Some notion of the rapidity with which the flames traveled may be gathered from the fact, that by the time we had arrived at Elm street, the roofs of the houses at the South-west and North-east corners of Chestnut and Lasalle streets had caught the flame.

We stopped to look at the rescued girl who had not yet come to consciousness. There was a deep cut on the forehead, a very pretty forehead it was, too, half concealed by the fair hair, which fell back in a bright shower over John's shoulder. But a stream of blood was staining the long tresses, and little drops were dripping over John's coat. "The poor lassie!" he cried, "George, lend me something to bind up this ugly cut, the poor thing will bleed to death." I gave him the muffler I wore round my neck; indeed, it was a plaid muffler which Neilson had given me himself, and which now came in useful. He bound up the wound in a barbarously clumsy manner—for John was little gentler than a bear in such matters—and we proceeded on our march, with the fire thundering behind us, and the crowd rushing before us. Then John had his pocket picked, but encumbered as he was, he could do nothing, and bore his loss philosophically. I felt a violent tug at my watch-chain, but it was found of very strong links of silver, in imitation of a chain-cable, and resisted the strain. I turned upon the thief instantly with my revolver cocked, and he disappeared in the crowd at once. If it had not been that I feared to injure some one else, I should certainly have shot the villain that dared to ply his trade under such circumstances.

We did not get beyond the reach of the flying sparks until we had got as far as North avenue, and even there, the sparks fell nearly as thick as ever. John had an otter-skin cap on, which he had brought from Canada with him, and it caught fire from a falling spark. I snatched it off his head, and put out the tiny flame, but I could not get him to put it on again.

The girl recovered when we were traveling towards Fullerton avenue, and struggled a little in John's arms before she remembered what had happened. "Let me down," she said, very gently. "I can walk now." "No, no, my lass," answered John, "you must not walk for another week at least, keep still and don't talk, I'll take care of you." I think she was quite reassured by the expression of John's rough good-humored face, blackened as it was with soot and smoke, for she laid her head on his shoulder and remained as quiet as a sleeping child.

Neilson swore that he was going to walk to his uncle MacPherson's farm, which was at least ten miles off, that same night, and I insisted that he should do nothing of the kind, but rather come with me to a friend's house on the outskirts of the city, a little beyond Clayborne avenue. But John was as obstinate as most Scotchmen are, and I verily believe he would have carried his pretty, but heavy burthen, all the way to MacPherson's, were it not that just then a whip-lash was laid gently across his

DESPERATE ATTEMPT OF A FATHER TO SAVE HIS CHILDREN.

shoulders. He looked up with a frown, which speedily gave place to a broad grin, as he recognized Stephen Phillipson, an old English friend, who was guiding his buggy slowly through the crowd of fugitives. "Hallo, Neilson," he exclaimed, "you're Samaritanizing, are you? Jump up here with your girl. I'll take care of you both. How are you George? Burnt out I suppose. Sorry I have no room in my vehicle for you. Never mind, you just come out to my house as fast as you can walk, and I'll make you comfortable for a night or two, anyhow. By George! this is awful, isn't it? I was near being burnt up myself. Came into the city to see a friend and I only just had time to get the harness on Billy before the stable was burnt up."

And so the good natured Mark Tapley chatted on until we got clear of the crowd, when he touched up the horse, and drove, shouting, "we'll be waiting for you. George, old boy, come on as quick as you can."

Well, this is nearly all I can tell you about the fire, that you have not already heard in the papers. I have only to say that we are getting on as well as before the fire, nearly, only we have removed to St. Louis. But I am afraid I am going to lose my room-mate, for John has been making fierce love to Gertrude Petterson, (the name of his protege,) who turns out to be a Swedish girl from Stockholm.

Yours Affectionately,
GEORGE BURKINSHAW.

P. S.—If you wish to publish this, as you hinted in your last, you must invent a "*nom de plume*."   G. B.

A YOUNG LADY RELATES A ROMANTIC INCIDENT OF HER EXPERIENCE.

DEAR KATE:

*   *   *   *   *   *   *   *

Mary and I heard the bells strike the alarm that night, but on referring to the card, which we always kept hanging over the mantel-piece in our bed-room, we found the fire was a full mile away, and we determined to stay indoors. It was then a little after 9 o'clock, and father had gone over the river to see a relative. Mary opened the window of our room—which was on the third floor, you know—and exclaimed, "Oh Gussie! it must be an awful fire, I can see the light quite plain from here!" I looked out and saw a great red light in the direction of the fire, with great yellow flames leaping up now and then above the roofs of the houses. We liked to go to fires, but the night was cold and stormy, and we thought that by the time we could reach the scene the fire would be well nigh extinguished. So in a little while we went to bed.

It was a very windy night, and the rattling of window frames, and banging of shutters, kept us awake until we heard the general alarm booming over the city. We were so tired and sleepy, having been at a ball the night before, that we did not even get up. Of course we never imagined that we were in the least danger, although we could see that the light of the fire was growing brighter through our windows, and I believe we were asleep in ten minutes from the time the fire bells had stopped ringing.

It must have been between eleven and twelve o'clock, when we were awakened by a tremendous banging at our door, and before we could get up to unfasten the lock, it was burst wide open, and in rushed father with his great coat on and a huge bundle under his arm. "Get up at once, girls," he cried, "if we are not out of the house in two minutes we shall all be burnt up." Just then I heard a curious crackling sound above our heads, the plaster began to break and fall from the ceiling, and the room filled with smoke. Outside we could hear a deep booming roar as of steady continuous thunder. We knew, immediately, that the house was on fire and there was no time to wait. And how terribly careless we girls are about our clothes, we could not lay our hands upon them at the moment, but we would not have had time to put them all on in any case, especially in that stifling smoke which was growing denser every minute. There was an old pair of brother George's trousers, which I had been mending for him, hanging on a hook behind the door, and I pulled them on at once. I caught hold of the first articles in the way of footgear I could lay my hands on, and threw a water-proof cloak over my shoulders, which completed my traveling costume. Mary had only time to throw on a gown loosely, and snatch up a few clothes, when father suddenly seized us both by the arms, and almost flung us outside the door. Just as he had done so the crackling above our heads deepened into crashing roar, the ceiling fell in, and the whole room was blazing in an instant like a furnace. Father hurried us out the back way, through the alley, and we found brother George with the horse and wagon all ready for us. The poor animal was terribly frightened, and prancing in terror, for the sparks were falling on him in a perfect rain of fire, but he became quiet when father spoke to him, and patted him, although he continued to tremble like an aspen leaf. I did not find that I had two left shoes on till we were in the wagon.

As we drove along at almost a gallop we had a plain view of the fire, and a more awful sight cannot be imagined. The flames

THE COURT HOUSE BELL, AFTER IT FELL.

seemed to touch the very sky, and some of them were of the strangest colors—deep, rich crimson and azure; and on one occasion I remember seeing a jet of greenish fire burst through the roof of a great building far to our left. The roar of the fire became so terrible that we could hear nothing else for a time, it seemed to fill one's brain, and we could hardly distinguish what each other said in the tumult of the Hadean hurricane.

It was strange to see the rats fleeing through the burning streets and alleys, and dogs and cats rushing to and fro. Several stray cows were dashing about wildly in their mad teror, and one of them knocked down and ran over a little girl right before us. Father jumped down and picked her up, George holding the reins meanwhile, and found the poor little thing so bruised that she could not walk. We were pretty closely crowded in the little wagon, but I took her upon my lap. She had nothing on her but a thin night dress, and was severely bruised and cut. George took off his coat and wrapped it about her, and I happened to have a handkerchief in the pocket of my cloak with which I bound up an ugly cut upon her poor little arm.

The crowd seemed to be full of thieves, pickpockets, and roughs, of the worst description, who robbed, swore, and fought, even in such a time of danger. Of course the police could do nothing except to club a rascal now and then, and I remember seeing one scoundrel snatch a rich fur cloak from a lady's shoulders and escape with his booty.

We stayed at cousin Phillip's house that night on West Randolph street. At one time, on Monday, we were afraid that the fire would spread even to our temporary refuge, but it came no nearer than Jefferson and Adams streets. Father and George had been lucky enough to save some clothes, but we would have been rather at a loss for wearing apparel, had not cousin Phillip been able to lend us some for the time being. In a few days, however, we received some from our sister Jane in St. Louis, and we soon expect to be comfortable again, as we are about to have a new house built very near the old residence. Our little protege is with us still, and has quite recovered.

       Heartily yours,   Gussie.

P. S—.I have discarded the pants, although they were not so very bad after all. I can testify that they did excellent service while I wore them, and, if in the course of time I ever see occasion to don them again, I shall at least know how the thing is done.

RUNNING THE GAUNTLET OF FLAME—INCIDENTS OF PERSONAL EXPERIENCE.

I went to bed pretty early that Sunday, feeling unaccountably dull and tired—I had a couple of handsomely furnished chambers in the quietest portion of Franklin street, my bed-room being separated from the sitting-room by huge folding doors which I always closed at night. In the sitting-room I always placed a rug near the door for Milo, a gigantic bloodhound of the purest breed, whom I had purchased when a pup from a French planter in Martinique, and is the best and truest friend a man could possess, having saved my life on more than one occasion. Milo scarcely ever barks or bays, he never makes too free by placing his paws on your shoulders and licking your face—he is what I might call a philosophically phlegmatic dog, never making a noise without good reason.

My landlord had gone over the river with his wife and daughter to visit his brother who lived on the West-side. And thus with no company but Milo, I went to bed, Milo lying down as usual outside the door.

I did not fall asleep for nearly an hour after getting into bed, but lay awake listening to the moaning and shrieking of the wind about the tall chimney—its weird whistling through chinks, keyholes, and the ghostly noise it made by shaking the window-frames and swinging the creaking shutters. I began to think of the strange theory that wind was in itself a living intelligent essence, and that there might be a vital principal controlling its movements far more subtle than oxygen or nitrogen. And as I listened to its strange whisperings and moanings, I fell into a doze, dreaming that the wind had found a tongue and was talking very strange things through the keyhole. Then I dreamed that Ethel (we were engaged) was sitting by the fire in the parlor, with a little bell in her hand, and a strange troubled look on her face. She called Milo, and tried to tie the bell about his neck with a black ribbon, and after much trouble she got it on. Then I thought that the bell began to ring, although Milo did not move, the sound being sweet and soft at first as though faintly distant—then to grow clearer, and deeper, and louder, swelling in volume until the walls of the house thrilled in unison with its thunder-vibrating tones. Then Milo looked up in Ethel's face as if wondering, and Ethel patted his neck with an anxious face, and then the tones of the bell seemed to change into rushing thunder, and I awoke with a short and strange sense of fear—which increased when I really heard the deep sound of the fire bells, rolling out their deep summons on the night air. I sat up instantly, bewildered for the moment, and then I heard Milo give one long deep bay and throw himself against the folding doors. I leaped up and opened them to find the room filled with the lurid light of a vast conflagration several blocks away Northward. Vast serpents of flames reared their quivering tongues upward as though to lick the stars, a fiery rain of crimson sparks was being carried far over the surrounding buildings by the fierce wind which wrestled horribly with the pythons of fire that were enveloping the buildings before me in their glowing sinuous folds. The streets were filled with a hurrying, struggling, panic-stricken crowd, and above the muffled thunder of myriad feet, the cries and exclamations of the fugitives, and the shrill shriek of the well-nigh useless fire-engines—above all boomed the roar of the advancing sea of flames, far more awful than the thunder of the Atlantic wave tempest upon the rocky shore.

That there was not an instant to be lost I could see at once —building after building sinking in the fiery waves even as I looked on. Dressing myself with all possible haste and securing the few valuable trinkets that lay within reach. I stood up on the threshold and cast a lingering glance upon the richly furnished chambers which I had decorated in the style that German students love. To save even my portmanteau would be impossible—my library, furniture, clothes, pictures, silver-mounted hookahs, and meerschaums—what could I save? I looked again at the towering, quivering wall of flame now only about five hundred yards distant, and taking the only article of value I had yet time to seize—a silver-mounted Smith & Wesson's revolver, rushed down the stairs and gained the street, Milo giving a deep rolling bay of relief.

We were not an instant too soon. Scarcely had we advanced half a block when a vast tongue of flame rose to an enormous height and then seemed suddenly to hurl itself forward like a stream of yellow lightning, piercing the brick walls of the house we had left as though it had been smitten by a thunder bolt. In about five minutes, as near as I can calculate, the whole structure tottered and crumbled into the Gehenna of flame that surged around it.

Of course, Ethel Summerfield was my first thought as I fled over the wooden pavements with the furious flames in rapid pursuit, and the wind showering a hail of sparks upon me and Milo. Ethel surely must be out of danger, I thought, yet the memory of that dream filled me with a ghastly fear as I hurried toward the residence of the Summerfields, on Wabash avenue. I am not superstitious—in fact I am rather skeptical, but the strongest minds are liable to be impressed by trivial incidents at such times, and I felt unusually anxious. I have often thought since that there is some truth in the beautiful theory of magnetic sympathy, the strange odic telegraph of thought, by which the mind in trouble calls for aid to the distant one it loves best. Thoughts like these flitted through my excited brain with the rapidity of lightning as I rushed over the smooth pavement, with Milo by my side.

Everywhere I beheld dense crowds of fugitives rushing towards the lake with bundles, furniture piled upon little vehicles, mattrasses, valises every species of household goods—while the sidewalks were frequently piled up with valuables, the owners of which had entertained the vain hope of being able to hire a vehicle in which to convey them away, and which they were finally compelled to abandon to the all-calcining flames which rapidly swept onward in a gigantic crescent, like an organized host of fiery spirits, while the white-faced moon looked down over all from a canopy of clouds crimson-fringed in the light of the conflagration, and seemed to marshal the towering spectres of flame.

A few moments later I arrived at Wabash Avenue. The fire had not yet reached any of its splendid marble palaces, although its fiery serpent arms went quivering over the dark housetops of yet uninjured blocks which lay between me and that ocean of scorching flame, standing out in ebony-black relief against the blinding brightness. I almost fancied that the griffin-tongued flames rose higher over the distant roofs and bent over the darkness as though to watch me with their awful glare.

Had Ethel's father returned from Boston whither he had gone for a few days on some commercial business, or had she a better protector than a few servants of questionable integrity, I should have felt less anxious as I stood beneath the gloomy marble portico, and rang the silver-toned door-bell as it had probably never been rung before. To my great relief I heard a sound as of little feet pattering down the great staircase and the next moment Ethel was in my arms.

"O, George! I have been so frightened at the great fire; papa has not come back, and the servant's left the house two hours ago and have not returned." "My God! did they not tell you, Ethel? Did you not know the danger you are in? In twenty minutes this house will be on fire. Is Mesty in the stable?"

"Yes."

Mesty (short for Mephistopheles) is the name of the splendid black horse who saved us that night.

"Ethel, there is not an instant to spare. Run up stairs at once and get whatever warm clothes you can lay hands on while I harness Mesty. Quick, and wait for me at the door. Good heavens!" I exclaimed, as a giant tongue of fire shot toward us from a distant building and seized upon a house but a few hundred yards away, "it will be a close race between life and death."

Ethel was as brave and noble a little woman as man ever **loved** She did not become faint or dizzy, or ask useless questions—although the news of her imminent danger, of which she had had but a faint suspicion, and must have been a voilent shock to any nerves—but darted off at once, while I rushed to the stable-door. The house being situated in that part of Wabash Avenue from whence we could not have obtained a good view of the terribly rapid advance of the fire in its earlier stages. Ethel's ignorance of her situation could be accounted for—especially as the servants had been to much occupied with their own safety when the news was brought to them by a fugative from Van Buren street, to attend properly to the rescue of their employer's daughter. I afterwards learned that they had gone to Ethel's room, and not finding her there, fled, without further search, calling on her to save herself at once, a summons which she never heard. Upon finding herself alone, she concluded that the servants had merely gone to look at the fire, whose real extent and fury she knew nothing of—certainly a strange proceeding on their part to leave the house unguarded—and would shortly return.

I had to pass through an alley at the rear of the garden to reach the stable. The crimson sparks were falling in vast showers, intermingled with fragments of blazing shingles, and timbers, borne towards me in a slanting, fiery rain, by the fierce wind which blew upon me, heated by its wrestle with the rushing fire, hotter than the breath of the red simoon. And even as I reached the door of Mesty's stable a burning brand lighted upon the roof, and the next instant the yellow serpent flames were dancing a demon dance among the dry shingles and inflamable roofing. No coachman was to be seen, and the great door was securely fastened with a stout wooden bar, that would defy human strength to break it. The side door was, however, fastened only by a lock, the bolts being rarely drawn. This I blew open with my pistol, and Milo and I rushed in together, just as the blazing hay began to fall from the loft. I quickly unfastened the halter, Mesty whinneying with joy, while he trembled in every limb as I hitched him to the light buggy and flung the great doors open, and scarcely had I leaped into the seat, when the flimsy buildings on both sides of the alley burst into flames. Mesty, however, shot through uninjured, save where the blazing hay had fallen on his sleek black skin, and almost leaped to the door of the house, where Ethel stood awaiting, well wrapped in her grey cloak; and as she sprang into the seat beside me, a bright flame ran like lightning along the cornices, and we knew that the house was beyond hope.

Desirous of gaining the prairie as soon as possible I directed our course to the southwest, intending to gain some distance by pursuing the diagonal course of Blue Island Avenue, provided we were fortunate enough to reach it. Mesty shot through Madison street and turned the corner of La Salle, like a race-horse, Milo running ahead with his long, untiring gallop. It was not until we were rushing along the white pavement that we saw the terrible danger before us. The houses upon the left side were a mass of burning timbers and glowing brick, and upon the right the flames would soon gain a foothold. Far away beyond Jackson street the flames were stretching their fiery arms across La Salle, barring our advance with an impassable rampart of the destructive element. Mesty stopped, rearing in terror. There was no retreat. The fire was behind us, and it were madness to approach the roaring hell of flame in the distance. Ethel clung closer to me, shuddering as we watched towering steeples and giant domes sink like fantastically-shaped fragments of coal into the terrible furnace beyond.

But Jackson street stretched away to the right and left, only a few hundred feet ahead. If we turned up to the right two or three squares, and then made a turn to the left, a hard gallop might save us. I patted Mesty's coal-black flank and spoke to him coaxingly as we turned the corner and sped along Jackson street. As we passed the first square, we beheld the red flames leaping across the streets far away to the right and left; and thus the fire glared upon us at every street opening in the vast blocks until we came to Canal street, stretching widely to right and left of us,—the hurricane of flame came roaring up on the left, but away to the right the buildings remained intact, and Mesty shot down it like the goblin steed of the Wild Huntsman in the German legend. And now it was truly a run for life or death,—a fierce conflagration on three sides of us, advancing with the terrible swiftness of a prairie fire, and the remorseless flames rushing to cut off our only chance of escape in front. The voice of the fire bells had been drowned in the fiery waves, and the terrible earth-shaking roar of the flame-tempest thundered nearer and nearer, drowning all other sounds, while the blood-red glow before us brightened into flame on the western side. In another instant the many-tongued fire was licking up the walls of the houses on our right, and ahead it was stretching its long arms across the splendid thoroughfare, and should it seize upon the opposite side ere we could pass, escape was impossible. We were scarce a hundred yards from the fire, and its hot breath, spark-laden, flew in showers about us. "Now, Mesty, your best," I cried, urging him forward with a stroke of the whip. He answered by laying himself out like a grey-hound, and dashing through that fiery blockade with almost the rapidity of the bright tongues of flame. And as we shot beneath the arch of fire, with bent heads and hard-held breath, the tower of a church just before us tottered in the folds of the anaconda flames, and scarcely had we passed when it hurled a mountain pile of ruins upon the spot touched by our wheels but an instant before. We had thus passed the great belt of fire, and I therefore pulled Mesty down to an honest trot, which was now sufficient to enable us to keep in advance of the whirlwind of flame.

Neither of us spoke verbally, but we drew a long breath as we heard the crackling roar grow fainter behind, and Ethel rested her head on my shoulder weary with the terror of that awful ride: we must have felt as Perseus did when persued by the Gorgons over sea and land, and the thunder of the pursuing element sounded not less fearful than the roar of the brazen wings of the mythical fiends.

But whoever gazes upon such a conflagration must feel a sentiment of superstitious awe akin to that of the Oriental fire-worshippers, and the ghastly fancy that there may be some truth in the Gheber's creed—that fire is a living intelligent being, invariably grows upon the mind as one follows the merry dance of the flames over roof and tower, along cornice and gable—or its serpentine embrace of the tall steeple from whose summit it streams in tresses of fire—or its triumphant roaring rush, through every window of the huge building once deemed fire-proof—or the weird manner in which it bends and stretches its fiery neck over great distances to lick up dwellings, one would fancy beyond its reach. And when it fails to leap the gap which separates it from what it seeks to devour, how angrily it will often recoil, only to rear itself upward and backward, as though to gather all its subtle python strength for another giant leap of a few hundred feet. Surely at such a sight we have all felt a horrible suspicion that there might be a terrible truth in Poe's personification of fire in the "Bells." And as the eerie verse comes to our mind, we feel that the strange thoughts therein are but the utterance of a wild fancy that has haunted many a brain.

> Hear the loud alarm bells,
> Brazen bells,
> What a tale of terror their turbulency tells,
> Too much horrified to speak,
> They can only shriek, shriek,
> Out of tune.
>
> In a clamorous appealing to the mercy of the fire,
> In a mad expostulation with the deaf and frantic fire,
> Leaping higher, higher, higher,
> With a desperate desire,
> And a resolute endeavor,
> Now, now to sit, or never,
> By the side of the pale faced moon.

The sublimely terrific grandeur of such a spectacle of lightning flames as pierced the black vault of the North-western heavens on that awful night, could perhaps be properly described but by one pen—that of the author of "The Last Days of Pompeii." The only scene that could surpass the horror of this stupendous conflagration would be the destruction of a city by a mighty volcanic eruption.

Marble fronts, huge structures of iron and brick, temples of hewn stone seemed to crumble, into sand in that glowing flame hotter than the famed seven-times-heated furnace of Nebuchadnezzar. Church spires vanished in awful light to give place to pinnacles of flame; vast stone slabs were calcined or split as though by lightning The huge dome of the court-house long towered darkly against the fiery horizon, like the vast helmet of some genius of fire in Oriental story; yet at length it, too, bore its garland of serpent flame and sank in a hell of fire-billows which hurled their red spray to the very clouds. What fireproof building could withstand a heat in which iron became as wax?—the very pyramids of Egypt could scarcely be relied on as places of safety if exposed to such a flame.

How we drove over the river before the "Red Death" in our rear, which rushed after our flying wheels, had devoured all the bridges in its hungry rage, I can scarcely tell. It was all like a terrible nightmare, of which I can recollect little but the wild tumult of panic-stricken crowds before and the roar of flames behind, the rush of feet followed by the mad rush of the demon fire—oaths and curses mingled with prayers and sobs, shrieks of hideous fear and the wild laughter of women whom horror had converted into maniacs—the cries of helpless children and tender girls, flying, half nude, from death—the neighing of horses, maddened with fear, and the roaring of terrified oxen—the mad shouts of reckless men crazy with drink, and the groans of fugitives knocked down and trampled upon in the torrent throng of struggling men, women, children, horses and vehicles, that poured along the ash-strewn pavements and bridges under the storm of fire-flakes. Many a fair girl lost her wealth of beautiful hair, many rich dresses and poor ones as well, were riddled with pellets of flame that terrible night. It seems a miracle that the loss of life by fire was not at least ten times greater.

Barrels of explosive oil piled in storehouses burst like shells and their fiercely blazing contents ran streaming along the gutters. Huge distilleries burnt fiercely, and the sheets of azure-tinged flame that rushed through windows and doors to wrestle with the less subtle tongues of yellow fire, showed that alcohol was feeding the conflagration. But when the fire had leaped the river in pursuit of its victims, and had licked the huge gasometer with its flickering tongue, then as the earth seemed to vomit forth a vast sheet of lightning toward heaven, and miles of blazing edifices trembled to their heated foundations at the concussion of that dull, awful thunder, it seemed as though the horrors of the vast catastrophe had culminated

The fire engines had long given their last despairing shriek ere we found ourselves in safety. The water-works buildings had crumbled in upon and paralyzed the giant engines that had supplied the water-veins of the great city now in flames. Men who had tried to save their houses toiled with all the vigor which human bone and brawn and muscle can endure, sweating at every pore in an atmosphere of stifling heat, and suffering a thirst which they could find no water to alleviate, swallowed glass after glass of the strong liquor that stupified them into forgetfulness of the approach of the remorseless element, and fell intoxicated upon the scorching pavement to be withered to little mounds of black ashes by the victorious all-devouring demon of flame.

Near Jefferson street we missed Milo, and paused an instant to look after him. We had seen him dart safely through the fiery gauntlet far ahead of us, yet shortly after he had dropped behind and we had not perceived him since. I uttered the well-known cry, and above the roar and crash of the approaching flames and the muttering thunder of the flying crowds, I heard the bell-like voice of the giant hound roll in answering diapason. While wondering what could have detained our faithful friend so long, Milo appeared toiling after us with a great bundle of something partly on his neck—partly in his mouth. He bayed again as soon as he beheld us, but ran wearily as though tired out. It is needless to say that I immediately hastened to relieve him of his burthen, when I found to my astonishment that said burthen was—a little girl! Her little arms were clasped around his great neck, and she lay partly upon the dog's great shoulders, he retaining hold of a fragment of her dress, as though fearful of losing his precious freight. The noble dog must have carried the child at least a mile without our knowledge, but our carelessness in his regard was chiefly owing to our knowledge of his wonderful powers of speed and endurance with his calm courage, wonderful even in a dog of his splendid breed. I gave the little girl, half dead with fright and exhaustion, into Ethel's care, and making Milo spring in and lie down at my feet, I shook the reins and Mesty trotted on bravely. I patted and petted the noble dog, tokens of affection which he only received with a wag of the tail and an upward glance from his great dark eyes, as much as to say: "It's nothing, I have only done my duty—"

Milo was never violently demonstrative in affection or gratitude. As soon as our little charge recovered sufficiently to speak, she threw her arms around Ethel's neck with a cry of joy and kissed her. "Why, George," exclaimed Ethel, "it is little Mary Williams," and I looked round at the child's face to recognize the golden-haired blue-eyed little daughter of Fred. Williams, our mutual friend and neighbor.

Little Mary told us her story, as soon as she was able to speak between her sobs of terror. It appeared that Fred and his wife had been obliged to leave their house and fly with such haste that they had not even time to take their clothes with them, but were compelled to hurry along in the throng of fugitives, Mrs. Williams taking little Mary in her arms. In a sudden rush of the crowd mother and child fell, and were separated by the panic-stricken crush of fugitives. The little timid girl was soon left far behind the fleeing crowd. She ran on and on, while the flames thundered behind, with a sound like the continuous roar of unearthly artillery, until exhausted with terror and weariness, she sank down upon the pavement which smoked in the breath of the fierce heat. The next thing she remembered was the touch of Milo's cold muzzle against her cheek, and the deep bay of the hound calling for help. She knew the great hound well, and put her little arms around her great neck. We never heard Milo's summons for aid in our blind anxiety to save ourselves, but the brave dog seized the helpless little child by its dress, and having encouraged her to get upon its back, galloped after us just as the fiery breath of the vast fire began to singe the hair on his tawny skin. I always looked upon my pet almost as a human friend, and, indeed, he has since been doubly dear to me.

Ethel tried to soothe the little sufferer, assuring her that papa and mamma were quite safe, and that she would soon see them again, till the poor little child sobbed herself to sleep in Ethel's lap.

Not knowing but that the whole of the West-side as yet but partly injured might shortly be swallowed up in flame. I deemed it best to drive to the prairie at once rather than seek for any temporary shelter. The vast elevator on the river behind us burst into a tempest of flame as we drove slowly through the flying torrent of vehicles and human beings that surged through the streets glowing crimson in the awful glare. The burning elevator was truly a grandly awful sight standing like a shadowy Typhon in the storm of fire, and vomiting a column of smoke, tongues of flame, and clouds of crimson sparks to the glowing skies. Even situated as we were then, we found the atmosphere almost suffocationg with smoke and heat, until it seemed that the very air had caught the fire and was burning behind us.

Mothers were calling for their children, children for their fathers, husbands for their wives, and lovers for their sweethearts —all separated from one another on that terrible race for life or death. Delicate women and children were, in many instances, walking barefoot along the crowded streets with but the scantiest clothing on their limbs, and I particularly remember noticing a very pretty young girl, who must have had barely time to leave her bed ere the room took fire, as she was clad in nothing but her night clothes and a thin shawl. I felt relieved when I saw a good-hearted policeman, who was escorting his wife and children to a place of safety, rap his great warm coat around her shivering limbs and take her under his special protection.

Women and men were conveying great bundles away in wheelbarrows; their bundles would get knocked off every now and then by some rough passer by. A few had been lucky enough to save their stores, but the greater number had barely time to save more than a bed or a quantity of clothes, bundled roughly together, and tied up in a huge parcel.

Daylight had not yet broken when we drove out on the prairie, over which the vast fantastic shadows of the awful fire lengthened and contracted weirdly in the lurid light which gleamed far over the level plain, and tinged the crests of the ripples on the troubled lake with a ruby glow. I intended to drive Ethel at once to Evanston, where she had many wealthy friends, and where I had myself purchased a little dwelling for our future home.

But seeing the prairie crowded with shivering groups of fugitives I though it would be as well to look about us and endeavor to find Mr. or Mrs. Williams, that they might feel at rest about their little girl. I felt certain that Milo could assist us in this, knowing that he would find our friends if in the crowd at all. So I drove Mesty slowly among the groups of homeless fugitives, and motioning to Milo to jump out, I gave the well-known signal,

WEDDING AMID THE RUINS. A ROMANTIC INCIDENT FOLLOWING THE FIRE.

and he started off at once as if perfectly aware of what I wanted him to do.

Soon after I heard Milo's bark, and as I turned round, Fred Williams and his wife came up pale and weary. To describe their delight on finding little Mary safe, or the manner in which Milo was petted and hugged would weary the reader. I proposed to take the child to Evanston with us that night, but as they were going to Calumet almost immediately in a friend's carriage, Ethel resigned her charge to them.

Then as we drove towards Evanston we cast many a look behind at the flames which roared to heaven, until the lurid light grew into a fainter red in the distance, and the grey dawn broke over the scene of devastation. And the giant pillar of smoke mingled itself with the clouds behind us as Mesty's iron-shod hoofs rang musically over the pavement of Evanston.

I soon placed Ethel in the care of her relations, and drove Mesty down to my new house in the suburbs.

Old Mary Delany, to whom I had given the charge of things in my absence, threw open the door as I checked Mesty and leaped to the gate.

She was delighted to see me safe, and was terribly frightened at the account of our narrow escape. I put Mesty in the new stable, curried and combed, and washed his graceful black limbs, and having procured some corn and oats, and given him a good meal, I went into the house where Mary had a good hot breakfast waiting for me, which I did full justice to, while I detailed to her the particulars of our race through the burning city.

Neither Ethel's father nor I had lost seriously by the fire, his real estate property being situated in the suburbs which the flames had spared. What city property we had lost was fully insured—and unless the companies should fail, the catastrophe would finally only occasion us a temporary inconvenience. Two days after the conflagration he met his daughter, and the meeting was—what every such meeting ought to be.

Ethel's father determined that the marriage should come off next Sunday as had been intended—since Ethel would not permit him to send East for any wedding gifts. So we had a quiet little wedding in Evanston, unattended save by a few old friends, among whom were Fred. Williams with his wife, and little Mary who had quite recovered her health and spirits. We had no white robes, or orange blossoms, or jewelry, or fashion, or gorgeous dinner **party—but** Ethel looked as pretty in her calico dress as she **ever did** when famous as a drawing room belle at the parties in ——— Avenue—and what was **very shocking, Ethel** allowed two large burned holes **to remain** unmended in said **dress —one on** the sleeve and one **on** the shoulder—asserting **that** they were mementoes of the great fire, and that she would **not** permit them to be mended on any consideration.

COMMENCEMENT OF THE REBUILDING OF CHICAGO.

THE FIRE MARSHAL'S GRAPHIC STORY OF THE GREAT FIRE.

STARTLING INCIDENTS FORCIBLY DETAILED.

A reporter for the daily press called upon the Fire Marshal for his version of certain matters connected with the fire, and obtained, in a few pointed words, the best history of some of the most startling events yet given to the public. We are indebted to the Chicago Evening *Mail* for the following graphic "interview" which will be found intensely interesting, and more exciting than any other account occupying double the amount of space:

Reporter.—Some of our exchanges have hinted that members of the Fire Department were drunk during the fire, and I have called on you, as one who had the best opportunity of knowing, to have the facts in the case.

Marshal.—Well, sir, I don't know how it was elsewhere, but I did not see a drunken fireman that night.

Reporter.—What is the character of the firemen in this respect?

Marshal.—They are a tolerable steady set when on duty.

Reporter.—Who appoints them?

Marshal.—The Board of Police. I have not had the opportunity of choosing a single one of my men.

Reporter.—What may have given rise to the report of drunkenness?

Marshal.—I don't know exactly, but I did see a drunken bummer with a fireman's hat on, and I took it away from him. He begged me to let him keep it, but I refused to. I took it to the engineer of No 6 and told him to take care of it, and it wasn't long before I saw another fireman's hat walking off with a drunken fellow under it, and I took it away from him also. It may have been that others saw these two thieves and swore that the firemen were drunk.

Reporter.—Very likely; but these witnesses say they saw the firemen working at the engines, and that they were staggering.

Marshal.—But bless your soul (and here the Marshal got interesting, not to say excited, and raised up on his elbow and threatened the reporter's nose with his finger) the heat was awful; 'twas like hell, and the firemen's eyes were red with the dust and fire, so that many of them were most blind. The hair was scorched off their faces, and they stuck to their machines like bull dogs, and worked them till they couldn't stand it any longer. Yes, sir, and they did stagger, for they were clean beat, and many of them, had to go home for the exhaustion from the heat. They were tired, too, from the fire of the night before, and then to give the same men such a long pull again, why, an iron man couldn't have stood it.

Reporter.—I hear the firemen were demoralized.

Marshal.—Well, now, it is pretty hard work for flesh and nerves to gain a victory, and then have to go to work again, and again, and again, and fight it all over. But that is just what the men did. And after they heard the waterworks were burned down they didn't give up; and they never quit working till all the water in the reservoirs and mains was used up. I don't think that was being demoralized; not much.

Reporter.—How was it that they got the victory? It looks to me as if it was a defeat worse than Waterloo.

Marshal.—'Twas water low, that was what hindered us from saving a large part of the North Division. But I tell you we got the fire under; and if it hadn't been for that awful gale, we would have been all right.

When I got down to the fire Sunday night, I got the engines all around it, and had hemmed it in so that it wouldn't have lived very much longer, when one of the men came and said, there is a church on fire north of us; and, sure enough, there was a church steeple all in a blaze two squares off, so I sent down an engine and pretty soon got two more to work on it, and had saved the long line of cottages just east of it, and the drug store across the road, and though the heat was awful, we had got it right under our thumb, when some one told us that the fire had caught still farther north. So I went down and there was the match factory just blazing, and the brick factory was smoking, and Bateham's shingle mills' yard was covered with shavings and cinders and flakes and flashing boards, just raining down on it so that it was on fire in more than a dozen places at once, and just beyond was the hardwood lumber yard, and everything dry as a bone, and as greedy to burn as gun-powder.

I hadn't more than got this surrounded when the Canal street people had kindled a new fire right in the middle of the street, though they didn't mean to, for they had piled up beds and bedding and furniture in the street, and it took fire and then it went away like feathers, for the wind would take up a blazing mattrass and fling it against a house, and that house went right down before you could get there. But I was just thinking that we would run the fire into the burnt district and stop it there, when they told me the fire was on the South Side. So I told the Fred Gund to get out of that right away, as the fire was coming awful heavy on her, and went across to Conley's Patch. The fire had then got well started, in two small buildings south of the Armory, and it just tore up Wells street, under those houses set on posts, and sidewalks raised up from the streets. Then I saw we should have heavy work before us.

Vandercook wanted some powder, but I told him we had none, and he went off to get some.

I had just got two engines to work when Jack said: "My God, she's ahead of us." So we went down, and you remember that carpenter shop behind the Oriental building and them low wooden sheds? Well, sir, they were blazing. I ordered up the Chicago and broke out the glass in the lower front window (that's where I got my hand hurt, you see,) and took the hose right through the basement, but the flames drove us out, and it wasn't long before the Oriental Hall was just rolling in flames. Why, if that building had iron shutters on her she wouldn't have burned; but the wind was fearful now. I saw a blazing board go right through the back window of a building in the block facing north on Washington, and pretty soon it was blazing fearful.

BLOWING UP.

Vandercook then came with the powder, and put it in the basement of the Union Bank building, but it just puffed and never jarred the block a bit, and before they could get ready to give her another lift they could not live inside of her. You see I thought we could save Sheridan's headquarters if we could only blow down the block across the street, but it was too late. Just then the Court House took fire, and I sent an engine to the Sherman House, hoping to save that, for I thought that the tower of the Court House would fall inside, and with the wide open space we should have some chance left yet. But the wind was just tremendous. I saw it blow a man against the lamp-post at the Pittsburgh and Fort Wayne ticket office, across the street from the Sherman House, and the post and the man came down together. A. H. Miller's store caught fire in six places from the awnings rolled up, and they served as pockets for the fire to lodge in. Then the old Tribune building got on fire, but I hoped yet to save the Sherman, when I found that those old wooden buildings on the south side of Lake street, and the sheds just south of them were just roaring with flame. Why the fire just roared like a lion, and I saw the Sherman House was gone up. Then I thought of my family in Thompson & Templeton's block, and I found that my wife had got all ready to go; but before we could get out anything but the piano and one chair, the house was too hot to hold us.

Just then some one said the Water Works were on fire. R. B. Crane said he didn't believe it. So he drove up with a horse and buggy, and he says before he got there the flames were coming out of all the windows. It caught from some cinders from the Court House or the Board of Trade. (They say cinders were on the crib, but I don't believe that, interrupted the reporter). Yes, sir, they were, and if you go out there you will see the marks on the roof, and it was life or death with the keeper and his wife, and they pumped water and put out the sparks, or the crib and they too would have gone, and perhaps you won't believe it, but a man was plowing up at Evanston, and that's 10 or 12 miles, and he saw sparks falling all around him; oh, you have no idea how the wind blew that night, and then there was something, I think, I don't know, I shouldn't like exactly to say it, but there must have been fire below ground as well as in the wind overhead. Two strangers came to me the next day and said they were strangers from the East stopping at the Sherman House, and when they saw that was going they went to the next street, and while standing there they saw a blue flame coming up through the iron gratings at the corner, and on looking in saw the whole basement on fire, and not a spark in the rest of the building. You saw at the corner of Wells and Randolph the road hove up; well, I followed that down to the gas-works, and it was raised up in half a dozen places; that was where the gas took fire and burst in the sewers. When the gas-works took fire, they let off the gas into the sewers, and the enormous gasometer fell down to the ground; and I think perhaps the buildings were filled with gas from the sewers and private drains, and took fire inside as well as from the roof overhead. People seemed stupified and crazed, and instead of putting out the sparks on their roofs, just let them burn, and the wind would take up pieces of blazing felt as big as half a sheet, and carry it up to a wooden cornice, and then that building was gone. And I didn't know but Allen was helping us on the West Side, when he and ten or twelve more were cut off, and they made up their mind they would have to swim for life. Allen had just stripped to his shirt and drawers when a tug and two vessels came along and took them aboard; and while they held up long enough for that the masts and rigging of the boats took fire. The tug cast them off below Van Buren street bridge and put Allen and his crowd ashore. Here Allen saw a fire on Quincy street, and says that if the houses had been covered with kerosene they could not have burned so fast while he was going only two squares. So, with everything making against us, no wonder we couldn't get ahead.

Reporter.—But had you engines enough?

Marshall.—All the engines ever made couldn't stop her at the Oriental Building. She kept a jumping over our heads all the time so we couldn't get ahead. We had only fifteen engines in all. Two were at the repair shop, and only one engine was burned, for we saved all of the engines that were being repaired.

Boston has 21 engines, but she hasn't half the territory; and look at her buildings. New York has twice as many as we, com-

WORKMEN HAULING SAFES FROM THE RUINS.

OPENING BANK VAULTS, CORNER LAKE AND DEARBORN STREETS.

pared with her size. I wanted the Board to let me have six floating engines last year, but they wouldn't, and if we'd had them the night of the fire we could have saved the elevators, for the fire crowded us so that we couldn't work but a mighty little while till we had to move. One of our engines didn't have time to unscrew her coupling, so they took an axe and broke down the hydrant and took it along with them, and even then the hair was singed off the horses.

This account reads like the veriest romance, and yet there is no question of its correctness, for the Marshal is not only a man of known integrity, but his account is authenticated from the mouths of scores of witnesses, equally reliable and wholly disinterested.

How Valuable Records Were Saved.

Scarcely less exciting than the foregoing, is the account given by Mr. John G. Shortall, of the manner in which he saved his numerous abstracts and indices of real estate transactions, which, as the records of Cook County were destroyed, are invaluable as evidences of title to Chicago property. Mr. S. had returned from church to his residence, in the Southern part of the city, but, from some unaccountable impulse, went down to the fire and watched it from 10 to 12 o'clock, when he began to fear that his office, in Larmon block, might be in danger. From this point we give the account in his words:

"On reaching the office, I found great danger existing from the awnings, which were outside the building, the embers dropping down very thickly on the roofs of the buildings, and on the front, and signs, and awnings. I ran up stairs, got into the office and tried to cut away the awnings in front of our building, and that of the building adjoining; but, owing to the absence of anything adequate, I had to give that up, and simply press them up close to the wall, that the embers might drop off them, and not be caught in them. Even then I scarcely believed it possible that the Larmon Block could take fire, and I requested the men in the upper portion of the building, with buckets of water, to put out any embers that might fall there and endanger the building. In another half hour I felt more apprehensive, and went in the street to find an express wagon. This must have been an hour and a half before the building actually burned. I stopped, probably fifteen different trucks and express wagons, offering them any pay to work for me in saving the books. Seven of them at least, I engaged, one after another, they faithfully promising me that they would come back when they had carried the load and done the work in which they were engaged, but no one came back. At this juncture I met my friend Mr. Nye, who was looking out, as I was, for the danger. I told him that I needed him, and he answered me promptly that he was at my service. We both watched some time longer for express wagons, but could find none. At last, when the Court House cupola took fire, I told my friend that we must have an express wagon within the next five minutes or we were utterly lost. He stood on Clark street and I on Washington street, determined to take the first expressman we could find. The first one happened to come along on his side. He seized the reins with one hand, and, taking a revolver from his pocket with the other, "persuaded" the expressman to haul up to the sidewalk, notwithstanding his cursing and swearing. When I came back from my unsuccessful watch I found the expressman there, and my friend, handing the lines and revolver to me, went up stairs to help our employes, who were then in the office, to carry down the volumes. We got round with the wagon to Washington street entrance, and, after filling the wagon, found that we had but about one quarter of our property in it.

Just at that critical moment a two-horse truck was driven up to where I was superintending the packing of the books, and my friend, Joe Stockton, whose face was so covered with smut and dust that I did not recognize him until he spoke, turned over the truck and driver to me, with the remark, "I think, John, this is just the thing you want." I never felt so relieved or so thankful as I did at his appearance with that substantial aid at that moment. We unpacked our impressed expressman immediately and set him adrift with $5 in his pocket for his five minutes' work, and commenced to pile our property on friend Stockton's truck. Meanwhile the flames were roaring and surging around us. Six of our boys were carrying down the volumes as rapidly as they could, and I, standing on truck, was stowing away the books economically as to space. About that time they told me the Court House bell fell down. I lost all idea of time. It must have been about 2 o'clock. I never heard the bell fall, I was so excited. Toward the last, when we had got our indices all down safely, and were trying to save other valuable papers and books, many of which we did save, it was stated that Smith & Nixon's building was about to be blown up. Our truck was headed toward that building. The sky was filled with burning embers which were falling around us thickly. As soon, I think, as the information was given that that building was to be blown up, the crowd rushed past us down Washington street, toward the lake, terribly excited, shouting and warning everybody away. My driver was very nervous, and on one pretext or another would start his horses up for a rod or two, swearing that he would not be blown up for us or for the whole country;

but I succeeded in stopping him eight or ten times during the excitement. In the meantime our men were coming down the stairs laden with our property and returning as rapidly as they could. I was standing on the books, packing them in the truck, and the embers were flying on them, and I picked them off as they fell and threw them into the street, until, a rod at a time, we reached the corner of Dearborn and Washington. Messrs. Fuller and Handy were the last to leave the office, and they did not leave until Buck & Rayner's drug store was on fire. The store, as we believed, was full of chemicals and explosive matter. At that time the Court House was a mass of flames, and our own building was burning, and other buildings in the immediate vicinity entirely destroyed. Three of us then started with the truck for my house, which we reached about 3 o'clock that morning. I had our property unloaded and placed securely within; and, after giving the driver and others some refreshments, I started again for the fire to see what aid I could give other sufferers.

WHAT A WOMAN RELATES—THE EXPERIENCE OF A REAL SUFFERER.

"We had a nice little cottage on the north side, near Indiana Street Bridge, with a little yard in front, where I had planted the rose tree mother gave me from our dear old home. Mother is dead now, and the homestead sold. We had plants in the window that grew well from the loving care bestowed on them. Geraniums and heliotropes, and even the orange tree that furnished flowers for my hair on my wedding night, while the honeysuckle over the door came from a far-away sister's grave at the East.

The mementoes on the mantel, the pictures of those gone before, the playthings of some little ones that are lying still and peaceful in Rose Hill, the golden locks cut from their curly heads, and the little clothing they wore—where is it all? What a horrible dream! We didn't save anything, because my husband said the fire wouldn't come so far, so we waited and I packed my trunk with all my nice things, and in a moment, before we could think, the distillery and coalyards and lumber were all on fire, and our house was in a great cloud of flame.

I took my boy and ran across the bridge. My husband dragged the trunk to the bridge, but left it a minute to help me over the river, and went back, and an engine had struck the trunk, burst it open, and not one single thing was left in it. Then my husband came and told me, and I didn't care whether I died or not. I wished I could die. And I looked across the river and saw all my things burning up in the house, and I just laid down under the sidewalk and tried to go to sleep. We slept under there all Monday night, and we had not a mouthful all that day. The rain came in the night, and I was soaked to the skin. Toward morning I took a chill. Then I hoped I should die for certain. I kept getting chilly, and I knew I was going away from all I loved here.

Some one came along Tuesday and said we should get into a church. Somebody carried me there, and gave me dry clothes and a room by myself and something to eat, and then I was afraid I should not die. Then I went to some hospital, for I was about to be confined, and the smell, the crowd, the sickness and deaths made me sick, and my husband brought me here. For weeks I stayed here with neither a door or window, and all the carpenters pounding till I thought my head would burst. Just a week ago to-day I had this little baby. Some ladies gave me some clothes for it. More than twenty of them have come here with pencil and paper and asked me what I needed and that was the last I have ever seen of them.

I have never asked for anything, but I must have blankets, and my husband wants shoes and drawers. He can get no work at his trade. He says he would walk two miles and back every day to get at his old work."

And this is her simple, truthful, terrible story!

A TOUCHING HOME PICTURE.

Here is a picture from the story of a lady whose home was burned:

"There came a strange sound in the air which stilled, or seemed to still, for a moment, the surging crowd. 'Was it thunder?' we asked. No, the sky was clear and full of stars, and we shuddered as we felt, but did not say, that it was a tremendous explosion of gunpowder. By this time the blazing sparks and bits of burning wood, which we had been fearfully watching, were fast becoming an unintermitting fire of burning hail, and another shower of blows on the doors warned us that there was not a moment to be lost. Call E——' (the invalid;) do not let him stay a minute, and I will try to save our poor little birds!' My sister flew to wake up our precious charge, and I ran down stairs, repeating to myself to make me remember, 'Birds, deeds, silver, jewelry, silk-dresses,' as the order in which we would try to save our property, if it came to the worst. As I passed through our pretty parlors how my heart ached. Here the remnant of my father's library, a copy of a Bible printed in 1637, on the table; on another, my dear Mrs. Browning, in five volumes, the gift of a lost friend. What should I take? What should I leave? I alternately loaded myself with gift after gift, and dashed them down in despair. Lovely pictures and statuettes, left by a kind friend for the embellishment of our little rooms, and which had turned them into a bower of beauty—must they be left? At last I stopped before our darling, a sweet and tender picture of Beatrice Cenci going to the execution, which looked down at me, through the dismal red glare which was already filling the rooms, with a saintly and weird sweetness that seemed to have something wistful in it. I thought, 'I will save this if I die for it;' but my poor parrot called my name and asked for a peanut, and I could no more have left him than if he had been a baby. But could I carry that huge cage? No, indeed; so I reluctantly took my little canary, who was painfully fluttering about and wondering at the disturbance, and, kissing him, opened the front door and set him free—only to smother, I fear. But it was the best I could do for him if I wished to save my parrot, who had a prior right to be considered one of the family, if sixteen years of incessant chatter may be supposed to establish such right.

Incidents are practically exhaustless, and altogether beyond computation. Thousands upon thousands of cases, even outside of the losses of life, are utterly irretrievable, tidious, pitiful and heart-rendering. As it is impossible to treat of them in detail, they are summed up in a comprehensive recapitulation in the proper place.

ORIGIN OF THE FIRE.

The committee appointed to investigate the origin, progress and devastation of the fire, have made their report. We take from it the following interesting items:

The board find that the fire originated in a two story barn in rear of No. 137 DeKoven street, the premises being owned by Patrick Leary. The fire was first discovered by a drayman by the name of Daniel Sullivan, who saw it while sitting on the sidewalk on the south side of DeKoven street, and nearly opposite Leary's premises. He fixes the time at not more than twenty-five minutes past 9 o'clock, when he first noticed the flames coming out of the barn. There is no proof that any persons had been in the barn after nightfall that evening. Whether it originated from a spark blown from a chimney on that windy night, or was set on fire by human agency, we are unable to determine. Mr. Leary, the owner, and all his family prove to have been in bed and asleep at the time. There was a small party in the front part of Leary's house, which was occupied by Mr. McLaughlin and wife. But we failed to find any evidence that anybody from McLaughlin's part of the house went near the barn that night.

If any person set the fire, either by accident or design, he was careful not to give any alarm. The nearest engine-house was six blocks from the fire; the next nearest one was nine blocks away. The nearest hose house was located eleven blocks from the fire, and at this hose house the watchman had seen the fire before the alarm was given from the Court-House, and the company were on their way to the fire before the alarm was struck.

In consequence of this early sighting of the fire, the hose company (the America) went eleven blocks and attached their hose to the fire-plug and got water on the fire before any engine did, although two engines were located considerably nearer the fire. It would require five minutes for the nearest engine to go to the fire, a distance of six blocks. From three to five minutes more would be required in which to unreel and lay out the hose, make connection with the plug, and go to work. Intelligent citizens who lived near the place of the fire testify that it was from ten to fifteen minutes from the time they first saw the fire before any engines came upon the ground. It is proved that the engines repaired to the fire, after getting the alarm, with the usual celerity. When they arrived there from three to five buildings were fiercely burning. The fire must then have been burning from ten to fifteen minutes, and, with the wind then blowing strongly from the southwest, and carrying the fire from building to building in a neighborhood composed wholly of dry wooden buildings, with wood shavings piled in every barn and under every house, the fire had got under too great headway for the engines called out by the first alarm to be able to subdue it.

Blowing up buildings in the face of the wind was tried, but without any benefit. The Court House and the Water Works, though a mile apart, were burning at the same time. Gunpowder was used in blowing up buildings with good effect, the next day, in cutting off the fire at the extreme south end of it, and preventing it backing any further.

We believe that, had the buildings on the West Side, where the fire commenced, been built of brick or stone, with safe roofing (the buildings need not have been fire-proof), the fire could have been stopped without doing great damage, and certainly would not have crossed the river. After it did cross the wooden cornices, wooden signs of large size, the cupolas, and the tar and felt roofs, which were on most of the best buildings, caused their speedy destruction, and aided greatly in spreading the conflagration. The single set of pumping works, upon which the salvation of the city depended, were roofed with wood, had no appliance by which water could be raised to the roof in case of fire, and was one of the earliest buildings to burn in the North Division.

ANOTHER THEORY

Concerning the origin of the fire, is constructed out of the fact, that in March 1871, three enterprising men visited Chicago for the express purpose of laying before the city authorities a plan for extinguishing fires by means of carbonic acid gas. This gas was to be generated and saved from the same coal that made the illuminating gas. The pipes were to be laid side by side with the others, and the whole theory of the plan was, that when a building took fire, the people were to rush out, the doors to be closed, the carbonic acid gas to be turned on, which would at once extinguish the fire, without any injury or damage to house or furniture by water, which often does more damage than the fire itself.

These men received some encouragement that their plan would be favorably received and accepted by the city. Expensive works were accordingly constructed, and time and money freely lavished while all through the summer months the men waited, hoping soon to realize immense wealth from their grand project. Late in September they learned that as a final decision the city declined to have any thing to do with the new extinguisher, refusing even to try experiments or allow them to be tried.

On Saturday October 7th those three men passed through New York on their way home—and in a few moments conversation with a friend at the depot, one of them remarked, in a tone half dogged, half reckless, "we have tried our best to do something for Chicago, she has kicked us out, and now she may bear the consequences."

"Where's Harriet and the children?" asked the friend.

"I brought them out to L—" (about twenty miles from the city) and they will remain there until I go or send for them."

A bell rang, the train started, and three hard, desperate cases were lost sight of in the crowded car.

The next morning the whole country thrilled with the news of the Great Conflagration, and two days later Chicago had passsd through the fiery furnace.

STILL ANOTHER THEORY.

There is another theory regarding the origin of the fire, to which many persons attach importance, and it is therefore worthy of record. It is the startling theory that a secret organization conceived and matured the diabolical plot for the destruction of the city, and sent their agents here to execute it. We therefore transcribe to these pages what purports to be the confession of one of the prime movers in this fiendish work. We give it without the expression of any opinion as to its authenticity. Though it appears at the first thought to be utterly romantic and improbable, there are not wanting confirmatory circumstances. For example, the original explanation of the origin of the fire has been denied by two persons on oath, which is sufficient to disprove the statement in a court of justice. There is abundant evidence going to show that the fire was set in more than one place. A well known lady who resides in the vicinity of the Franklin school, on Division street, states positively that while the fire was progressing north in the North division from the river, she saw a man walk up to the side of the primary school, a frame building in the rear of the Franklin school, turn out a lot of shavings from a bag, and immediately after saw the shavings flaming up. With these observations, the alleged confession is given in the precise language that it was received, as follows:

CONFESSION OF A MEMBER OF A SECRET ORGANIZATION.

The headquarters of the organization is in Paris, and its ramifications extend all over the world. There are branches in London, Edinburgh, Manchester, Liverpool, Dublin, Berlin, St. Petersburg, Naples, Florence, Vienna, and other cities in Great Britain and on the continent, and in New York, Boston, Washington, New Orleans, Baltimore, and Chicago, in this country. Its members are bound by a fearful oath never to divulge any of the plans of operations of the society, and were it known that I was about to relate the story I have commenced I should never live to finish it, while if the author of this ever becomes known I will die a death more horrible than that which met any of the victims of the inquisition. It is, therefore, with fear and trembling that I sit down to write the true story of the origin of the Chicago fire, and nothing but the sternest sense of duty, and a desire to clear my conscience, of a load that is too heavy for endurance, would induce me to pen these lines.

I fancy the sneer of incredulity with which some will greet my announcement that the destruction of Chicago was accomplished by this organization, but, when I have unfolded the details of the plot and the motives that prompted its conception, incredulity will give place to astonishment that human beings could be found who were so blinded by fanaticism as to become parties to so great and overwhelming a crime. The events of the past two weeks have awakened me from a dream so wild and improbable that were it not for the dreary evidences of its reality that I see about me, I could scarce believe, and still more reluctantly can

SWIFT JUSTICE. FATE OF THIEVES AND INCENDIARIES.

I believe, that in the terrible tragedy that has been enacted I was one of the principal actors; that, though blinded by a fanaticism more fearful than the worst form of lunacy, I permitted myself to become the cause of so much misery and woe.

To begin at the beginning, I must revert to its extent—its objects and its plans.

The society was organized during the troubulous times that preceded the election of Louis Napoleon to the Presidency of France. A commune, in which all should have equal rights and privileges; in which the poor should be equal with the rich and the rich equal with the poor, was much talked of at that time, and this organization was formed with that object in view. The election of Napoleon to the Presidency, and his subsequent *coup d' etat* by which he seated himself upon the throne, for a time defeated the plans of the socialists. Notwithstanding the fact, however, the organization was not abandoned, but was rather more closely cemented and more widely diffused. The evils of the reign of the third Napoleon seemed to add fuel to the fire that was smouldering in France, and the society drew into its ranks all the elements of discontent throughout the empire. The result of the late war between France and Germany was to incorporate a more dangerous element into the society, and it was determined to seize upon the opportunity offered by the withdrawal of the Prussians from Paris for putting the principles of the society into execution.

Emissaries were dispatched to all the commercial capitals of the world, and, together with those who had fled from the Versailles government, formed branches in all the leading cities, not only in Europe, but in America. There was not lacking those who were so deeply imbued with an insane desire for the triumph of communistic principles that they were willing to undertake any desperate plan that gave promise of success, even though attended with infinite misery and suffering.

The long existing conflict between capital and labor had prepared thousands of persons in every large city, and especially in manufacturing districts, for any desperate work that would avenge the real or fancied wrongs they had received at the hands of the monied aristocracy. In this field the emissaries labored with a zeal that would have done credit to a better cause. The utmost care was exercised to prevent any disclosure of the plans of the organization.

While in Paris I became a member of this organization, and it is not surprising, therefore, that on its first organization in Chicago, some eight months ago, I was selected as one of the prime movers. Since I had returned from France I had been in correspondence with some of those prominent in the movement there, among whom were M. Henri Martin, who was among the first to fall a victim to the Versailles troops at the capture of the city; M. Assi, whose tragic fate is so fresh in the minds of all, and M. Julius Garadine, from whom I learned the progress the society was making, and many of its future plans.

The organization in Chicago was formed under the direction of two members who had fled from Paris, and myself. As elsewhere, none but the most daring and trustworthy were admitted. The avowed purposes of the society were harmless in themselves. They were to endeavor to elevate the workingmen to the level of the rich; that everybody should enjoy equal benefits, and poverty and want should be unknown. To these declarations there was a codicil binding the members, if it were found impossible to secure the results by peaceable means to resort to whatever measure should be deemed advisable by the directors of the organization.

The first two months of the existence of the society were consumed in fruitless attempts to stir up strife between the mechanics of the city and their employers. But the disastrous consequences of the eight-hour strikes in 1867 were yet fresh in remembrance, and for once the labor unions refused to do the bidding of their prompters. This was a discouraging blow, but the members of the society were determined; for colossal fortunes were being amassed in an incredibly short space of time, and an aristocracy of wealth was springing up that threatened to become so strong as to defy overthrow. Plan after plan was suggested, and abandoned as impracticable. Finally, the

BURNING OF THE BUSINESS PORTION OF THE CITY

was suggested. Appalled by the thought of working such desolation in the fairest city on the continent, I at first shrank from participation in the transaction. I protested that instead of promoting the objects of the society it would only retard them. But all the others were firm, and, weakly, I yielded. Gradually the insanity produced by being a promoter of a calamity that would shake the world to its centre, took possession of me. Sleeping or waking, my thoughts were filled with the plan.

To mature the details of the plot required the utmost caution. The project of raising a mob by means of some popular excitement and to burn and pillage the city was debated at length, but at last abandoned because of its hazardousness and the inevitable loss of life that it would involve, for to take life was not our object—it was only to humble the men who had waxed rich at the expense of the poor. The incendiary's torch was finally fixed upon, and on the ninth day of August preparations were actively begun to carry it into execution.

Several times a day was fixed for the awful tragedy, but as often abandoned. The co-operation of the elements was needed. The torch was first applied to the warehouse on the corner of State and Sixteenth streets on the gusty morning of the 30th of

A LADY BETWEEN TWO FEATHER BEDS ABLAZE.

September. It was hoped that the high south wind then prevailing would carry the flames to the row of frame buildings to the Northward, but a sudden change in the wind defeated the project by enabling the fire department to quench the flames. Again on the Saturday night preceding the catastrophe a match was applied on Canal street, and for a few hours all seemed to be working well, and but for the failure of one of the petroleum mines to ignite, Sabbath morning would have seen Chicago in ashes.

But the doom that was overhanging the city was delayed but a day, and that day came near proving fatal to our plans, for then and only then were we in danger of betrayal.

All day long we had been in secret conclave where no mortal could spy out our doings. Petroleum mines had been laid in a score of places, and trusty men were stationed at each of them to apply the match at the proper moment. The plot had been arranged that all should appear as accident, our part being mainly to assist the progress of the flames, for we knew that, once beyond a certain limit, no agency could stay them. The place above all others in the city which promised the great measure of success was in the barn on DeKoven street. No "old Irish hag" was milking her cow at the time, as the reporters of the city press are determined to have it. A human being of a different sex was there, however, but had disap ared, as if by magic, before any mortal eye had remarked his presence.

Before the arrival of the jaded firemen at the scene of the conflagration, half a dozen mines had been touched off, and their efforts to subdue the flames were as futile as the effort of a child to stem the raging cataract of Niagara. When the flames had reached the river, work began on the South side. Simultaneously a mine was sprung at the gas-works, and another near Van Buren street bridge, and two whole blocks were a seething hell of flame in less time than it takes my unaccustomed pen to tell it. From thence onward the fire was assisted by a mine set on Wells street, near Monroe, another a block and a half further east, and still another in Farwell Hall. Few on that eventful Sunday night suspected that they were sitting over a magazine that needed but the touch of a match to involve them in a perfect hell of flame.

From that point the destruction of the South side, with its massive granite piles and well-stored warehouses, was assured. Onward sped the flames, and wherever they appeared likely to skip, a new magazine was fire, and ruin with his fearful front involved the fair city.

I had been delegated to explode the powder magazine on South Water street.

Our only fear of want of success was that the authorities, failing to stay the mad current of fire by ordinary means, would resort to the last and only hope—lay a few blocks in ruins by means of gunpowder. To guard against this a train had been laid communicating with the magazine, and required but a spark to destroy it. When the work had been fully inaugurated, I hastened to the point to which I had been assigned, wild with a frenzy more terrible than any I had ever before experienced. I reached the spot where the match should have been applied. A huge coal lay within a few feet of it. A slight kick from my foot would have placed it over the hidden fuse, but the streets were thronged with people, and I shrank from committing the act that would have plunged hundreds of human beings into eternity.

That moment's hesitation was their salvation. The powder brigade arrived almost upon the instant, and the explosive was removed from the building. Among the first barrels removed were those with which the train communicated, and although a stray spark afterward fired the fuse, no explosion followed.

Hardly had I recovered from the momentary flash of humane feeling that overcame me, than I was placed in imminent peril of my life. The flames had advanced Northward on both sides of where I stood, and were rushing toward me with fearful rapidity. Dazed by the various conflicting emotions that had filled my breast, I had not noticed this, and when I awoke from my trance the most horrible of deaths stared me in the face. Hemmed in on every side in a crucible of fire, I for a moment gave way to despair. But despair gave me strength, and, breaking down a heavy door, I rushed through a store to the river and plunged into its waters. A boat moored at the dock assisted me to cross, although I did not waste time in getting into it, but pushed it before me as I swam. Reaching the North-side, I ran with all my speed through the streets toward the city limits, seeking to escape.

In the meantime, my co-workers in crime had not been idle. As the currant of fire passed northward from Van Buren street, it appeared that a large tract bounded on the north by Madison street, and on the west by Dearborn street, including a valuable section of the city, would escape the terrible destruction that had visited the remainder of the city. The flames had proceeded along Harrison and Van Buren streets to Fourth avenue, and here seem to have spent their force. It was a terrible moment. A few brave men battled with the demon and but for the omnipresence of the league would have stayed its progress. But a man rushed into a house that had been abandoned by its occupants, ostensibly for the purpose of saving some household utensils that had been left, and returned laden with goods; but a moment afterward the rear of the building became a mass of flame, and a gust of wind carried it eastward to the lake and northward over the district that had thus far been spared, thus completing the universal ruin.

ON THE NORTHERN SIDE

it had been intended to destroy but few buildings, and these the business headquarters and residences of the affluent. As during the progress of the fire on the South Side, mines were sprung in various localities as the flames advanced, but only where the natural course of the flames was likely to leave the work but imperfectly done.

The fire progressed too slowly. The water-works were in full blast, and there was danger that through their agency some of the buildings doomed to demolition would be saved. The works had been prepared for destruction, but the time had not arrived, as the fire was several blocks away. But, notwithstanding this fact, the match was applied, and the workmen were obliged to fly for their lives. In their flight the man who had fired the mine was overthrown and badly injured, and as the fire advanced he fell a victim to its fury.

This ended the work of the incendiaries. The elements completed the destruction, and the loveliest portion of Chicago was a wasted and dreary ruin. The results are more than had been anticipated, and not yet satisfactory. Many buildings that had been doomed escaped the fiery ordeal, while a large tract that it had been determined to spare is now a ruin. Retribution is not long in following the perpetrators of great crimes. Two of the original founders of the organization in Chicago met death in the terrible conflagration they had instigated, and I alone am spared to suffer worse than a thousand deaths from the stings of conscience. Seven of the men delegated to assist the fire in its progress also perished miserably in the hell they had conjured up, while two others are probably maimed for life.

As for myself, I have little hope of escaping vengeance. The oath to which I subscribed carries with it the penalty of death in a form more horrible than any that has been visited upon mortal since the sun first rose over chaos. The organization is omnipresent, permeating every circle of society, each member being bound to mete out the penalty of the oath to any one who may divulge its secrets. This, its greatest of secrets, has been written under the load of a guilty conscience. Life has lost all its attractions for me, and I scarcely care to live, save to see the damage caused partly through my instrumentality repaired. But if it shall appear that I cannot escape from those who have already involved me in so much misery, I will yet not die at their hands, but will prefer to lie in accursed ground.

P. S.—Let me add one word of warning. Other cities, both in this country and Europe, have been threatened with fire."

That many of our prominent citizens believe in the genuineness of these revolutions, is demonstrated in their daily conversation; and it is by no means impossible that they are founded in truth.

SCENE IN THE GERMAN CEMETERY. THE LIVING SEEKING SAFETY IN THE CITY OF THE DEAD.

Call for Help for Chicago.

BY N. S. EMERSON.

For years our beautiful city
Has grown in her strength and pride,
  Strong as an Indian warrior,
Fair as a hunters bride;
  But up from her hearts quick throbbing,
List to our pitiful cry.
  "A Demon has been among us,
Help! or we surely die.

"A Demon whose power was stronger
Than the strength of our puny hands,
  "Who paused not to ask for favors,
But took the wealth of our lands:
  We fought him with desperate courage,
He laughed at our fruitless pain,
  We begged him to spare **our treasures**
Alas! that we begged in vain.

"Spare us McVickers **temple**,
Home of dramatic **art**."
  The demon shrieked **and** McVickers
Was booked for its **closing** part.
  "Spare us our Tribune building,
Stately and high and strong,
  "Whence the Messenger birds fly daily.
To battle against the wrong."

The demon crept over the pavement
And clutched at the pillars fair,
 And only a heap of embers
And a wreath of smoke were there.
 "Spare us then Colyers pulpit,
He has fought in the Lords good fight,"
 "And every word he utters
Is an anvil stroke for the right."

 "I am no respecter of person,"
Quoth the demon grim and dread,
 "And Collyer can preach next Sunday
With God's blue sky o'er head."
Thus hath the red browed Fire Fiend
 Stolen our treasures dear,
Sucked out our hearts best life blood,
 And left us to famish here.

Gone are our shrines and altars,
 Gone are the hopes we cherished,
All in one hot breath wasted,
 All in a moment perished,
Lost is the grain we garnered,
 Harvest of years gone by.
Help us, for we are starving,
 Help! or we surely die.

ERIE RAILROAD DEPOT, NEW YORK CITY. PROMPT RELIEF FOR CHICAGO.

Starting of the First Lightning Train

WITH RELIEF FOR CHICAGO.

BY N. S. EMERSON.

    From the desolating power,
      Of the fire fiend, hour by hour,
We could see the stricken city, crushed and smothered as she lay,
      We could hear her children crying,
        Homeless, helpless, weary, dying ;
And we answered, "Of our bounty we will share with you to-day."

    So the engine dumbly waited,
      With its strong hot breathing bated,
While the twice ten thousand packages and bales and boxes came,
      Brought in every form and fashion,
        By our wide awake compassion,
For the sufferers who were writhing 'neath their fierce baptismal flame.

    Since the earliest flush of dawning,
      Through the busy Autumn morning,
Food and clothing had been gathered, and one quaint big box we found,
      Hustled in among the others,
Labelled "For our starving brothers, In the care of J. F. Jr.,
      God's Expressman ! Westward bound."

    "God's Expressman !" Each rude letter
      Told of labor's clinging fetter,   [fraught,]
On the clumsy hand that traced them, but the heart with love was
      And we gave our tribute cheery,
        Honor to the Prince of Erie,
Blessings from the weak and weary, on the generous work he wrought.

    But the cars were packed, overflowing,
      And the engine puffing, blowing ;
While, with hand upon the throttle, stood the stern faced engineer;
      Tall and strong, all nerve and muscle,
        Heedless of the noise and bustle,
Seeing well the work before him, with no sign or thought of fear.

THROUGH THE FLAMES AND BEYOND.

"Ready Sam?" The grey eyes brightened,
And the brawny hand clasp tightened,
"Ready Colonel! every man is at place to-day, I know."
Said the Colonel quick and clear,
To the waiting engineer,
"What's the fastest time on record from New York to Buffalo?"

"We have made it in Twelve-twenty!"
"Do it now in 'Leven-twenty!"
"Aye! Aye! Colonel!" came the answer with a hearty vim and power
"Start her Sam!" and cheers were sounded,
And the first long curve was rounded,
And beyond our sight and hearing,
Mid the blessing and the cheering,
Westward flew the train of treasure, Forty, Fifty miles an hour.

Westward still! We hear the echo!
"Here is comfort for Chicago;"
And through busy towns and villages, the laden coaches fly.
Many a voice cried out "God speed them,"
And the pitying angels heed them,
As upon their Heaven sent mission, quick as light they hurry by.

"In the Smithfield light the fires,"
Said the message on the wires,
And we fancy swarthy fireman twice a hundred miles away,
Listening for the long, low humming
Of the "James Fisk Jr." coming,
Making fastest time on record, on that memorable day.

Ye who mourn the lessening stature
Of our modern human nature,
And the wickedness and weakness of our cultured lives deplore.
Cease your scoffing and your scorning,
Think of that bright autumn morning,
Think of all the generous wishes which the train of treasures bore.

Heart and hand had wrought together,
Knowing not nor caring whether
Friend or stranger would be succored by the bounty of their store.
Every Iron horse was ready,
Every driver firm and steady,
Every whistle rang a rally,
Through the Susquehanna valley,
And the lightning train sped onward, Forty, Fifty miles an hour.

GENERAL DEPOT OF SUPPLIES FOR THE SUFFERERS BY THE FIRE.

RELIEF.

HEAVENLY CHARITY—SUBLIME SYMPATHY. THE GREAT HEART OF THE PEOPLE AROUSED. IMMENSE DONATIONS FROM ALL PARTS OF THE COUNTRY, ETC.

On the morning of the 9th of October, 1871, the telegraphic wires flashed to every part of this nation, and to nearly every portion of the civilized world, the shocking intelligence that Chicago was in flames, hundreds of lives had been destroyed, and ten thousand families were homeless, shelterless, scantily clad, and suffering intensely with cold, hunger, fatigue and fright. The whole world was appalled. The thrilling horror chilled every heart, and for a moment paralyzed every hand. Men stood aghast at the startling and terrific announcement, that acres of buildings were in embers and men, women and children terror-stricken, were fleeing for life, from what, but yesterday were comfortable and happy homes. It was difficult to realize the awful calamity. It seemed to be an exaggeration, and all hoped, at first, that it would prove such. But later dispatches more than confirmed the previous intelligence; and, ere mid-day, Mayor Mason of the doomed city, had telegraphed to the Mayors of the principal cities in the country, the fact of the utter destitution of the people, and appealing for food, clothing and other necessaries of life.

His touching appeal aroused the people to their senses. The great heart of humanity throbbed with the emotion. Heaven born charity, that divine principle in man, which most resembles the author of his being, and which blesses the possessor no less than the recipient of his favors, in a moment was quickened newness of life in every heart throughout the nation and even across the broad Atlantic; and a sublime, human sympathy, limited to no section, nation or race, to no party, creed or social condition, instantly was displayed in active word for relief. A portion of humanity, was suddenly and sorely stricken and afflicted, and purse-strings were loosened everywhere. In a brief space of time, the Mayors of cities had issued orders for the assembling of councils; Presidents of Chambers of Commerce, and Boards of Trade,

Officers of Masonic, Odd Fellows, Temperance and other societies and Ministers of different religious sects had notified their respective bodies to assemble for the purpose of taking immediate action in regard to providing for the sufferings of the distressed people of the burnt district of Chicago. With alacrity the members responded to this call and when assembled, although hearts were overflowing with generous sympathy and tongues were let loose in eloquent portrayal of the necessities of the people of a sister city, impoverished in a single night, by the destructive ravages of the fiery element, yet no unnecessary words were spoken, for all felt that not a moment should be lost, if they would succor those in distress, in the hour of their direst need. Action, action, prompt and efficient action was the soul-stirring eloquence on those occasions. In accordance with the object of the gathering, in each case respectively, when some generous member would lead off with a resolution donating a sum, which under other circumstances would have been deemed a most exorbitant demand upon their treasury, ere the member had fairly pronounced the sum, another would spring to his feet and move to amend, by doubling the amount; a third one would treble it, when a half dozen, all at once, would amend the resolution by naming a sum at least four times as large as the original motion, so unselfish and generous had they become under the inspiration of this unparalleled calamity. Cities and towns all over the country, in their corporate capacity, made haste to vie with each other, both in the amount of their donations, and the speed with which they should forward both money and supplies to the unfortunate, though brave and deserving city.

FIREMEN FROM ABROAD.

As the news was received that the firemen of Chicago were entirely overcome with fatigue it became necessary that brave and skilful firemen in other places should volunteer their services in this time of fearful need; and hundreds of these unselfish, couragous, and noble men, with their splendid steam fire-engines, from the principal cities within several hundred miles, were quickly on their way to lend their utmost aid to stay the further progress of the devouring flames; and, to encourage and assist the suffering citizens in every other way within their power. As delegation after delegation arrived, they were welcomed with loud cheers and heartfelt thanks by the terribly afflicted citizens, who hailed them as friends indeed, because friends in need. But when these noble men, with that cool bravery and discriminating judgment, so peculiar to tried and experienced firemen, stationed their engines, steamed up and commenced their attack upon the devouring element, they were enthusiastically cheered by the people, who greatfully acknowledged their efficiency and important and praiseworthy efforts.

Each delegation of firemen also received public acknowledgement of their invaluable services.

UNEXAMPLED LIBERALITY OF CITY GOVERNMENTS AND CORPORATIONS.

City councils everywhere throughout the country, convened with the utmost promptitude and voted and forwarded donations of money and necessary articles, with unprecedented liberality and extraordinary dispatch; their hearts seeming to lie in their hands and their hands thrust deep into the treasury of the people, who, for once, not only approved of the lavish expenditure, but were ready to urge their councilmen to give still more generously. Every Chamber of Commerce probably in the Union, on receipt of the frightful intelligence of the terrible fire, immediately held a special relief session and voted large sums of money, which were promptly forwarded to the proper authorities.

Boards of Trade all over the land also convened with alacrity and poured out their treasures abundantly; swelling greatly the funds which were to partially relieve the distresses of those who had thus suddenly lost their all, and were afflicted, as were never before so many persons in so short a time.

Committees from the City Councils, Chambers of Commerce and Boards of Trade of each city, were generally appointed to co-operate with each other in the distribution of their donations, so that their charities would be the more effectual and speedy in relieving distress.

The overflowing sympathies and munificent charities of the people all over the country, sublimely portrayed the generous impulses of humanity, and the grand fact that an occasion only was needed to show that much of the angel still inhered to man. Majestically did the American people, upon this occasion, portray their relationship with angels. Masonic societies all over the country, prompted by the ties of brotherhood and holy principles of charity, were not tardy in convening nor niggardly in their donations of relief, and not dilatory in forwarding them to the sufferers, with brotherly assurances that those were but an earnest of what they would do in the future, in case of need. Odd-Fellows Lodges, inspired by the heavenly principles of "friendship, love and truth," responded nobly in behalf of the sufferers, sparing no efforts, and making no delay in dispatching their abundant contributions, while offering words of consolation and hope, and expressions of earnest and tender sympathy. The societies of "Good Men," "Red Men," Order of Pythias, Son of Temperance, Good Templars, and mutual benefit societies of every other name, all made generous donations, forgeting, for the time being, all selfish ideas and feelings, and having before them only the idea of a whole city in dire distress, appealing for succor. They all offered words of cheer, flanked by grand donations of money, or what was equivalent. Corporations, for once, if never before, proved that they were not devoid of souls, but stirred by human and generous sympathies, alive to the sufferings of humanity, and ready and willing to give liberally to relieve their distress.

Though thousands of our citizens were houseless and hungry on the desolate prairie, yet so utterly were we paralyzed by the stupendous shock, that people at a distance seemed to comprehend our situation more readily and thoroughly than we did ourselves.

We knew not what to ask for, but hundreds and thousands seemed to know by intuition what to give, and assistance flowed in from the most unexpected sources and with the most unparalleled munificence.

As early as daybreak on Tuesday morning the farmers and merchants from the towns near, as well as from the unburnt portions of the city, emptied their cellars and storehouses for our relief, and right grateful were we for their prompt and generous bounty. All day long car-loads and wagon-loads of provisions were being brought in, while the active Relief Committee, organized as by magic, received and distributed with wise discrimination these truly wonderful gifts.

Soon contributions came from greater distances: for days and weeks the tide flowed in, bearing almost unlimited supplies of food, clothing, and money, and for two months every day brought its quota. The whole amount from the different states may be summed up in round numbers, as follows:

LIBERAL CONTRIBUTIONS FROM THE VARIOUS STATES.

Massachusetts, five hundred and fifty thousand.
New York, four hundred thousand.
Pennsylvania, two hundred and fifty thousand.
Maryland, two hundred thousand.
New Jersey, one hundred and eighty thousand.
California, one hundred and sixty thousand.
Connecticut, seventy thousand.
Rhode Island, fifty thousand.
New Hampshire, forty thousand.
Ohio, fifty thousand.
Illinois, fifty thousand.
Virginia, thirty thousand,
Kansas, twenty-eight thousand.
Indiana, twenty-five thousand.
Minnesota, twenty-five thousand.
Tennessee, twenty-four thousand.
Maine, fifteen thousand.
Louisiana, fifteen thousand.

And every other state and territory in the Union gave proportionately, until the amount of money received by the Chicago Relief and Aid Society, up to December 1st, reached the grand sum of three millions.

ILLINOIS LEGISLATURE.

Governor Palmer called a special session of the Legislature, to convene on the 13th of Oct. According to the constitution of the State the Legislature could not appropriate more than $250,000, but that, in addition to the millions outside, added much to relieve the terrible distresses of the people. They passed a bill to relieve Chicago of taxes for the present year, to the amount of $3,000,000. As this amount would have to be made up by other portions of the State, it is creditable to the State that there was no more grumbling from the press and people; and that they generally so cheerfully acquiesced in such a law.

RAILROADS.

MAGNIFICENT LIBERALITY.

The railroads gave free transportation to all who wished to leave the city, and thousands of people availed themselves of the privilege thus offered, either to find shelter under friendly roofs, or seek relief elsewhere.

All our Railroad corporations did noble and generous work.

Railroad companies in every part of the country, through their officers, at once announced to the public, that their roads were ready to transport goods of all descriptions, donated for the benefit of the sufferers, together with the properly appointed committees for their distribution, to Chicago, free of cost. And they all promptly and faithfully fulfilled their promises.

ACKNOWLEDGEMENT.

The Committee on Subsistence and Railroad Trains on behalf of the General Chicago Relief Committee desire to return thanks to J. McCreighton, Assistant Superintendent of the Pennsylvania Railroad, for the interest taken by him in relieving Chicago sufferers, he having passed through, free of charge, over one thousand persons, and expressed a willingness to aid the Committee in every way he could. They were also indebted to Mr. Unger, Manager of the Union Depot Hotel, for kindness shown and assistance rendered in taking care of the sufferers, he having furnished meals to over one hundred free of charge, and provided many others with meals at a rate merely covering cost.

JOHN MOORHEAD.
Chairman.

REUBEN MILLER,
Secretary.

All the roads leading out of Chicago, for days, carried free of charge such of the homeless as had friends in other places. And in every way possible for them to facilitate the distribution of charities, by carrying either donations, or authorized persons connected with the Relief Committees, to or fro, they responded promptly and liberally. The same should be said of all the express companies, they promptly aiding in transporting goods to Chicago from all points of the country. Indeed, they were mighty auxilliaries in the gigantic work of feeding, clothing, and otherwise rendering comfortable a hundred thousand people, who in one night were stripped of their all.

VIEW FROM THE COURT HOUSE LOOKING SOUTH.

THE RUSH FOR LIFE OVER RANDOLPH STREET BRIDGE.

At sunrise, the Eleventh of October, only two days after the fire, Col. James Fisk, Jr. mounted one of the splendid express wagons connected with the Erie Rail Road, and gathering up the reins, drove six in hand about New York City, receiving contributions, which were freely offered, and the more generously given as the personal magnetism of Col. Fisk inspired every one he met with something of his own enthusiasm.

At ten o'clock that morning, seven cars heavily laden with supplies of all kinds were ready to start from the Erie Depot. It was there that the mammoth box was found marked, "Care of James Fisk, Jr., God's Expressman."

Mr. Crouch, who went with the train as super-cargo, as well as the engineer, Samuel Walker, testify that all along the route crowds of enthusiastic people gathered at the principal depots, bidding the train God speed, and even attempting to throw parcels upon the cars as they hurried by. This was the first lightning relief train, and made unprecedented time.

The name of the engine used on this occasion, in starting from New York, was the "James Fisk, jr." On the evening of that day, Col. Fisk wrote to the Mayor of Chicago as follows :

"We have received, since the departure of the Lightning Relief train this morning, over ten thousand consignments for the sufferers at Chicago.

It is quite impossible to enumerate either the contents or the value of the packages gathered, but a person competent to judge, who inspected the goods forwarded by that train, estimated their cash value at not less than one hundred thousand dollars. We have, from appearances, as much, if not more, to receive to-morrow, which we shall forward by our regular express trains.

MUNIFICENCE OF NEW-YORKERS.

On the next day, the people of New York, not in the least having abated their interest in the Chicago sufferers, poured in contributions from every quarter. Immense supplies were furnished for consignment by the railroads, large numbers of persons of every age and both sexes came to the railroad depots with packages of various sizes and descriptions. At the Erie depot clothing came in bundles, bales, trunks, valises and cases. Boxes and barrels formed by far the largest part of the offerings. Provisions were also contributed in abundance of every kind. One firm in Williamsburgh, a sugar refinery, gave one hundred and four barrels of crushed sugar. The contributions received by the

Erie company alone amounted to about $100,000 per day for several days.

At a meeting of the Chamber of Commerce of New York City, held on the 11th of October, $109,243.50 were raised, and $32,082.00 reported for the day before, making a total of $181,325.50.

Five thousand dollars were contributed from the funds of the Gold Exchange, and in addition the members subscribed quite liberally, especially, as many of them, as members of the Merchants' Exchange had previously subscribed large sums. Their contributions and those through the Drug Exchange Committee, were $12,086. The Wholesale Coal Traders, at a meeting on the same day subscribed $4,300 and a Committee was appointed to obtain further contributions. The total subscriptions by the Exchange up to the 10th, were $27,000, and of the Cotton Exchange, $14,000. The Jersey City Board of Finance and Taxation voted to issue one year bonds for $50,000 for the relief of the sufferers.

In the Academy of Music, Brooklyn, a mass meeting was held for the purpose of raising means for the relief of the sufferers.

The amount of all the subscriptions, from every source, thus grandly commenced, reached an enormous figure.

In thus giving some of the initial work in raising funds for the Chicago sufferers in the Metropolis of the country, we give only what was done in every other city of the country, in proportion to its size, population and commercial and manufacturing importance. The total amount raised by the Chamber of Commerce Committee of New York, reached the enormous sum of $905,095.46.

DONATIONS BY THE PRESS.

Robert Bonner, publisher of the New York *Ledger*, presented $10,000 to the publishers and news dealers of Chicago who had suffered by the fire, and Street & Smith of the New York *Weekly* sent a private agent with $10,000 to seek out and assist individual dealers who had lost their all.

Such generous deeds can never be forgotten. They merit and receive reward. These large-hearted men will find that they sowed seed in good ground, which will bring forth fruit a hundred fold.

When the news of the fearful catastrophy reached Philadelphia, Geo. W. Childs, proprietor of the Ledger, was absent, not

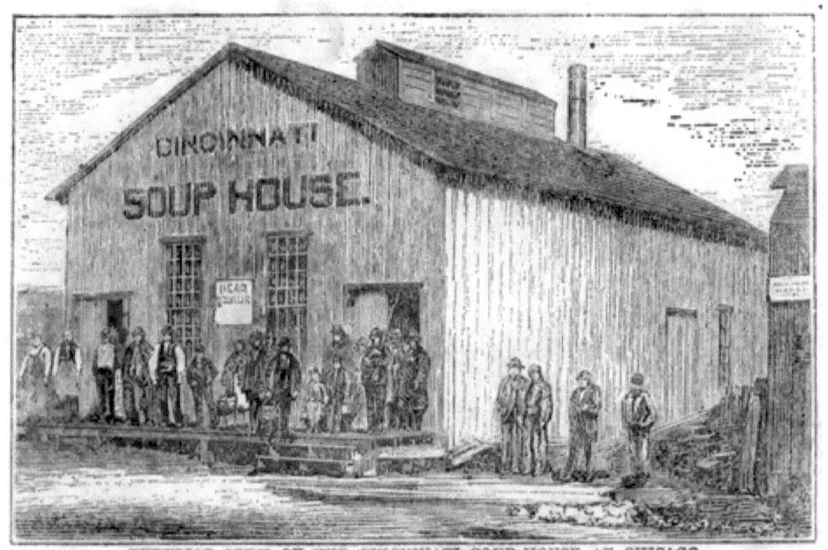

EXTERIOR VIEW OF THE CINCINNATI SOUP-HOUSE AT CHICAGO.

INTERIOR VIEW OF THE CINCINNATI SOUP HOUSE, ON PEORIA STREET.

having returned from his tour in Europe. His friends, however, knowing his benevolent nature, subscribed $5,000 in his name. A few days thereafter, Mr. Childs returned, and his first act was to ratify the act of his friends in respect to the donation. Few men are so proverbially liberal, that friends would dare to display such generosity in their names during their absence. But in this case it was perfectly safe, there not being a shadow of doubt but he would approve of it. All honor to Geo. W. Childs.

MUNIFICENCE OF CINCINNATTI.

Cincinnatti, agreeably to her generous antecedents, on the occasion of the great calamity, sounded the depths of her benevolent impulses and munificently poured forth her charities to alleviate the distresses of the suffering citizens of Chicago.

Her city council was immediately convened by order of Mayor Davis, and with noble generosity voted to appropriate $100,000. The Chamber of Commerce held a special meeting, as did the Board of Trade, to institute measures of relief, at which the members subscribed generously, which, together with the donations of citizens in their private capacity, reached the splendid sum of $125,000.

Immediately, on the receipt of the terrible news that their sister city was in flames, several of her best steam-fire engines were dispatched to Chicago, with a competent force of experienced firemen to manage them, under the efficient management of Miles Greenwood, which on their arrival did admirable service. Then, with all possible celerity, twenty car-loads of provisions were forwarded, with an efficient committee to superintend their distribution. In order to make their contributions more efficient and lasting, so as to serve during the entire winter, they erected a spacious soup house at the rear of the freight depot of the Great Eastern Railroad. To convey to our readers an idea of this splendid charity, we give below a description of the CINCINNATTI SOUP HOUSE.

The Cincinnatti soup-house, was located at the cor. of Green and Carroll streets. The building, a plain frame structure, 30x50 feet, erected at a cost of $2,500. The machinery essential to its operation was simple and cheap. The soup was cooked in six large tubs, each filled with pipes, through which the steam was admitted. The ingredients of the soup were beans, rice, barley and vegetables of all kinds. The cooking was thorough, and the soup produced was not excelled by that of the same kind furnished at the best hotels in the city. The establishment has a capacity to furnish 16,000 gallons daily.

The rule was to give each person one-sixth of a gallon. About 3,500 were daily served. This soup-house was the only point of supply. There was, however, another point of distribution at the barracks, corner of Centre avenue and Harrison street, where about half the amount was dealt out. Another place of distribution was established on the North side. At the central soup-house it was furnished from 7 in the morning until 7 in the evening. At the barracks from 9 until 5. Seven-eighths of all those who applied were women and children whose husbands and fathers were, to a certain extent, occupied in the various industries of the city.

The low rates at which people were fed will perhaps astonish most people when they learn it. The entire cost of running this establishment was only $241.60 per week, including all contingents. For this sum they furnished 24,500 rations a week. This makes the soup about one cent per ration, or six cents per gallon. By increasing the amount it can be furnished for four and one-half cents per gallon, making the entire expense of feeding one person for a day not more than four cents, supposing the diet to be entirely of soup.

The institution was under the especial superintendence of Rev. R. Frankland, formerly connected with the Cincinnati Bethel and many other worthy charities. It was supported by a fund of $25,000, set aside for that purpose from the special appropriation made for Chicago relief by the Cincinnati Council. The advisability of selling this soup at a very moderate rate to those who do not desire to receive it as a charity, has been considered and it is possible that some plan to accomplish that end may be adopted.

It will thus be seen that the charity of Cincinnati was not only upon a grand scale, but conducted with intelligence, and upon such economical, and wise principles, that their benefits were timely, effectual and likely to continue as long as the necessity for them existed.

ST. LOUIS NOBLY GENEROUS.

The people of St. Louis, also proverbial for their generous sympathies, came up gloriously to the work of relieving the distressed.

Mayor Brown promptly convened the city council which voted to appropriate $50,000. But this sum was but a fraction of what her liberal citizens contributed. The ladies of St Louis, with commendable earnestness and indefatigable energy, set themselves to work in every way in their power to alleviate the distressed. They gathered large quantities of clothing and other necessary articles, and promptly forwarded them under the charge of a committee of ladies.

SISTERS OF MERCY.

The executive committee received a letter from the Sisters of Mercy, residing in Twenty-third and Morgan streets, offering to accommodate one hundred girls, seeking situations, if beds were provided by the committee. This was referred to the Ladies Executive Committee.

The following correspondence ensued by telegraph :

MEMPHIS, Oct. 12.

HON. JOS. BROWN, Mayor :
Persons rendered destitute by the Chicago fire will be passed free, from Humboldt to Memphis, on certificate issued by your authority, or by the superintendent of the Iron Mountain or St. Louis & Cairo Short Line railroads.

J. F. BOYD, Supt.

LEAVENWORTH, Oct. 12.

HON. JOS. BROWN, Mayor, St. Louis :
Thanks for your dispatch. Have sent to Chicago four car loads of provisions and clothing. Committee leave immediately with ten thousand dollars in cash. All classes are at work in behalf of the sufferers, and I can promise with safety that Leavenworth will swell her contributions to twenty thousand dollars.

JOHN A. HALDEMAN, Mayor.

REPLY.

OCTOBER 13.

JNO. A. HALDEMAN, Mayor, Leavenworth, Kansas :
Your dispatch received for the Chicago destitute. You are doing nobly. You are fully up to St. Louis in proportion to your population. Every one is now realizing that it is more blessed to give than to receive.

JOSEPH BROWN, Mayor.

GEO. FRANCIS TRAIN.

LEAVENWORTH, Ks., Oct. 12.

Mayor BROWN, and Citizens' Committee for Chicago Sufferers :
Will lecture 19th. Dollar tickets, donating entire proceeds to Chicago.

GEORGE FRANCIS TRAIN.

ANSWER.

Oct. 13.

GEO. FRANCIS TRAIN, Wyandotte, Ks. :
Your dispatch received proposing to lecture for benefit of Chicago sufferers, at one dollar each, signed Geo. Francis Train.
The executive committee desire me to say that our people are in no mood to listen to lectures, but will gladly receive and forward any money you may wish to donate.
JOS. BROWN, Mayor.

The work thus promptly begun in St. Louis, was continued for days until the most pressing necessities were passed, she nobly doing her full duty.

LOUISVILLE.

Louisville did not fall behind her sister cities, Cincinnati and St. Louis, in active deeds of charity, but through the action of her city council, public meetings, benevolent societies and efforts of her generous hearted citizens, made large contribution, meriting and receiving the public thanks of the authorities of Chicago.

If it were not to repeat, in nearly the same language in each case, we might donate several pages to each city in the Union, in presenting to our readers the grand uprising of the people in this hour of frightful need.

Every city did nobly, and of course, to a great extent, carried out nearly the same programme, bringing into requisition the municipal governments, Merchants Exchanges, Benevolent Societies, Theatres, Ladies' Relief Societies, etc.

As so terrible a catastrophe tended to demoralize everything, and produce the utmost confusion, by request of the Mayor, General Sheridan assumed command of the city, and through his wise, prompt, and energetic movements, brought harmony out of discord. We give below an order of the general:

"HEADQUARTERS OF MILITARY DIVISION OF MISSOURI, CHICAGO, October 12.

To his Honor, the Mayor.—The preservation of the peace and good order of the city having been intrusted to me, by your Honor, I am happy to state that no case of outbreak or disorder has been reported, that no authenticated attempt in incendiarism has reached me, and that the people of the city are calm, quiet, and well disposed. The force at my disposal is ample to maintain order should it be necessary to protect the district devastated by fire. Still, I would suggest to citizens not to relax in their watchfulness until the smouldering fires of the burned buildings are entirely extinguished. P. H. SHERIDAN,
Lieutenant General.

HOUSES OF WORSHIP.

As most of the houses of worship were destroyed, and funds called for to rebuild church edifices as well as to relieve individual cases of distress, an appeal was made to the Churches in all parts of the union and nobly responded to.

At St. Patrick's Cathedral, New York, the very Rev. Dr. Starrs, Vicar General, read the following circular addressed to the Catholic Clergy:

To THE REVEREND PASTORS OF CATHOLIC CHURCHES IN THIS CITY.—The cry for help which comes to us in such piercing tones from the thousands of our fellow beings in Chicago, seated amid the ashes of their desolated city, without food or shelter, appeals so forcibly to every human heart, that there is not one, I am sure, having in his power to give relief, be it much, or be it little, that will not promptly do so with willingness and generous hand. In order that greater facilities may be offered to all the members of our flock, for the expression of a great act of Christian charity, I hereby recommend that a collection be made in all the Churches of the city on Sunday after next, 22d inst.; due announcement to be made on next Sunday. The sums collected should be sent immediately to the chancery office, that they may be remitted without delay to succor the distressed.

† JOHN, Archbishop of New York.

Given at New York, this 10th day of October, 1871.

The Churches generally, throughout the country, did good work in this hour of dire necessity.

BOOKSELLERS ROW, STATE STREET

KERFOOT'S BLOCK AFTER THE FIRE.

The American Bible Society generously signified its intention to supply all sufferers from the fire with a copy of the Holy Scriptures, gratuitously.

Rev. Dr. O. H. Tiffany's Church, St. Paul's, Newark, sent $1,500. Mrs. Tiffany coming to Chicago to assist in the distribution.

The Ladies' Relief Committee of Philadelphia sent six large boxes of clothing, and two containing women and children's shoes.

Philadelphia sent $500,000 to Chicago, and Quincy, Ill., $20,000 and a train load of provisions.

Quite a number of the students at Yale College are from Chicago. One student of the College is said to have lost $200,000, which he owned in his own right, while another, an orphan, has been reduced to penury from opulence.

ACTION OF THE OFFICIALS AND CITIZENS OF WASHINGTON.

WASHINGTON, Oct. 11.—The following was telegraphed to Boston to-day, viz:
EXECUTIVE MANSION, Washington, Oct. 11.

To the Hon. Samuel Hooper, Boston, Mass:
Would it not be well for the good people of Boston to dispense with the ceremony and expense of a public reception on the occasion of my visit to your city, and to appropriate such portion of the fund set apart for that purpose as is deemed advisable for the relief of the sufferers by the Chicago disaster? I am, yours
U. S. GRANT.

The following was received here to-day:

CHICAGO, Oct. 11.
To E. D. Townsend, Adjutant-General, Washington:
There was some excitement here yesterday and last evening, but it is now quieting down. Some of the troops from Leavenworth and Omaha are coming in. I have taken all the necessary steps to meet the condition of affairs here.
P. H. SHERIDAN.

Supplies of tents from Jeffersonville, Ind, on Gen. Sheridan's requisition, were forwarded. Gen. Van Vliet sent at $7\frac{1}{2}$ this morning Major Hodges, of the Quartermaster's Department, in charge of a special train from Philadelphia, with blankets. They will reach Chicago on Thursday, and Gen. Sheridan has been advised that there are more tents at Jeffersonville at his disposal.

Every effort was made at once to prevent any delay in mails for the North-west. George S. Bangs, Superintendent of the Railway Mail Service, one of the oldest and most efficient Post-office men in the country, reached Chicago, and everything possible was done to reorganize mail service at once.

Several Thousand dollars were raised to-day among the clerks and employees of the Treasury and other Departments.

The Secretary of the Treasury, this morning, received telegrams from London and Canada, inquiring if clothing, blankets, &c., for the people of Chicago, would be admitted free of duty. The Secretary immediately replied that such goods would be admitted free, and gave the necessary orders to Collectors.

Acting-Governor Stanton issued a proclamation convening the Legislative Assembly at once to legalize a loan of $100,000 for the relief of Chicago. Twenty-five thousand dollars on that account was at once forwarded. The amount contributed in the Post-office Department, July 11th, was $2,400, the Post-master-General and First-Assistant Smith heading the list with liberal subscriptions. The Board of Supervising Inspectors contributed $220, being $20 for each member of the board. Various measures were taken to increase the subscriptions by benevolent associations, churches, concerts, theatrical performances, &c. There seems little doubt that the District of Columbia will, in the aggregate, contribute not less than $150,000.

THE TYPOGRAPHICAL UNION.

At a Special meeting of the New York Typographical Union, the sum of $2,000 was appropriated for the relief of the members of the Chicago Printers' Union who were left destitute by the fire. A resolution was also adopted requesting the President of the National Typographical Union to call on the subordinate Unions under his jurisdiction to take immediate action for the relief of the members.

The Typographical Unions elsewhere did their proportion of Charitable work, although we have not the data to present to our readers the amount, or even an approximation to it, which the Unions in the country contributed in the aggregate.

JUVENILE GENEROSITY.

At one of the schools in Pawtucket, R. I., the children were given a recess to go home and bring whatever wearing apparel they had to spare, to be forwarded to the Chicago sufferers. One of the little girls on going home for her share, found that her mother had stepped out. Overflowing with generosity, she concluded that it was all right and she would help herself. She accordingly packed up all her dresses and every other article of apparel of which she was in possession, save those she was wearing, and with a countenance beaming with joy because she deemed that she had performed a praiseworthy act, presented them to the Committee, who, of course, packed them with the rest and sent them away.

LADIES DISTRIBUTING CLOTHING TO THE SUFFERERS.

GETTING WATER FROM THE ARTESIAN WELL.

When the little girl's mother came to look for a change of clothes for the child after school, the discovery was made of what had been done, when the consternation of the family can better be immagined than described. The little girl, with the utmost *sang froid* imaginable, said she "had been sent home for the clothes and guessed she wasn't going back without them." We opine that the mother of so generous-hearted a child was not herself deficient in kindly and charitable impulses; and, therefore, although put about for the time to obtain a re-supply, within her inmost heart she blessed her little darling for the noble deed.

Had a tithe of interesting incidents like the one just related been brought to light a volume much larger than this could be filled with them alone, which would be a monument of glory to the nation that produced so many angelic natures, so exhalting to humanity and so creditable to the race. The pure gold will show itself at intervals, the diamond will sometimes come to the light and display its luster, though hidden for years.

RELIEF SOCIETIES.

Hundreds of Relief Societies were specially improvised in every part of the country, all doing noble and efficient work. During the week of the fire meetings were called in nearly all the churches to take action in regard to the sufferers; and, on the following Sunday, nearly all the pastors of churches in the land delivered sermons upon the unprecedented calamity, some of which were eloquent in the extreme; nearly all breathing the true spirit of benevolence, and giving an earnest exhortation to their congregations to give liberally to those so suddenly reduced from affluent and comfortable circumstances to penury. To the credit of their hearers those appeals were responded to majestically, and large sums of money were raised in the churches. In addition to the money raised for general relief the churches took action in regard to relieving the distresses of individual members of their respective denominations who were in want, and too sensitive to make their wants known to the General Committee.

HONOR TO THE LADIES.

The ladies, ever foremost where real suffering demand their symathy and attention, promptly formed Relief Societies, within and outside of their church organizations, and solicited donations of money, clothing, bedding, and every other article which could be forwarded to, **or used, in** the ill-fated **city.** They also contributed and solicited donations of different materials to be made up, and **with their** sewing machines and dexterous fingers, soon converted **them into** wearing apparel for men, women and children, or into articles of bedding, which by their own committees were speedily **dispatched** by rail; and, in some instances, brave and philanthropic women left the comforts of home to assist for days **in the** distribution of those articles, to those they deemed most deserving and needy. A more sublime spectacle of true charity was never before enacted in so brief a space of time.

The outpouring of money, food of every description, and every nameable article of human necessity, was inconceivably enormous. **It was indeed a magnificent** display of generosity. There was **something grand,** magestic, almost God-like, **in it.** The fire was mighty in its devastation, but the people of the country, mightier still, **in the** marvelous promptitude and rapidity with which **they** furnished **and forwarded the grand** relief.

A STRIKING INCIDENT OF GENEROSITY.

The following, individual **case,** so beautifully **exemplifies** true charity and large-heartedness **on the part** of Mr. Hudson and his wife, that although **they may not thank us for thus publicly** using their names, **we feel impelled, in justice to true benevolence, to thus far offer our tribute of appreciation for their generous deeds:**

E. A. Snively, of the **Macoupin Enquirer, has this story concerning Ed. Hudson and the Chicago fire:**

A day or two before leaving Peoria, we heard a good **one** on Mr. Ed. Hudson, superintendent of the P. P. & J. Railroad and a gentleman well known to railroad men. Upon hearing of the burning of Chicago, his first act was to telegraph to all **agents** to transport free all provisions for Chicago, and to receive such articles to **the** exclusion of freight. He then purchased a number of good hams and sent them **home** with a request to his wife to cook them as soon as possible, so they might **be** sent to Chicago. He then ordered the baker to put up fifty loaves of bread. He was kept busy during the day until five o'clock. Just as he was starting for home the baker informed him that the hundred loaves of bread were ready.

"But I only ordered fifty," said Ed.

"Mrs. Hudson also ordered fifty," said the baker.

"All right," **said Ed.,** and he inwardly blessed his wife for the **generous** deed.

Arriving at **home he found** his little boy dressed in a fine cloth suit, carrying in wood. He **told him that** would not do, he must change his clothes.

"But **mother sent all** my clothes to Chicago," replied the boy.

Entering **the house he** found his wife clad in a fine silk dress, superintending the cooking. A remark in regard to the matter elicited the information that she had sent her other dresses to Chicago.

The matter was getting serious. He sat down to a **supper** without butter, because all that could be purchased had been sent to Chicago. There were no pickles—the poor souls in Chicago would relish them so much.

A little "put out," but not a bit angry or disgusted, Ed. went to the wardrobe to get his overcoat, but it was not there. An interrogatory revealed the fact that it fitted the box real well, and he needed a new overcoat any way, although he had paid $50 for the one in question only a few days before. An examination revealed that all the rest of the clothes fitted the box real nicely, for not a "dud" did he possess except those he had on.

While he admired the generosity of his wife, he thought the matter was getting entirely too personal, and he turned to her with the characteristic inquiry:

"Do you think we can stand an *encore* on that Chicago fire?"

But this generous sympathy in this sudden affliction was not confined to the United States. The neighboring provinces of the British Dominions were equally liberal, their people sending out donations in great abundance, of every description. Army tents and blankets in large numbers were supplied by order of the home government. Meetings were also promptly held in London and other cities of Great Britain, and in all prominent cities over Europe, and large amounts of money subscribed. The British People responded liberally, nobly, grandly; for which the American people will ever hold them in kind and grateful remembrance.

EFFECT OF THE NEWS IN ENGLAND—ACTIVE MEASURES TAKEN FOR THE RELIEF OF THE SUFFERERS.

LONDON, Oct. 11.—The chief topic of interest here in all circles, is the calamity which has overtaken Chicago. At Clubs, exchanges, news-rooms, in the parlors of hotels, everywhere where men were assembled, the appalling disaster was talked about, and the brief account transmitted through the cables discussed. At first the telegrams were regarded as greatly exaggerated; but as each succeeding dispatch confirmed and increased the extent of the losses, and private advices began to be received, a feeling of deep sympathy was aroused, and a desire was manifested to contribute in some effective manner to the relief of the sufferers. This disposition was quickly directed to the proper channel by prominent gentlemen and firms opening subscription lists and volunteering to receive and forward contributions. Hon. HUGH McCULLOCH, J. S. MORGAN & Co., and other American bankers, were among the first to take active measures in this behalf.

At Liverpool a Committee was organized and dispatched a cargo of food and clothing.

Mr. SCHENCK, the United States Minister, issued an invitation to all Americans in and near London to meet at the Langham

Hotel for the purpose of organizing relief committees. Gen. ADAM BADEAU, the United States Consul-General, sent a circular to all the Consuls and consular agents within his jurisdiction, requesting their active aid and participation in the work of collecting and forwarding contributions from their respective territories.

The *Times* had a leader on the subject, deploring the fire, and hoping the dispatches magnified the loss; expressing faith in the energy of Americans, and in the resources of Chicago, and earnestly wishing that the unfortunate city and its suffering inhabitants might promptly recover from the effects of the disaster.

Other journals made the same topic prominent. Several of them recalled the munificence of America to the starving people of Lancaster, and declared that Englishmen must not only repay that generous kindness, but must aid to restore the city which has been regarded as a monument of American enterprise.

The English papers, immediately after the fire, came to us with copious accounts of sympathetic meetings held in the principal cities of the United Kingdom.

Birmingham was the first in the field, and, while the flames were still ravaging the unfortunate Garden city, held a meeting in their splendid Town Hall, presided over by the Mayor, attended by a large number of the most public spirited citizens.

The generous action of the meeting was moved by Mr. Goodman, and seconded by Mr. Gem. Gems of goodness they certainly displayed, and they have scintillated across the board Atlantic, and sparkle still with such brilliancy that there is no probability that their luster will fade, or their light cease to illuminate the paths of humanity, so long as the world stands. Such gems of goodness, more precious a hundred-fold, than diamonds of the first water, are rich jewels upon the brow of our sister nation— or, perhaps, more endearing, our mother country—and will draw and bind us to her with an indissoluble tie.

On the 11th of Oct., the Home Government sent a cable dispatch to the authorities in Canada, to offer to Chicago all the military tents and blankets in the Dominion.

The subscriptions throughout the kingdom were very extensive, and evinced the earliest and most generous and sympathetic feelings of the English people toward the people of the ill-fated city, and, in fact, toward the entire people of the country.

THE CAPITAL OF THE GERMAN EMPIRE CONTRIBUTE $25,000 TO THE CHICAGO SUFFERERS—INTERESTING CORRESPONDENCE BETWEEN U. S. CONSUL KREISMANN AND MAYOR MASON.

The German people responded also in a generous manner, large sums having been raised and promptly forwarded. We append the following:

On the 17th of October, only eight days after the great fire, Messrs. Hardt & Co., of New York city, forwarded to Mayor Mason, of Chicago, their draft for $15,000, contributed by the people of Berlin, Prussia, in aid of the sufferers by the fire. This splendid gift was duly acknowledged by Mayor Mason in a letter to the Chairman of the Chicago Relief Committee at Berlin, as was also the subsequent donation of $10,000 more from the same source. Still later the following letter was received from the United States Consul at Berlin:

BERLIN, Oct. 20, 1871.

To His Honor the Mayor of the City of Chicago:

SIR: The appalling calamity that has befallen our beloved Chicago, involving such destruction of use and beauty, of commerce, civilization and progress, as has never been recorded in human annals, has awakened earnest and genuine sympathy throughout all Germany. The burning of our great and beautiful city, the grandest and most conspicuous monument of the genius and enterprise of the American people, under free and liberal institutions and government, is justly considered a national, not a mere local calamity. It is felt that a long and cruel train of horrors and sufferings must follow the awful destruction that has swept over the ill-fated city; and everywhere funds have been and are being raised for the relief of the vast necessities of your destitute and stricken people. Being one of your citizens, allied to Chicago by many associations of public services and friendship, and glorying in its marvelous growth, prosperity and splendor, the horror of the announcement of its sudden destruction by fire unspeakably shocked and overwhelmed me; but feeling that I must do whatever little there might be in my power toward aiding and assisting my fellow citizens in their dire distress, I promptly took steps to organize a relief committee here, and, thanks to the ready response to my appeals, we have thus far given orders to Messrs. Hardt & Co., of New York, to pay to your order the sum of $25,000, which the committee trust you have promptly received.

Among the contributors to the fund are found the Emperor and Empress, the Queen Dowager, and the Crown Prince and Crown Princess. The Empress, to quote the language of the letters transmitting me the donations, given in "grateful remembrance of the sympathy displayed by America during the late war," and the Crown Prince and Crown Princess "in grateful acknowledgement of the friendly feelings which America most efficiently manifested for the German warriors during the conflict with France, and in heartfelt sympathy for the inhabitants of Chicago smitten by terrible misfortune."

Our collections are still going on and promise additional results. To enable the committee to properly account to the contributors for the sums received, I am directed to respectfully ask your Honor to make suitable acknowledgement of the receipt of the amounts transmitted to you from Berlin. In the meantime we all here feel that the people of Chicago, though grievously tried, and well nigh overcome, have not and will not lose hope and heart, and with the help of God, and by their undaunted courage, enterprise, skill, and energy, will rebuild and restore their city to even greater wealth, usefulness and splendor—a consumation most fervently to be desired and hoped for. I have the honor to be, sir, your obedient servant.

H. KREISMANN, United States Consul.

CHICAGO, Nov. 21, 1871.

H. Kreismann, United States Consul, Berlin

SIR: Your letter of October 26, advising me of the remittance to Messrs. Hardt & Co., of New York, of $25,000 from the Relief Committee of Berlin for the use of the destitute of Chicago, is duly received. On the 21st of October I acknowledged to Messrs. Hardt & Co., and to the Berlin committee, the receipt of $15,000 of the above sum, and on the 2nd of this month acknowledgment was made of the remaining $10,000. For this proof of the active sympathy of the people of Berlin for those who were almost ready to perish, permit us to offer you, on their behalf, most heart-felt gratitude. The unprecedented calamity of the 8th and 9th of October, which stripped 100,000 people of all their worldly possessions, has still left upon the books of the Relief Society (which has now the management of this great charity) not less than seventy-five thousand men, women and children, dependent for their daily bread, for shelter, and sufficient clothing, upon public charity. To care for this multitude, with any efficiency would have been utterly impossible but for the generous sympathy and aid which this calamity has called forth from all parts of the civilized world. This wide spread beneficence, it is hoped, will help us to carry the people through the long winter before us without essential suffering; and your Relief Committee, will understand how thankfully their large contribution is received. A very large proportion of the sufferers by the fire are Germans, who, especially, will be deeply sensible of the kind exertions of yourself and the other members of the committee to relieve their excessive wants. I remain, very respectfully, your obedient servant,

R. B. MASON, Mayor.

The Empress Augusta of Germany, contributed a thousand thalurs ($800) for the relief of the Chicago sufferers.

THE CHINAMEN'S CONTRIBUTIONS FOR CHICAGO.

The San Francisco, Alta says that when the Committee in that city to solicit contributions from the Chinese merchants for the relief of the Chicago sufferers made known the object of their visit the response was a credit to the representatives of that race, who have been treated with indignity on so many occasions, and are liable at any time to be assaulted when passing through the streets. In one case an intelligent merchant said to the collectors: "Me leadee in Alta, Melican man town all same hap gone—burnee up. Melican man wantee dollas; some time poor Melican man strikee Chinaman with blicks; Chinaman no care. Alle people Chicago losee everything—wifee and childlen burn out. Chinamen say alle same my countree peoplee—wantee help. How muchee dollas you wantee? Hundled dollas? Allee light; you not find enough money commee again, give another hundled." The contributions thus given by the merchants reached $1,200. Not bad for the "Heathen Chinee."

CHICAGO RELIEF AND AID SOCIETY.

In order to facilitate and judiciously distribute donations for the relief of the sufferers, the Chicago Relief and Aid Society was formed at once. Wirt Dexter being made chairman, and

Geo. M. Pullman, treasurer. The society did noble and efficient work; and, through its instrumentality, donations from abroad were no doubt more properly, beneficially, and satisfactorily divided. This society had its various committees which co-operated with the committees for distribution from abroad, and generally working with great cordiality and harmony; all conscientiously laboring to relieve the distresses of those around them, which was nobly done by the prompt collection and disbursement of $2,051,023,56, with arrangements for extending this munificent sum to $3,000,000. This includes the funds in the hands of the New York Chamber of Commerce, amounting to about $600,000, and the balance of the Boston fund, about $240,000, both amounting to $840,000 not yet placed to the credit of this Society, but which may undoubtedly be relied upon to meet the demands of the future. As to our disbursements, we can only say that we are at present aiding 60,000 people at regular distributing points. Some of this vast number we relieve in part only, but the greater portion to the extent of their entire support. This is in addition to the work of the special Relief Committee for people who ought to be sent to the general distributing points, and which is largely increasing upon our hands. It is only in addition to the expenditures of the committee on existing charitable institutions.

The great matter pressing upon the committee is shelter for the coming winter. We may feed people during the mild weather, but where and how they are to be housed—permanently housed—we regard as the serious question. To this end we have been aiding those burned out to replace comfortable houses upon their own, or leased lots, where they can live, not only this winter, but next summer, and be ready to work in rebuilding the city. Of these houses—which are really very comfortable, being 16 by 20 feet, with two rooms, one 12 by 16 feet, and one 8 by 16 feet, with a planed and matched floor, panel doors, and good windows—we have already furnished over 4,000, making permanent homes, allowing five for a family, for 20,000 people, and with the 7,000 houses which we expect to build, shall have homes for 35,000 people. These houses and some barracks, in both of which there is a moderate outfit of furniture, such as stoves, mattresses, and a little crockery, will consume $1,250,000, leaving $2,200,009, with which to meet all the demands for food, fuel, clothing, and general expenses, from the 13th of October last.

By this statement we see the gigantic proportions of the work in which they were all engaged. That they conscientiously and faithfully performed their work there is no question. That they have been misrepresented and slandered, while doing their utmost for the good of the sufferers, is but the usual fate of true philanthropists; and we rejoice that, notwithstanding they have received abuses, which, in nearly, if not every case, were entirely unjust, they have pursued their work with an eye single to the great object before them, trusting to the future, to set their work and motives in the true light. As this Society is composed of high-minded, honorable, and competent men, whose reputation is dear to them, and who have undertaken this responsible and Herculean task voluntarily, working night and day to relieve the distressed, the public outside of Chicago may rely implicitly upon their faithfully and justly performing their whole duty; and performing it as well as it can be done by human instruments until their work is accomplished. Their ability to do the work before them is undoubted. Of their integrity there is no question. Some of the instruments they at first used in their mighty work no doubt were worthless and worse than worthless; but experience corrected such mistakes.

This Society established depots in different districts of the city for the reception of supplies, that they might distribute them to the needy with more facility. There was also a special relief Committee, doing their whole duty.

CHARITY OF THE RIGHT STRIPE—WOMAN'S INDUSTRIAL AID SOCIETY.

Some of the ladies and gentlemen connected with the various Churches of Chicago effected an organization to give relief, by light and agreeable employment, to women and children who had become straightened in their circumstances by the fire, but who prefered to acquire subsistence by their labor, rather than by the charity of others. This common sense, timely, and excellent movement, was inaugurated on the 28th of October, at the old building, widely known as St. John's Protestant Episcopal Church, Union Park. No Society was ever organized in Chicago so unselfish and devoid of sectarianism as this. Its platform broad enough for all to stand upon. The means of sus-

A NIGHT SCENE IN GRACE CHURCH. CITIZENS PREPARING FOR REST.

taining it was ample; the room well fitted for the purpose, and the superintendents overflowing with kindness.

Thousands of cultivated and refined women were thrown out of employment by the burning of stores, offices, and factories, and this society provided the means to enable them to still earn a livelihood, without being subjected to the humiliation of receiving charity. Many women who were heretofore obliged to work at starvation prices, to the shame of their employers, were by the aid of this Society able to earn remunerative prices. The Work of the relief society is enormous, extending over many miles, and in all its departments embracing from 50,000 to 75,000 people.

MISS BARTON AND CHICAGO.

Miss Barton, who has done so much for the suffering and helpless ones in this and the old world, but who was in Paris, France, when our fearful conflagration took place, wrote a letter full of sympathy and consolation.

Few persons better comprehend the terrible situation or would be more competent to labor in this needful yet noble work. Our people remember with pride and lasting gratitude the good work she did in the field and in the hospitals during our terrible war; and since the conflict of arms between France and Prussia, Miss Barton has often been heard of at Strasbourg, Metz, and Paris. In a letter from Paris, upon the receipt of the awful news from Chicago, she says:

"My soul was darkened and my heart wrung by the intelligence. For the last twelve months I have stood only in the ashes of burned and destroyed cities, working among the shelterless, naked, and starving inhabitants. In Strasbourg I found 20,000 people without a roof, or bread, or fire, or clothes, or work. I worked with them until all were housed and clothed. Forty thousand warm garments were made by their own hands, and they were saved from beggary. When I entered Metz I found 40,000 people too weak to riot. They stared vacantly, tottered, and fell, like old men and women, or little children. Seven months after this, when I stood among the smoking piles and vaults of Paris, and its twice ruined thousands, I felt it was time I found an end of such scenes and such labors. I thought I had learned my lesson."

The appalling news of a greater calamity than all these having reached her, the whole promptings of her sympathetic nature again tell her she must do and dare still longer for suffering humanity.

Her services are promptly offered to our citizens, if needed. Just now the people of Chicago are tolerably comfortable, owing to the large-heartedness and noble generosity of the people everywhere throughout the country. But a long, cold, dreary winter is before them, and if charities are not constantly kept up, before Spring there will be sufferings beyond all computation. Food is abundant in the West and very cheap, comparatively speaking, and if the Relief Committees judiciously expend the monies at their disposal, probably there is no necessity of any persons suffering from hunger. The greatest needs are comfortable shelter, clothing, and fuel. These must all be provided for thousands until next June, when the milder weather will naturally relieve many necessities. It is the work of this nation, to see that all these things are amply supplied. Everybody can help some. Miss Barton, possessing knowledge, and having had experience in this particular line, far beyond nearly all others, her services would be of the greatest value in organizing and conducting a grand system of benevolence having for its task the feeding, clothing and housing of thousands of men, women and children for many long and cheerless weeks. By all means, she and all other noble philanthropists like her, should be cordially and thankfully invited to help the good, though arduous work. There is no estimating the worth of the grand sympathies and glorious charities which this awful calamity has developed not only in this country, but all over Europe.

PERSONAL.

Robert Collyer, the celebrated and brave Chicago preacher, whom the fire left nothing but his courage and his opportunities, says he don't know anything about the story that the students of Cornell University have invited him to make a "first class horse shoe," for which they will pay him $2,000, the money to go to relieve the Chicago sufferers or towards the building of a new Unity Church. He seems to wish it were true, however, as must all his friends, and says:

"I write this to stop the thing if it be bogus, or to hurry it along if it be real; because I am now ready to go to work right off at the price named, and when I have made one shoe for the Cornell boys, price $2,000, and got the money into the treasury of the Relief and Aid Society, I will reduce my price one-half and make as many more as the whole world has a mind to order, and apply the whole income of the same to rebuilding first my church and then my home." There is a chance that Collyer's horse shoes may be in demand.

TOUCHING WORDS OF THANKS.

ONE OF THE BABIES BORN ON THE PRAIRIE.

Mr. John A. Nolan, formerly of Boston, writes to Mr. O. W. Newcomb, of that city, as follows:

"MY DEAR FRIEND.—You doubtless think of my family and self as dead. I am happy to inform you that my wife and my babe are now well. Our little daughter (our first born) was born in Lincoln Park on Sunday morning, the 8th inst. I made a home of my coat, a sheet that a neighbor kindly loaned me, and a high hat that I picked up near our location. We were boarding at the Sherman House, but had to flee and leave everything. I was even left without my hat.

"God bless the Boston folks! and but for a warm bed and clothing from your noble city, my wife would now have been dead. A pair of blankets from Boston was brought to us in our hour of peril, thus saving the life of my wife and little one. How acceptable the food has been, too; but hundreds about us have nearly died from over eating, as well as from exposure. The first thing I got to eat was a 'Boston cracker.' I enjoyed it better than I ever enjoyed a dinner. I had a little money in my vest pocket, which will keep us a long while. We have a tent now, and are very comfortable, and should be perfectly happy if we only knew the fate of our dear mother, who is missing. I presume we never shall.

"I trust you will pardon the writing, for it is accomplished under many difficulties. We shall always bless your people for their great kindness. Three cheers went up for Boston from our little crowd last night. A little bundle of baby clothes was brought to us last night, with a label: "From the Christian Union of Boston." In the bundle was everything, even to a nursing bottle, a very acceptable article, which we were obliged to use. God bless the hands that did up that bundle; a mother must have done it. We call our baby Eva Boston, and we hope she may grow up to bless the donors of the first outfit.

GEN. P. H. SHERIDAN.

The following notice being given in the New York *Herald*, so just to a brave and efficient officer whose promptness is one of his chief characteristics, with pleasure we make room for it in this volume:

In the terrible ordeal through which the ill-fated city of Chicago has just passed, there appeared one man, at least, who, while the fiery tide swept over the city, was calm, collected, and self-controlled amid the excitement prevailing all around him. That man was General Sheridan. As at Winchester he arrived in time to rally his army and infuse spirit in his retiring soldiers to renew the struggle which secured them a glorious victory, so his presence at Chicago, when the city was wrapped in flames, had the effect of inspiring the almost despairing citizens with the hope that all was not yet lost. Self-controlled, determined, and vigilant, the hero of the Shenandoah Valley played a part in battling with the flames in the Garden City of the West, which will add to his renown and cause his name to be still more warmly cherished in the memory of his countrymen. With his handful of men he accomplished wonders. Fighting fire with fire, destroying to prevent greater destruction, blowing up buildings, the ruins of which were to serve as barricades against the fast consuming flames, General Sheridan contested every inch of its advance. As if Heaven itself smiled on the resoluteness with which the brave soldier fought for the safety of the homes of the unfortunate Chicagoans, it let fall copious torrents of rain to aid the strugglers, and thus the conflagration was stayed. But the labors of the soldier were not ended. Thousands of homeless men, women, and children, were without a place to lay their heads and without food to appease the cravings of hunger. For a second time did Sheridan's thoughtfulness and army experience come to the rescue. The tents and army rations provided through his forethought afforded shelter and food for the sufferers. This temporary relief bridged over the interim between the first effects of the terrible calamity and the reception of the first bounteous offerings of the people of the whole nation; who have never yet been deaf to the appeals of suffering or misfortune.

INSURANCE COMPANIES.

Although heavily taxed, with commendable rivalry they telegraphed from every part of the country assurances of their solvency, and determination to pay every dollar to those holding policies; alas, the only thing left to thousands, who, but a few days before, were estimated to be immensely wealthy. All the great companies, immediately commenced to settle up, and assured the people of Chicago that all liabilities would be paid as quickly as they could possibly be adjusted.

Of course, many insurance companies, in and outside of Chicago, by their enormous liabilities were obliged to suspend business.

The following will give the reader an idea of the enormous losses of the Insurance companies, summing up about $90,000,000.

The *Insurance Spectator* on the 10th of Nov. issued a table showing the aggregate losses of companies by States, the number suspended and assessed, and the number unaffected by the Chicago fire. The total number of companies in the United States is 335; aggregate capital $47,939,216; total losses, $82,821,122; companies suspended, 57; number assessed, 28; number not in the fire, 87. The following are the losses of companies by States: New York, $21,637,500; Ohio, $4,818,657; Massachusetts, $4,481,550; Pennsylvania, $2,082,000; Illinois, $33,878,000; Connecticut, $9,325,000; Rhode Island, $2,072,500; Maryland, $397,165; Wisconsin, $290,000; Michigan, $175,000; Minnesota, $100,000; Main, $30,000; Kentucky, $6,800; California, $2,950,000. The losses of foreign companies are $5,813,000.

Of the 335 companies doing a fire insurance business in the United States, 249 experienced losses more or less severe; while of the six English companies, but one escaped loss at Chicago. The American companies show an aggregate loss of $82,821,125, and the English companies of $5,813,000; so that the total insurance covered by this great conflagation may be summed up in round numbers at $90,000,000. The aggregate insurance capital of American companies amounts to $74,930,216; while the total assets of all the companies both English and American, amounts to $145,879,521.

Deducting the losses at Chicago the companies have about $60,000,000 left, the impairment being not far from $25,000,000 on the total capital. Of the 254 companies affected by the disaster, fifty-seven have suspended, and twenty-eight of the remainder have already taken measures toward the filling up of their respective deficencies. Illinois has suffered the most severely, no less than fourteen of her twenty companies have already stopped. Connecticut loses seven of her eleven companies. Rhode Island five out of nine.

One of the most remarkable effects of the disaster is the increase in the number of insurers. Those who have regularly insured have largely increased their lines, and property generally was never so well protected in this regard as now. Rates of premium have generally advanced, and the increased income of most of the companies will aid the process of recovery very greatly.

The Great Northwest Fires;

FULL DESCRIPTION, WITH THRILLING INCIDENTS.

Simultaneous with the Chicago calamity, the most terrific general conflagration known in the history of the world, raged throughout various parts of the Northwest, spreading devastation and death in its lurid pathway. The loss of life was vastly greater than at Chicago, and the destruction of property very great, most of it uninsured, and therefore a total loss. It is said that 480,000 acres of timbered lands were burnt over, equal to 750 square miles, and that the timber burned was equal to that which would yield a product of 1,800,000,000 feet of lumber—enough to build a large city.

It is now conceded by scientists that the Chicago fire, and the fires in Michigan and Wisconsin, were produced by natural causes beyond human foresight or control, and the startling theory that "they resulted from the passage of a great atmospheric stream, which arose in longitude sixty-two degrees, swept with a cyclone Antigua and the Virgin Isles on 21st August, the Bahamas on 23d, and then moved slowly to the Northwest, striking Chicago and the forests," is believed by scores of intelligent people.

The Peshtigo Fire.

A VIVID PICTURE.

The Sunday of the fire was noticed as a chilly day, though the atmosphere was still and filled with a dense, blinding smoke. The smoke created no alarm, as the smouldering fires in the pineries about, sufficiently accounted for it. Toward evening the smoke increased, while the chilliness of the atmosphere perceptibly abated, and early in the evening gave way to occasional hot puffs from the burnt districts. Soon after 8 o'clock in the evening, the warmth of the atmosphere still increasing, and the smoke almost suffocating in its density, a low, sullen rumbling began to be heard far away in the southwest, while a painfully ominous stillness pervaded the immediate vicinity of the town. People asked each other what was the matter, and tried to appear unconcerned while trembling with undefined apprehensions. At half-past eight the far-off rumbling had increased to a steady roar like distant thunder, or the coming of heavy freight trains at full speed. Men felt their way through the smoky streets and congregated at the hotels, in front of the stores, and all other places of resort, and discussed the strange sounds. Anxious mothers nervously and hesitatingly put their little ones to bed, and then peered out in the dismal streets to see what they could see. Nine o'clock came, and with it an alarming increase of the unknown sound, which now resembled the roar of a dozen freight trains racing at full speed, the location of the sound being sensibly nearer the town. Suddenly there was a cry of fire sounding through the smoke-beclouded streets, and men rushed hither and thither through the impenetrable blackness, rubbing their eyes for sight, and stumbling against each other as they ran. But no fire was found, though the search extended out of the village and into the edge of the woods, and the excited people hurried back to their houses laughing at each others apprehensions, and trying to feel secure.

Scarcely, however, had the first alarm subsided when the appalling cry was again raised in another quarter, and the blind running and colliding and stumbling was again renewed as the terror-stricken citizens sought a second time for the flames that were not to be found. But while this confusion was at its height, and while the majority of the men were away from their houses groping through clouds of smoke and blackness, and with a roar that was almost deafening filling their ears, a change began to manifest itself in the atmosphere. The whole air seemed sensibly agitated, and angry puffs of almost burning heat came sweeping through the town, while at quick intervals a frightful glare penetrated the dense dark smoke from the southwest, and at times seemed playing high up in the heavens above. Even the very earth seemed to quake and tremble. Horrors impended on every hand. Mothers caught their children from their beds and hastily dressed them. A cry of terror filled the town. Men hastened to their houses and collected their families about them. Many bolder ones caught up their valuables and buried them. Even the dumb beasts were seized with fright and ran bellowing through the streets. Then came nearer, clearer, and more deadly than before, that horrible roar, resembling the din of a mighty battle, and with it the more eccentric and violent agitation of the atmosphere, a more continuous show of the lurid glare overhead and in the southwest; while, to add to the horror of the night, great balls of fire like flaming missiles shot from unseen artillery, began falling on the housetops, in the streets, and all through the doomed village. The scenes that followed were an aggravation if possible of Dante's wonderful description of hell. Men, women, and children, horses, oxen, cows, dogs, swine, fowls—everything that had life, was seized with panic, and ran wildly, and with equal uncertainty to escape the impending destruction. Children got lost from their parents and were trampled upon by crazed brutes. Husbands and wives were calling loudly for each other and rushing in wild dismay, they knew not where.

The day of judgment had certainly come, in the opinion of the great majority, and yet they all sought to escape its terror. The oppressive, burning heat seemed to be the most dreaded affliction, and, following the instincts of the animals, those who could, ran to the water. The majority of the residences were on the southerly side of the river, while the company's store, boarding-houses, warehouses, and shops, occupied somewhat isolated positions on the northerly side of the stream. Many people rushed to these for safety. The great boarding-house was soon filled with people. A number of the Company's employees sought shelter in the stores, taking their families with them.

But while the community were thus frantically seeking shelter anywhere and everywhere rather than where they chanced to be, the awful scene changed, and, with the howling of a tornado, against which seemingly nothing could stand, came a storm of fire, which an eye-witness likens to the heaviest snowfall of winter, with each flake of snow a coal of fire. The heavens rained fire on every hand, as if to consume the whole earth.

In an instant, nearly every building in the town was in a blaze. Then the fury of the tempest received additional strength and burst in one mighty effort, as if determined that the flames should not rob it of its prey. Houses crumbled like paper structures, and flaming roofs and sides were borne away like gigantic sparks upon the gale to spread the consuming element. The Company had but recently completed a very large warehouse, built with a special view to withstand the gales, which so frequently visit that region; but when this tornado struck it, it went to pieces like a child's playhouse built of cards. Whoever had not reached a place of safety found it impossible to move against this mighty storm. People threw themselves on the ground rather than be borne away by its violence, and perished where they fell. The next day a man was found hugging a tree, his body half consumed. The storm of falling cinders was succeeded quickly by a continuous blaze that licked up everything with which it came in contact. Those in the water only saved themselves by keeping their bodies submerged, only venturing to raise their heads at intervals for a moment to gasp for breath. Many were drowned in the effort to escape burning, while others, who sought to catch breath, inhaled only livid flame, and perished. Even the very fishes were reached by some mysterious agency and killed, so that the next day hundreds of them were found floating, dead.

IN THE FLAMES.

A correspondent furnishes the following thrilling incidents of this remarkable fire:

The tornado was but momentary, but was succeeded by maelstroms of fire, smoke, cinders, and red-hot sand. Wherever a building seemed to resist the fire, the roof would be sent whirling into the air, breaking into clouds of flame as it fell. The shower of sparks, cinders, and hot sand, fell in continuous and prodigious force, and did quite as much in killing the people as the first terrific sirocco that succeeded the fire. The wretched throng, neck-deep in the water, and still more hapless beings stretched on the heated sands, were pierced and blistered by these burning particles. They seemed like lancets of red-hot steel, penetrating the thickest covering. The evidence now remains to attest the incredible force of the slenderist pencils of darting flame. Hard iron-wood plow-handles still remain, and for the main point unburnt. When the hapless dwellers in the remote streets saw themselves cut off from the river, groups broke in all directions in a wild panic of fright and terror. A few took refuge in a cleared field bordering on the town. Here flat upon the ground, with faces pressed in the mud, the helpless sufferers lay and roasted. But few survived the dreadful agony. The next day revealed a picture exceeding in horror any battle-field. Mothers with children hugged closely and the poor flesh seared to a crisp. One mother, solicitous only for her babe, embalms her unutterable love in the terrible picture left on these woful sands. With her bare fingers she had scraped out a pit, as the soldiers did before Petersburg, and pressing the little one into this, she put her own body above it as a shield, and when daylight came both were dead—the little baby face unscarred, but the mother burnt almost to cinders.

SCHWARTZ, THE HERMIT.

About the first farm out from Peshtigo is owned by a one-eyed German, who is known the country round as Schwartz, the hermit. Some twenty years since, when this region was an unbroken wilderness, occupied almost exclusively by Indians, this man Schwartz came here, built a cabin, and ever since has lived entirely alone, apparently caring very little for the outside world, or for what other people thought of him. At that time, with the exception of the blind eye, Schwartz was a splendid looking man, and blessed with a very superior education. The story of the cause of his abandoning the world and adopting the life of a recluse, is the same as has been told thousands of times before. He fell in love with a handsome girl—the story would be spoiled if she was not beautiful—was engaged to be married, when she, like too many others of her sex, proved false and married another fellow, a major in the Prussian army. This was too much for our hero, who forthwith fled to America and found consolation for his blighted affections in the solitude of these pine forests. He dug, or rather burrowed in the ground, where he lived with his chickens, geese, cats, hogs and dogs, presenting as happy a family as can be found in any menagerie in the country. Schwartz

A FIRE SCENE ON THE PRARIES.

has been very thrifty and industrious since he came here, and was considered very wealthy, many even asserting that he had gold stored away in every corner of his filthy abode. When the fire came Schwartz and his family ran down to Trout Brook, into which they plunged and remained until the fire had spent its fury. The hermit has already commenced building another hut, where he will doubtless spend the balance of his days, little heeding what takes place elsewhere.

DOWN IN A WELL.

About half a mile beyond Schwartz's, on the right, and about two hundred yards from the road, are the remains of a dwelling which was occupied by a family named Hill. The family were all in the house at evening prayers, when they were suddenly startled by a loud noise, much resembling continuous thunder. On going to the door they found themselves entirely surrounded by fire, and as the only means of escape, the whole of them, eight in number, went down into the well. Here they remained in safety, until the wooden house covering the well caught fire, fell in, and burned the entire party to death. Another case exactly similar to the last was that of the Davis family, in Peshtigo, who were all smothered to death in their well, into which they had descended in the vain hope of saving their lives. I have heard of quite a number of such cases, but as the facts were not definitely given, I make no mention of them.

BURNED WHILE ESCAPING IN A WAGON.

A short distance on, we come to a lone stone wall, the foundation of a house, the former residence of a family named Lawrence, all of whom perished. Immediately in front of this place was the iron work of a wagon, which once belonged to Chas. Lamp. Lamp lived about a mile beyond, and when he found the fire approaching his house so rapidly, he hitched up his team, and with his wife and five children drove with all speed toward Peshtigo. In a very few minutes after starting he heard screams in the wagon, and looking back found that the clothes of his wife and children were all ablaze. It was certain death to stop, and he therefore urged his horses to still greater speed, but before he had moved many rods, one of the horses fell, and finding that he could not get him up, and seeing that all of his family were dead, Lamp started to save his life, which he did after being most horribly burned. He is now in the hospital at Green Bay, and is slowly recovering. When at the latter place I saw him, and had a full narrative of the bloody tragedy from himself. What little was found of the charred remains of the wife and five children were buried in a field not far off. Of the wagon not a speck was to be seen, excepting the half-melted iron work.

SUDDENLY EXTINGUISHED PROSPECT OF SAFETY.

We next come to the Lawrence farm, one of the best on the whole route, showing a very high state of cultivation, on which everything had been swept away. Lawrence, with his wife and four children, ran to the centre of an immense clearing. several hundred yards from any house or timber, with the idea they would be entirely safe there. The fire came, and rushed along on every side of them, yet they remained unharmed. At this moment one of the great balloons dropped in their midst, and in an instant they were burned up, hardly anything being left of them.

FIRE BALLOONS.

Your readers may wonder what I mean by fire balloons, and I confess that I hardly know myself, and only use the term because it was so frequently used by others in conversation with me. All of the survivors with whom I conversed said that the whole sky seemed filled with dark, round masses of smoke, about the size of a large balloon, which traveled with great rapidity. These balloons would fall to the ground, burst, and send forth a most brilliant blaze of fire, which would instantly consume everything in the neighborhood. An eye-witness, who was in a pool of water not far off, told us about the balloon falling right down on the Lawrence family, and burning them up.

A PATH THROUGH THE FIRE.

In returning, about a mile to the north we came to Adnah Newton's farm, where sixteen persons were burned to death. As soon as Newton saw the fire he started out to see what was best to be done. Running down to the road he found himself headed off by the flames. Turning back, he saw his family and workmen in the yard coming toward him, but when they noticed him turn back they also changed their course; in an instant more they were all on fire, and must have perished in a moment. Newton happened to notice on his right what proved to be a path through the flame about fifty yards wide, for which he rushed, and continued for three-fourths of a mile, when he came to a house still occupied by several persons. They all invited him to come into the house, but he declined saying he would rather trust to being saved in a small pool of water close by. In another instant the house was on fire, and before the inmates could get to him, they were all burned to death, while Newton escaped pretty well singed. I had a long conversation with Newton, and he declared he had no hankering after another such a race. The second day after the fire thirty-three remains were found on these farms.

THE ONLY TRACE.

The Doyle family consisted of the husband and father, Patrick, the wife, and seven children. The fire came, and not one single trace of any of them could be found, excepting a Catholic medal, some nails out of a pair of shoes, and some hooks and eyes. Of their bodies not one single thing was left, not even the ashes of their bones. Next to the Doyles lived the Pratt family, all of whom perished, excepting a small boy, who saved himself by jumping into the well. When the burial party arrived they found the large Newfoundland dog watching by the body of his mistress, and it was only by force that they could drive him away long enough to bury the corpse. The Hill family, consisting of ten persons, lived near by. They had working for them a half grown Indian boy, who was ordered down to hitch up the team. The barn getting on fire, the master ordered him to return. Not coming as fast as Hill desired, the order was repeated in a more peremptory manner, when the Indian looked up and said; "Its everybody for himself now," and off he started with the speed of the deer. Rushing through the fire, he reached a clearing half a mile away and was saved, while the entire Hill family perished.

THE ONLY HOUSE LEFT.

In the entire Upper Bush country there is only one house left, the home of "old man" Place. Many years ago this man settled here, soon afterward married a squaw, by whom he has had many children. He has always engaged in trading with the Indians, who have had his house as their headquarters. When the fire came, about twenty Indians covered his house with their blankets, which they kept wet down, and thus saved the house. One great big fellow stood at the pump for nine hours, showing an endurance possessed by very few white men. Strange as it may now seem, while there are about as many Indians as whites in this section, at least one thousand of the latter perished, and not a single Indian. This may seem strange, but it is vouched for by the very best persons here. Whether the Indians could smell the fire sooner than their more refined white brethren and escaped in time, I know not, but I do know that they were all saved. And the only ones I heard of being injured were the half-breed children.

HOW ARTICLES WERE SAVED.

Mr. Shepard, of Peshtigo, was aroused on Sunday night by the servant girl, after he had retired, with the information that there was danger from fire. He ran to the mill, attached the hose and commenced wetting down the mill. When the tornado came and he saw that all was lost, he ran to the house to save his wife and children, in which he succeeded. After the village was burned, when Mr. Shepard supposed he had not an article left but the clothes they had on, which were burned full of holes, the servant girl went to the site of the house and dug up out of the sand all his best clothing, the silver ware, and most valuable goods, that she had buried without his knowledge, while he was trying to save the mill. Mrs. Shepard lost some of her clothing, as the fire did not give the girl time to bury it deep enough.

HONEYMOON TRAGEDY.

On Thursday, the 5th inst., Mr. J. G. Clement, formerly a painter in Fort Howard, late of Peshtigo, was married to Miss Trudell, daughter of Theodore Trudell, of Menominee. The bride's mother visited them at Peshtigo on Sunday, the 8th, and left at 4 P. M. When the fire struck Peshtigo, Mr. Clement took his wife in his arms and started for the river. They met a man with a buckboard, going to save his wife and family, but seeing the task was hopeless he started to go back. Mr. Clement asked him to save his wife and he would do the best he could for himself. The man took Mrs. C., and Clement ran behind, holding on the buckboard, but finally fell in the road and died from suffocation. The bride begged to be allowed to get out, but was held in and taken to the river, where she arrived unconscious, but was restored and saved.

SUICIDE RATHER THAN TORTURE.

In the Lower Sugar Bush, Mr. C. R. Towsley was found lying on the ground, a child on each side of him, the throats of all three cut and a knife lying on his breast. The father had evidently, when he saw that escape was impossible, chose to die by the knife rather than endure the horrors of torture by fire. About ten rods from them lay Mrs. T. with an infant child on one arm and a Bible on the other, and a likeness of one of the other children on her breast.

P. M. Brown informs us that Miss Augusta Bartels, about fourteen years old, daughter of Fred Bartels, Peshtigo, was in the Sugar Bush, visiting her grandparents, Mr. and Mrs. Adam Newton. When the fire burst upon them she said there was no use in trying to live, all had got to be burned, and threw herself into the creek, that ran through Stephen Storey's farm, where she was drowned. The cries and lamentations of the old people were pitiful to hear.

FATAL MISTAKE.

A man in Peshtigo village started for the river with his wife. They stumbled and fell in the dense smoke, and springing up again he seized, as he supposed, his wife, and got her into the river. When the smoke cleared away, he was horrified to find that he had saved another man's wife, and his own wife was burned to death.

MINOR INCIDENTS.

Wm. Curtiss was found in a well with the bucket chain around his neck.

A man, a shoemaker, running for the river at Peshtigo, found a little girl four years of age and took her into the water. She lay across his shoulder and he swam with her about half an hour and saved her without injury, although he was considerably burned himself.

Mr. Dix got his family in the river, half clad. The baby had on nothing but a nightgown. Somebody brought a bundle of bed clothing to the river. Dix opened it and took out a sheet. The owner wanted to take it away from him for fear it would get burned, but he secured it, spread it over his family and kept it wet by throwing water on it with his hat. He thinks he could not have saved his baby without it.

Mrs. Heldenworth, a woman sick with a fever, was on a log in the river at Peshtigo, with a child. Her husband had gone back to the town for some purpose, and when he returned his wife and child were gone. The fact was that a cow came swimming along, and rolled over the log. She caught the cow by the horns, and the cow swam out with the woman and child. They were found and secured in the river again.

The scene after the fire, about daylight, in front of the company's blacksmith shop, where a heap of coal was burning, and the people had gathered to dry and warm themselves, was heartrending in the extreme. Men, women, and children, were crying, and wringing their hands, and such exclamations as these were common: "Where is my husband?" "Where is my wife?" "Where are my children?" Some finding their friends were dead wished they had died too.

S. V. D. Philbrook & Brother had a ship yard on the Island at Menekaune, at which the little schooner Stella was being repaired. Large numbers of people flocked aboard of her, and as the fire got uncomfortably close some were for cutting the lines and letting her adrift. Mr. P. seized a handspike and threatened death to any one who would cut the lines, and this held the vessel until many got on board, and in fact, our informant says, her lines burned off. She drifted off into the middle of the river, where she grounded on a bar and remained all night in front of the burning town.

F. Crickelair tells us how Charles Rubens, in the town of Lincoln, saved his family of six children. He had a house and store, and when he saw they could not be saved, he put his children in the well. Afterward he took them out and put them in the middle of a field and threw the goods from his store into the well. In saving the last child his face was badly burned, and his shirt burned so he tore it off. The goods put in the well were all burned but one piece of flannel in the water. He has been blind ever since the fire.

SCENE ON THE PRAIRIES.

A young lady ran for the river with a child in her arms; but, overcome by the heat and fright, fainted and was dragged by some one to the water and saved. In the morning she learned that her sister was burned.

One old man, after the fire abated, was found to be so burned in his side that his entrails hung out. His hands and face were horribly burned, and he begged piteously for some one to kill him and end his misery.

A little girl, as she clung to her mother's dress, looked up and asked, "Mamma, what shall we pray?"

If you suppose the worst snow storm you ever witnessed, and each snow-flake a coal or spark of fire, driven before a fierce wind, you have some idea of the state of the atmosphere at the time the fire struck the town.

Mr. Johnson, in the sugar bush, threw his money, with some bedding, into his well, covered the well with boards and piled dirt on the boards. The wind blew off the dirt, the boards burned, and all the clothing and money were destroyed.

Some one who saw the fire approach the town from a distance, says there seemed to be a vast cloud, streaked with blood, which went in advance of the fire in the woods, leaping over the adjoining timber, and fell upon the town.

There were many phenomena, which, aside from the fire, were similar to what have occurred during the tornadoes that frequently swept over the country. Roofs were lifted from buildings and windows burst in. Whatever was light and movable was caught up and carried forward and burned, so that the air seemed to be literally on fire. It was no more than what might happen in any timbered country, especially where the timber was principally pine, in time of drouth, with fires scattered through the woods, if a hurricane should sweep over it.

During the fire roofs and chimneys blew off with the force of the wind and showers of burning coals filled the houses.

Next morning many of the survivors breakfasted on raw cabbage—a field of cabbage having escaped. The first aid was a load of provisions from John Mulligan's railroad camp. Provisions from Marinette arrived about noon, and from Green Bay next day.

Every one had sore eyes, and all walked with their heads down, or bandages over their eyes.

The first ones to collect the dead and make arrangements for their burial, were John Mulligan and his wife. Mulligan (who will be remembered as the prize fighter, but whose heart is much larger than his fists), saved his wife by carrying her in his arms from Hale's place to and across the bridge and into the river, a distance of half a mile. There is the advantage of muscle.

The family of John Greyer, an old Frenchman in the bush, was found, the charred remains of three in the ruins of the house, and another still sitting on a stump near by.

A Swede sitting on a chair in the Peshtigo Company's boarding house, was urged to flee for his life, but sat there and was burned with the house.

John Plush died in his accustomed place by the tavern door. Another man died with his hands on the handle of Woodward's force pump.

A gentleman walking through the ruins in Peshtigo saw a burned pocket knife and a slate pencil and picked them up. In doing so he saw a line of white ashes the shape of a body, and a few teeth. This was the earthly remnant of a boy.

We learn that a woman in the Sugar Bush, seeing the impending doom, started with a team and wagon with her children for Peshtigo. On the road she found a tree that she could not get over and immediately cut one horse loose, got upon his back with her children and reached the river at the village, saving them all, but with clothing nearly burned off, and there on the bank of the river, she gave birth to a child.

THE NEWBERRY FAMILIES.

A Mr. May was found three quarters of a mile northwest of his house, his wife about the same distance north, and his little boy, four years old, the same distance north-east. The Newberry families, consisting of seventeen persons, were all lost. They lived near each other. They owned a mill and three farms. Old Mr. Newberry was not found, Charles Newberry ran about half a mile and fell, and his two little boys, running hand in hand, were found a little beyond their father, lying side by side, while wife and mother was found on the road near a bridge ; she, forgetful of her own suffering, tried to save her babe. Her charred hand was pressing the head of her child upon the ground so that it might not breathe the fire. The child's face was all that was uninjured. One of the Newberrys was found dead in the water under the bridge.

MIRACLES AND CHILD HEROISM.

Charles Lamb took his wife and four children in a wagon when the fire began ; the horse became unmanagable and ran away ; the children were thrown out one by one ; Mrs. Lamb was dragged into the corner of a field, and was the only one of that family saved. Mrs. Caroline England, expecting to be confined every hour, rode four and a half miles to Peshtigo, stood in the water five hours, saved three out of four of her sister's children, and gave birth to a daughter the day after. In the middle of Sugar Bush, a boy jumped into a barrel of rainwater that stood near the house, but seeing his father and mother in a green turnip patch, started to go to them, but getting badly burned as he tried to climb the fence, he went back and got into the barrel again. The father and mother were burned. The boy was found there alive.

One woman, with a baby ten days old, and four other small children, displayed more bravery than many a general on the battle field. She gathered her children around her and picked the coals off her family as they fell. She was badly burned, and one of her children has since died, but the babe escaped. Mr. Tanner tried to save his wife and two children; when his wife fell dead he took a child under each arm and started on the run. His children died in his arms, and then he drew a knife and tried to take his own life. After stabbing himself twice, and before he could accomplish his design, a limb of a tree knocked him insensible and thus his life was saved.

FURNISHING COFFINS TO BURY THE DEAD.

I will mention one case of a little girl, 15 years old, who saved her little sister from death, but who was advised by many to desist from the attempt lest she herself should perish. She heeded them not, but by the most heroic efforts she succeeded in rescuing her little sister from the merciless flames. Her father, mother, brothers, and other sisters perished in the devouring element. And after the fire had abated somewhat, she worked away back over hot ashes and burning coals, and dragged the dead bodies of her relatives out into an open space and then stood watching their charred remains all day and through that long and desolate night that followed. That is child heroism, the like of which was never before recorded.

One man was sick of typhoid fever; a young man stopping with him took the sick man out back of the house and buried him in the sand. He was saved, and is rapidly gaining his health.

The Manistee Fire.

ORIGIN, PROGRESS, AND EXTENT OF THE CONFLAGRATION.

Manistee Lake is a body of water nearly five miles long and from one-fourth to three-fourths of a mile wide, lying nearly parallel with, and about a mile or two from Lake Michigan. Near the northern extremity it is connected with the latter lake by the Manistee River, a large navigable stream, from 75 to 125 yards in width. On the north side of the river, between the two lakes, lay the First Ward of the city, and on the south side of the river (toward Grand Rapids,) and adjacent to it, divided nearly equally by Maple street, on which was the swing bridge, lay the Third Ward, next the Manistee, or as it is more generally called, "little lake," and the Second Ward to the west, next the "big lake," or Lake Michigan. To the southeast, bordering on the "little lake" was the Fourth Ward. The Third was the most populous and embraced the greater part of the foreign and poor population. The Second Ward was the best built part of the town, especially that part between Oak and Maple streets. Within the city limits, and directly south of the space embraced between the latter named streets, was a tract of about twenty acres of dead hemlock forest—the trees partly standing and partly lying upon the ground, but the whole as dry as tinder and nearly as combustible as gunpowder.

On the fatal Sunday, October 8, the fire-alarm sounded at about 9 A. M., and the Fire Department hastened with the steamer to the vicinity of Gifford & Ruddeck's mills in the Fourth Ward, where an old chopping was burning furiously, and threatening destruction to that part of the town. By the most unwearied efforts, continued all day, the fire was subdued, and that part of the town was saved. About dark the engine returned to its quarters. It was scarcely housed when the wind, which had been blowing furiously all day, rose to a perfect gale.

At about 2 P. M., while the fire in the Fourth Ward was burning, an alarm whistle was heard from the east side of Manistee Lake, and through the thick smoke it was discovered that the large steam mill of Magill & Canfield, on Blackbird Island, was in flames. In an incredibly short space of time, mill, boarding-house, stables, shops, docks and lumber were consumed.

As soon as darkness began to close in a lurid light appeared in the south-west on the shore of Lake Michigan, showing the pine woods that line the shore were on fire. About 9:30 p. m., just as the people were returning from evening service, the fire alarm again sounded, and every one now was on the alert, for the wind was blowing a fierce gale. Instantly a red angry glare lighted up the western sky near the mouth of the river. The fire department rushed to the rescue. At the mouth were located the large mill and interests of John Canfield, with boarding-house and about twenty-five or thirty dwellings. On the beach several acres were covered with pine sawdust, highly inflammable. Along the river near the piers were piled several hundred cords of dry pine slabs (fuel for tugs.) Down from the circling hills on the lake shore pounced the devouring monster. The burning sawdust, whirled by the gale in fiery clouds, filled the air. Hundreds of cords of dry pitchy slabs sent up great columns of red flame, that swayed in the air like mighty banners of fire, swept across the Manistee, 200 feet wide, and almost instantly, like great fiery tongues, licked up the Government lighthouse, built at a cost of nearly $10,000, situated 150 feet from the north bank of the river.

A large fleet of vessels, wind bound, lay opposite Canfield's mill, with four tugs, including the three large barges of Tyson & Robinson and the great steam tug Bismarck. Now commenced furious efforts to remove the vessels and barges. The wild puffing and screaming of the tugs, the hoarse hallooing of sailors, the loud roaring and crackling of the flames, the awe-stricken faces of the gathered multitude, luridly lighted, made up a scene never to be forgotten or adequately described. The efforts of the firemen were in vain—the engine became disabled, and the flames came sweeping all before them. But now a new source of terror arose. A bright light came up out of the south, directly in the rear of the town, and the fierce gale bearing it on directly toward the doomed city. Those who resided in that part of the town rushed to the new scene of danger, the full extent of which few comprehended. The fire had originated two miles south of the city, on the lake shore. It first came upon the farm of L. G. Smith, Esq., which it devoured. Eighty rods north the extensive farm and dairy of E. W. Secor shared the same fate, with all his barns and forage. Another quarter of a mile and the large farm buildings of Mayor Peters were quickly annihilated. Here the column of fire divided, the left hand branch keeping to the lake shore hills, and coming in at the mouth; the other taking a northeasterly course and coming in directly south of the town, as before described. Here a small band of determined men, fighting with the energy of despair to protect their homes, kept it at bay till past midnight. But all was vain. At half-past twelve o'clock the gale became a tornado, hurling great clouds of sparks, cinders, burning bark and rotten wood, through the air in a terrific fiery storm.

Every man now fled to his own house. The fire now came roaring on through the dead hemlocks south of the blocks included between Maple and Oak streets in the Second Ward. The flames leaped to the summits of the great hemlocks, seventy or eighty feet high, and threw out great flags of fire against the lurid heavens. The scene was grandly terrible beyond description. To us, whose homes and dear ones and all were in the track of fire, it was heartrending. Then came a deluge of fire, like that which rained on the cities of the Plains. The wooden town, the sawdust streets, the stumpy vacant lots, the pile-clad hills north of the river, all burst into a sea of flame, made furious by the most fearful gale of wind I have ever experienced. On, toward the river and the Manistee lake, spread the tempest of fire. Men, women, and children, in night clothes, half clothed or fully clothed—some bareheaded, on foot, in wagons, on horseback,—all fled for their lives. It was pandemonium on earth. Families were separated—husbands and wives, parents and children. The writer, when he gave over the unequal contest south of the town, rushed to his residence to find it destroyed, and for nine hours he could get no word whether his family were dead or alive. They had fled before the tempest of fire across the bridge, which burned behind them, only to be surrounded and almost to perish in the smoke and fire on the north side. Every thing went down before the storm—dwellings with their home treasures, mills with their machinery, stores and their stocks, warehouses and their contents, the fine swing bridge at the foot of Maple street, vessels and their cargoes, all mingling in common ruin.

From Fifth street, half a mile south of the river, to Cushman & Calkin's mill, half a mile north of the bridge, and from the foot of Oak street eastward to Tyson and Robinson's mill at the outlet of Manistee lake, three-fourths of a mile, was one surging sea of fire. The steam fire engine burnt in the street where it stood, the men and horses barely escaped with their lives. About three o'clock the wind abated, but the work of ruin was complete. When Monday morning's sun glared red and lurid through the heavy masses of smoke, where had stood Manistee, it beheld a scene of desolation, scarcely to be described. In the first ward three buildings remained—the catholic church, the Ward School house and a small dwelling—and I should add some small fishing shanties near the mouth of the river. The Third Ward was swept clean except a few buildings near Manistee lake. In the Second Ward the six plated blocks lying between Oak and Maple streets, and about thirty buildings near the mouth, were swept away. The Fourth Ward escaped nearly untouched, the fine residence of J. L. Taylor, banker, formerly the residence of M. Engleman, situated in the very corner of the ward, being the only one burned. His loss was great and almost total. The fire made thorough work. The buildings were built mostly on wooden foundations, and their very site was scarcely distinguishable.

A THOUSAND PEOPLE HOMELESS.

A thousand men, women and children, houseless, homeless, and many of them penniless, wandered sad and blinded in the black and smoking streets, or had taken refuge on vessels, tugs, boats and barges, to escape the devouring element. Nothing but the cleared fields of Messrs. Canfield and Peters, south of the western part of the Second ward, saved that part of the town from utter annihilation, and hundreds from perishing in the tempest of fire.

THE AFTER SCENES.

The writer of this, at ten o'clock the next morning, found his family three miles east of the desolated city, having barely escaped with their lives, with the scanty clothing snatched in the moment of flight. Then was seen a spectacle to gladden the heart. Every house that remained was opened to receive the sufferers. Hearts and hands were as open as the homes. We almost felt it worth while to suffer for the sake of witnessing how much of generosity was latent in human nature.

WHAT OF THE FUTURE.

Manistee will rise from her ashes. The work of rebuilding has already commenced. We have faith, hope, energy in the future, and some capital. We have a splendid natural situation, at the mouth of a beautiful navigable stream penetrating the interior through the pine forests, 200 miles, on whose banks stand four thousand five hundred million feet of good pine, most of which must be manufactured at and shipped from Manistee. Help us through this winter, and the future, though dimmed, is safe.

Ahnappe.

THE TERRIBLE STORY OF THE LAST WISCONSIN HAMLET THAT FOUGHT THE HURRICANE OF FIRE.

Compared with the facts of this unvarnished narrative, the wildest fiction is ame and common-place. Human annals do not record, in equal time and space, the immensity and intensity of suffering and death crowded into the meager epitome of one single hour. The scene of a thriving industry, and the home of nearly a hundred people; the place, though isolated from any human vicinity, had maintained a flourishing and tranquil vitality. The shingle mill, with its co-adjutant industries, gave employment to the entire people, women and children, dividing the easy labors of shingling and binding. There were but four buildings on the clearing—the mill, the general boarding-house, a store, and the barn. Economy and convenience, curious to say, had dictated the selection of this remote spot. The timber inexhaustibly covered the place, and it was of unequalled quality; a lazy little stream meandering through the gnarled roots and soft soil, offered a supply of water, enough with artesian wells to drive the mill machinery. It was cheaper to work the great logs into marketable shape here, where they were right at hand, than establish the mills on the lake or bay, and drag the immense timber over miles of wretched road. The fiery experience of the west shore—of the whole Northern Wisconsin—had been the experience of this wood-immersed hamlet. For weeks, incessant, laborious battle had been waged night and day, reliefs of men, and even women, taking turns in the exhausting contest. It was hoped that all danger had been warded off when a wide belt, fully a mile deep, had been burned outward from the clearing. The serenity of assured safety had come upon the people when this black circumvallation was complete—the very night before the calamity. On that fatal Sunday morning the mill operations suspended, and the men who had homes in the neighboring towns of Big and Little Sturgeon, made an early start through the woods. When night came, some kindly Providence detained them, and the massacre was so much less. The night came on tranquilly, the humid air gave grateful promise of coming rain, and the last lingering distrust was banished from the timidest inhabitant. Early in the night most of the little population in the hamlet were in-doors or in bed. It was still early when those casually astir outside saw a great glowing light shoot athwart the southern sky, and, spreading rapidly west and northward, continue with dazzling brilliancy. Presently a slender column of fire shot forward, and, caught by a whirlwind, came ploughing through the solid timber toward the mill. By this time the sleepers and all had rushed from the barrack in a wild, clamoring consternation.

Three brothers, Williamsons, owned the mill, and had in the colony, mother, father, sisters, wives and children. Hastily charging the women to care for themselves, the brothers set about saving the property if possible. But before the hose could be brought to bear, the saving of the life alone became the stake in the dreadful encounter. The brothers, as proprietors, seem for a time to have been full of calm, brave discretion, and, with the full realization of the sudden danger in the first rush of the tornado, attempted systematic plans of preservation. The women were directed, as far as possible, to put on men's clothes throughout, as offering less chance for the fire to catch. So far as known not a woman heeded the advice. Had they have done so their lives might not have been sacrificed on that ignoble pyre. Even if life had not been saved, the most revolting sights of the massacre would have been spared the heart-broken survivors. This was the last shred of coherent conduct among the frightened people. Swift whirling columns of flame had cut through the intervening timber, and fell voraciously on the light frame buildings. The whirlwind lashing the trees into fragments caught the fire in roaring surges and flung it about in billowy waves among the tree tops. Slender tongues of fire falling from above played in malevolent currents across the clearing. A desperation of terror filled men, women and children—a terror as natural as fatal, for had common fortitude led the group not a soul need have perished. With one impulse the frantic mass, battling and crowding, rushed to the potato patch. Here a rising ground was crowned by a shallow pit, not six feet around, and hardly, at the deepest part, two feet below the surface of the ground. Men now living, who came almost unscathed through that night of doom, tell how, before the evil time, when the fires were raging, this spot had been fixed on as a place of safety, because almost in the centre of the clearing, with no inflammable matter near, it seemed to promise a breathing in case of a general conflagration. There had been constant jocosities and banter about this "center of salvation," and some one actually attempting to enlarge the cavity had been driven off by good-natured ridicule. Even as late as Saturday it had been used as a place of refuge, notwithstanding, and, when the actual danger came, the credulous mass remembered the delusive pit. If that fatal spot had not been, if the whimsical belief had not obtained a firm hold, there is not the slightest doubt but the forty-seven that perished would have escaped in the neighboring woods. Into that crampled place, crowding. buffeting, cursing, imploring, praying, shrieking, men, children, and women, elbowed and fought in the frenzy of a hideous desperation and terror. Not large enough to admit a dozen by the closest packing, nearly fifty wrestled and crowded in and about the fatal spot. With ostrich instinct, in the abjectness of their unreasoning fear, men plowed their burning heads under the living pyre. An inextricable pyramid of bodies, in all sorts of conceivable postures, stood in the flame-swept place.

There were a few in this awful time that preserved an amazing equanimity. The engineer of the mill, Byron Merrill, a young fellow of marked character and intelligence, battled resolutely till the last chance to save his employers' property, and only when the futility of the effort and the danger of life became obvious was his self-imposed duty resigned. A bit of romance tinges the glaring picture. His sweetheart was the relative of the mill-owners, Miss Maggie Williamson, a girl of rare beauty and attraction. The young fellow, bright and cultured beyond his kind, regarded with favor and affection for many a mile around, had won her heart, and the two were to have been married. The girl, with her kindred, had fled to the potato patch, and here, suffocating with smoke, their garments in flames and writhing in awful agony, the young fellow found the chief part of the people. He tried to scatter the infatuated group. With his hat pressed closely over his mouth and nostrils, he directed the group to break and take shelter in the edge of the timber. Hopeless! the roar of the hurricane, even the blood curdling shrieks of the sufferers, drowned his voice. He tried by main force to tear the hideous mass asunder, but the best strength of a giant could not have broken the maddened clutch of the wretched sufferers. The group was immovably fixed to the fatal spot, and rose from burning sand a fiery Laocoon struggling with the coiling flames. Merrill hastily fetching wetted blankets, threw them over the nearest sufferers, meantime shouting to them to break for the timber, not twenty steps away. Useless. With the skin hanging in shreds upon his hands and forehead, he carried water and poured it on the infatuated group, while the ignoble crowding went on madly among the swiftly roasting crowd. The tumultuous struggle had been from the first a loathsome, unreasoning fear. A moment's coolness—a moment's cessation of the frightful effort to wedge downward would have given life to all. The time came, however, when the faithful Merrill, stripped almost of clothing and burned beyond recognition, had to give up the heroic effort, and plunging through the darting flame dashed his burning body in the well. Earlier in the catastrophe a half dozen heavy sleepers had found tardiness their salvation from the potato patch, and they darted into the timber belt, which had been carefully burned out long before, to keep the fire from the houses. Here, prone on the ground, they protected themselves, while the mad crowd, not ten yards away, roasted in their blindness. The falling trees could be guarded against, but nothing could save from the encompassing fire in the clearings. One came, too, whose frail chance of life the meanest creature struggling in that hot pit would not have refused, an old tottering, half blind, trembling woman, mother to the owners of the mill. She must have been forgotten in the first rush, for when she came toward the potato patch it was filled with a swarming crowd thrown down upon their faces in the shadowy depths of the potato pit. Seven of her kindred writhed in that hideous knot. Passing on with decripped step, the venerable mother, whose eighty four years had not worn out coolness and discretion, came upon a great boulder near the edge of the timber. Climbing on this although half suffocated, she covered her head with her skirts, and, with clothes carefully tucked up from the running flames, kept for hours on the back of this unique salamander The only son that came out of the fire with his life, it is said, did not forget his duty, and aided his mother to this forlorn refuge. Be that as it may, with a thick blanket, well wetted, over her body and her skirts out of reach of the hot incendiary sand, the brave old lady perched on that rock through the long night of agony, every shriek of her roasting kindred splitting her ears, and their burning bodies almost within reach of her helpless arms. Twice through the night she received succor, once from her son, who came up and wetted her covering, and once from the barnmaster Bush, who also bathed her head and gave her cool water to drink. Through the whole unspeakable tragedy of piteous cowardice ran this vein of simple fortitude and heroic endurance.

The mill blacksmith, Michael Adams, stands out as though of antique mould. He was a man of gigantic figure and grave, rough reserve. When the danger came, he gathered his three children and baby in his great strong arms, and with his wife strode to the centre of the clearing, where he calmly placed them on wetted blankets, and, covering them with his coat, quietly brought water in buckets and saturated the frail protection. The flames hissed and roared about him, but he never desisted. Resisting the hot torrents with wonderful endurance and even when his hair was ablaze, his hands fleshless, and the coals eating into his flesh, he continued his efforts for wife and child. The young engineer and the barnmaster shouted to him to fly to the woods. He seemed to hear them, but calmly shaking his head remained at his post. As his strength and sight began to fail, he looked with unutterable yearning toward the helpless group at his feet, then glanced anxiously toward the wood. Whether he saw that there was the better chance of safety can never be known; he reeled suddenly and dropped like a shot in his tracks. When help came to that group the next day, an unscarred babe lay in the arms of its dead mother, the father's arms about both. They were, of course, all dead, but the father alone, with one arm burned off, was unrecognizable, save by his giant frame. Even the dog that howled, smothering in the hot air, and kept in restless motion to prevent being roasted on the hot sands, seemed impressed by this man's devotion. Wagging delirious inquiry with his tail, and interjecting sharp barks, he seemed to plead with his obdurate master. Hopeless of recognition, then he would poke his nose under the wet blankets, and, after a thorough cooling, emerge dejectedly, as though deprecating the weakness, while his master was exposed. The sand growing hotter and hotter, the forbearing dog made for the woods, but in mid career, and almost in the performance of a jig—his legs were kept moving so briskly to keep his feet from burning—he turned longingly, as if reminding the man that that was the way to safety. No heed was paid him, and with painful limps and piteous whines he returned, and settling his feet on the blanket, stared eagerly at his master. His poor, singed body was found in the attitude of love and duty.

At the well, which stood nearest the house, a wretched group had taken refuge —not only at, but in it. Six people flung themselves into this last resort, counting confidently on it as a place of security. Finally, when crippled by the fire, and exhausted by his long efforts, the young man Merrill threw himself into that crowded pit also: the place was packed. Even here his presence of mind was all that saved a life where life had very little chance. The frail wooden curbing above the mouth had taken fire, and the flames began to run downward fiercely. The paralyzed group dared not put out their heads, lest the flames should smother them. But Merrill, without an instant's hesitation, uprose and flung the dangerous thing away, and the barn master, hovering about the edge of the woods, presently refreshed the smothered victims by a bucket full of water. The well was, notwithstanding, a place of death. The flames, sweeping savagely over the clearing, lurched and spit down hatefully into the crowded pit, and soon the steady blaze from within indicated the fate of its inmates. Merrill still held his mind and resisted the flames. In this he was aided by Brush, who helped him to his final deliverence. He aided all who would listen to him, and to his presence of mind and heroic efforts, the few that were saved owe their lives. He brought water from the creek to aid the group on the potato patch, and kept the sheltering blankets saturated as long as he dared venture inside the line of fire. It must not be supposed that outside the clearing there was a fair chance of safety. On the contrary, the ceaseless explosions of breaking trunks and splintered branches, were so terrific, mingled with volumes of flame in the tree tops, that the greater part of the people preferred to risk the dangers of the open ground. But the thick wood had its security, and with care the people that lay down near the edge found themselves, when the frightful morning came, comparatively uninjured.

Here the climax comes ; the tragedy is complete in this one terrific picture ; the light of the new day revealed only the machinery of the horrid master-piece. The red glare of night had changed into the bleak dawn, and the dawn had changed into high noon before a helpful hand broke into the black Golgotha. The barnmaster Bush, when silence had fallen upon the place an hour or two before dawn, took a horse and attempted to make his way to Little Sturgeon ; as well try to ride through a stone wall. Leaving his horse behind he struggled on by the bright light of the burning pines, and, after incalculable trouble in the way and out of the way, some time about daylight he came upon the ruins of a lumberman's cabin, which by the regular path was not more than two miles from the mill. He had been hours in reaching it, and, **worn out by the** labors and agony of the **night**, he sat down to rest. Presently the owner came, and together the two started **back** to the settlement. They went **first to the** well. Merrill, apparently quite dead, was taken out first. Six **more after**, all dead, save a child crowded below its mother at the bottom. Merrill soon gave feeble evidence of life, and was cared for **at once.** Bush ran to the stone to aid the old woman. The blankets were rolled away. **The stone was bare, and no** vestige of Mrs. Williams could be found. Then they came upon **the pit.** An indistinguishable heap of arms, legs and bodies, perfectly still and wholly naked, was all that remained of the mass that came there in abundant **life a** few hours before. They were all dead, and few of **them** recognizable. Seven Williamsons perished in the group, among others the young girl whose long black hair was found clutched in masses in her uncharred hands.

The darkness of a new night threw **a** pitying **veil** over the scene **when the** first relief from the outside had **succeeded** in cutting a **way** through. **The** work of burial began next morning, **and fifty** were accounted for in the fatal clearing. The venerable mother was found on **the road to** Big Sturgeon the day **after the** terrible exposure, very feeble and worn out. **She was tenderly cared** for, and **is in** a fair way to recover what she **can** count but little—**her health.** One son out of three **was spared.** Her husband laid his grey hairs in the terrible holocaust; her whole kindred passed away in the ravages of that deadly night. For many a day the woods were not clear of the dead. Bodies in every stage of decay were constantly brought in by the committees, and the grand total can only be a matter of conjecture.

ST. CHARLES.

AN EVENTFUL EXPERIENCE.

Mr. James Langworth, of St. Charles, Saginaw county, **Michigan, thus details** his experience concerning the fire in that district:

Mr. Langworth states that he lived about four miles south of St. Charles, owning **a farm** of ninety acres. He had four stacks of hay near his barns, six acres of corn **in the** stock, a stack of wheat, thirty bushels of threshed wheat, and various farming implements, all of which were converted to ashes.

During the greater part of **the** week previous to the fire, the smoke in Langworth's locality was **so dense and** stifling **that he** was at times unable to discern any object twenty feet away. Two weeks before he sent his wife and children to friends in Canada for a short visit, and this fact probably saved their **lives.** The **husband was not** apprehensive of danger to his property until Sunday, when the **flames were within a** mile **of his place,** with **the** wind rather driving them away **from him.** Great clouds of smoke settled down on every thing, making it danger**ous for** even one familiar with the locality to wander far from home, every object taking on a strange look to mislead his steps. The farmer had a cow and several herds of young stock, and these was suffering so terribly from the smoke that he **turned** them loose on Sunday afternoon to care for themselves. They started off in the direction of the village, but probably perished in company with scores of other domestic animals. Langworth's well had been without water for a week, and his only resource was a small creek about forty rods from the house. By digging a hole in the bed of the stream about a barrel of water would collect during the day, and this he was using for drinking and cooking purposes.

Just before dark Sunday night, Langworth states that his yard was almost overrun with rabbits, **woodchucks,** coons and other **small** animals, while more than a hundred squirrels were to be seen about the house and barns. The animals moved about in a stupid way, blinded by the smoke, and would hardly move away when approached.

There was no sleep for the farmer that night. It was as much as he could do to breathe, the smoke creeping in and filling the room until his lamp could scarcely be seen across the room. Soon after midnight he ascertained that the wind had changed and freshened, and in an hour more he could hear the hoarse roar of the fire and the terrible crashing of the giant trees as they toppled over. Between his place and the fire was a swamp nearly half a mile across, and he had great hopes that this would act as a guard to prevent the further spreading of the flames. In one sense it did. The fire did not sweep across it, but ate its way around it, the wind seeming to fan the flames each way, and when the farmer's clock marked the hour of six Monday morning, the smoke was so dense and the roar and noise of the fire so loud that he decided to leave. Having little money to care for, and being poor in household goods, he decided to make the attempt to save some of the bedding. Taking some small articles, as photographs, a small picture or two, the family Bible, and his faithful clock, Langworth placed them on a feather tick, wrapped this up in a blanket, and was ready to go. Stepping out of doors to take an observation, he could not see ten feet in any direction, and the air was as hot as the atmosphere of an engine-room.

As he stood near the door, peering this way and that, a great flame suddenly shot up from his barn and haystacks. As he returned for his bundle, thousands of sparks and scores of burning twigs and branches swept in at the open door, and he leaped out and ran for his life. There was a wagon-road from Langworth's place to the village, and he sought this means of escape. Behind him were the roaring flames, sweeping everything before them, and traveling so fast that he had to strain every nerve to keep ahead. Where the fire met with an open space or a small swamp, its progress was checked for a moment, and the farmer could get clear of the flying sparks, But no obstacle could long stop the progress of the flames. What they could not burn they would leap over until they caught a mass of grass or a heap of leaves, and in a moment the fire was eating each way and progressing forward nearly as fast as a man could run. Almost stifled, his throat so parched that he could not swallow, and his lungs feeling as if a knife was at work there, Langworth stumbled forward, scarcely hoping to make his escape. What he expected soon occurred. The flames which had been sweeping down from another direction, suddenly jumped across the road in front of him, half a dozen trees flaming up at once. Behind was the main fire, to the right was a solid sheet of flames, and the only avenue of escape was to plunge into the woods, already taking fire on the left side.

It was now a race for life, with the chances against escape. Turning to the left the farmer hoped that by making a sharp run for it he might head off the fire, turn its path and again reach the road. He had almost accomplished this object, when he encountered a "swale" of considerable extent, and found that he must turn toward the main fire and endeavor to work around the "swale" before the flames could reach it. Sparks and cinders were falling all around him. The ground was covered with dry leaves, the wind sweeping through the trees in gusts, and several times Langworth had to leap over the running flames. In one of his leaps he tripped and fell, plunging headlong into soft mud and water. This was a most fortunate occurrence for him, as his clothing had already been scorched by the flame. He ran forward at his greatest speed, hearing the fire roaring on all sides, and when he reached the end of the marsh the flames blistered his cheeks as he passed around the swamp and struck the high ground.

In turning and twisting, and bewildered by the smoke, he had lost all knowledge of the country, and now he ran forward with but one idea of keeping in advance of the fire. As the forest was here more open, and the leaves had been well cleaned off by the wind, he was not so closely pressed. Almost every moment he ran across wild animals, all fleeing for a place of safety, and losing their fear of man in the general desire to escape the more relentless foe pressing behind. At length Langworth passed beyond the roar of the flames, and felt that he had escaped the fate which for a time seemed certain. He knew not which way he was traveling, and cared not so long as he could keep in advance of the fire. The smoke was so thick that he had to press forward like one blindfolded. Falling into holes, stumbling over logs, he pushed on, and was at length clear of the woods. He found the fire everywhere. Swamps were blazing, logs smouldering, trees and shrubs burning, and the short grass and dry turf was being eaten up as if it were dry peat. He had to pick his way between and around the lesser fires, making detours where the fences were blazing, and at last arrived at the outskirts of St. Charles, to find every man and woman at the limits, to fight for the salvation of their property and lives.

Every dollar possessed by Langworth, except in real estate, was swept away by the flames. The clothing he had on was so scorched that it could be picked to pieces with the fingers, and he had at least a score of blisters on his face and hands. But his loss was small compared with that of others. As he states, the flames have swept for miles, burning barn, fences, haystacks, houses and sheds, reducing many a farmer from wealth and plenty to almost absolute beggary. The flames stopped at nothing. They traveled with the wind, against it, and made a scene of desolation in their route. Hundreds of cattle and sheep have been smothered or roasted, and the fury of the flames has almost blotted some localities out of recognition.

THRILLING NARRATIVE.

A FIGHT FOR LIFE THROUGH A FLAMING FORREST—DEATH STRUGGLE WITH A MANIAC—A RAIN OF FIRE—THE RESCUE, ETC. STORY OF MRS. MECHAND.

On the morning of the 11th of October, just as we were sitting down to take breakfast, Mr. Richardson, a neighbor of ours, came running into the house and told Mr. Mechand that he must come out immediately and see what could be done. During the night the wind had risen, but not so greatly as to amount to anything like a gale, but rather did it resemble the ordinary fall wind. Mr. Mechand did not seem at all uneasy, and leisurely swallowed his breakfast before following Mr. Richardson who had disappeared as soon as he had stuck his head into the room and called my husband. Mr. Mechand went into the woods and stayed until about noon, when he came running back and said that he had climbed up to the top of Brown's Hill, where the wind was blowing a gale, and from there had seen the fire, which was coming towards us at a rapid pace. Indeed I had feared as much, and had been exceedingly uneasy all the morning, for the smoke which for days had been in the valley where we lived had become more and more dense, and occasionally hot puffs of wind had blown down over the hills, driving the smoke in a dense cloud before it. I asked my husband if he thought there was any danger to be feared; he shook his head and answered "No," yet I knew from his face that he was far from being devoid of fear. He ate his dinner hastily, and then ran out again, and was met at the door by a neighbor who said the fire was advancing with frightful speed. Indeed the air had now become sultry as it never had before except on some hot days in summer immediately before the coming of a thunder storm. The air was stifling, and the smoke got into one's lungs and nostrils in such a way as to render it exceedingly unpleasant. Mother sat in a corner holding little Louis in her lap, and I noticed that she seemed restless, and that her eyes shone with a light such as I have sometimes seen in the eyes of a wild beast, and had only seen in hers in the old days when she was about to have an outburst of fury. I was frightened and fidgety, and didn't do anything in the right way. I went and took the boy away from mother, who relinquished him readily; and then, as I had afterward terrible reason to remember, although I had hardly noticed it at the time, she went to the cupboard and secreted something in the bosom of her dress. Mr. Mechand stood at the door speaking hurriedly with the man whom he had met, when a burning branch of pine fell at his feet. Instantly the air darkened, a violent puff of wind rushed upon us, and smoke poured in volumes about the house. Then, following the gust, a bright sheet or rather wall of fire, seemed to be pushed down almost upon us, and instantly everything was in flames. Mr. Mechand cried out to me to bring Louis with me, and seized mother by the hand, and we all four ran out into the woods ahead of us. I ran on blinded and choked by the smoke, and carrying Louis in my arms. He was pale with terror, and did not utter a single cry, but clung to my neck as I hurried on, stumbling and tripping at nearly every step. So sudden had been the rush of the fire that we had no chance of saving anything but our lives, even if we had cared to do so. I kept calling to my husband to keep in sight, but, poor fellow, there was no need of doing so, for I could see that mother was a great worry to him, and that he had almost to drag her along. She kept looking from side to side, and trying to break away from him; even then I thought how terrible it would be if she should become furious again. What on earth could we do with her?

We must have gone on in this way for at least three miles, and I was almost exhausted, for Louis was a boy six years old and large for his age, and I had been carrying him all the way. The trees were compact, and in some places the undergrowth was close and stiff as wire. Mother kept getting worse, and Mr. Mechand, who was a short distance ahead of Louis and me, had the greatest difficulty to make her obey him. Presently he stopped, and evidently was waiting for me to come up. So I took Louis down and told him to keep alongside of me, at the same time taking him firmly by the hand. The fire had come much slower than me, and I believe we must have been at least two miles ahead of it, although there was no telling, for I could see nothing behind or far before me but smoke curling like a mist in and out of the trees. Behind us, indeed, it was heavier, and looked a sullen, dirty white.

We could not have been six feet from my husband when my mother broke away from him, and with a loud cry darted off into the woods, and then I knew that what I had dreaded had indeed come to pass, and that excitement and danger had brought back an old sickness upon her. She was a maniac. Mr. Merchand darted after her, and in the terror of the moment I forgot all else and followed him, leaving poor little Louis behind. I must have been crazy to do so, but on I rushed, and soon saw that mother was cunning enough to escape by doubling on her tracks, for I saw her dress dart past the bushes at my side as she ran diagonally away from me. I sprang after her, and after running for about five minutes, found to my horror that I had not only lost her, but Louis and his father. Madly I tried to retrace my steps, but there was nothing to guide me—no path, no blazes on the trees. The wind shook the trees, and almost bent them double; the sultry air filled with smoke, and all the horrors of **my terrible** condition made me frantic. I rushed about helpless, crying, and screaming, "**Louis! Louis! Father!**" But that last word made me calm for an instant and I felt that I was not alone—not utterly lost in the burning woods, for the spirit of my dead father was near and there were guardian angels. I knelt down, took my crucifix from my neck, and prayed. In kneeling down I found to my great joy that my dress was wet. I had knelt near a spring. I bathed my face and hands, and soaked my hair and the upper portion of my dress. But then my boy—my little Louis. I sprang to my feet, and called on the Virgin to direct me, dashed on in the direction of the fire. I had not gone more than a quarter of a mile when I found my darling, standing with head erect, and his flashing eyes filled with angry tears, trying to beat away some wolves, which, hungry though they were, seemed bent only on flight. I cried, "**Louis! Louis!**" and clasped him to my heart. It was my boy, and he was saved. He had not seen his father though once he heard a man's voice calling, but the voice seemed to have come from an immense distance. "Oh, Louis," said I, "we are lost unless we find him. We must run for our lives." The boy began to cry, and then I was ashamed of what I had said, and tried to cheer him up. The fire must have been very near us then, for I could not only feel its heated breath, but above my head, among the tree-tops, sparks and firebrands were whirling in the air. I took Louis in my arms, determined that never again should he be separated from **me**; **and** pressed onward with the idea that I would soon reach Wolf River.

Night **was** coming on, and since noon **we had had nothing** to **eat.** I did not feel hungry, but was tormented with thoughts of what might happen if we should not soon reach some place of safety, **for I feared** that Louis would give out, and that was **one** of the reasons which made me carry him. My arms ached, and my limbs were scratched, bruised and bleeding. Still I made good headway, and soon came to a natural clearing, on the thither side of which we sat down to rest. By this time night had come on, and what a night! No moon, no stars, but the cloudy heavens lighted up afar with the horrible fire of the burning woods. The clearing in which we sat was the dried up bed of a stream, which for some unaccountable reason had not thickly wooded shores, and we were at least two hundred feet from the forest in flame. All this time, Louis, manly little fellow, that he was, had not even asked for food, nor had he cried since I myself foolishly frightened him.

We sat there a long time while I was trying to think where we were, but I could come to no conclusion. I had heard **my** husband speak of a stream which had **run** dry, but that was in a northeasterly direction from our house, and, notwithstanding the fact that I was lost, yet **I had a** general notion that I was approaching the Wolf River. The stars could **give** me no information, for I could not see them. What to **do** I scarcely knew, **but** when the heat of the fire became such that **I could not** doubt that it was near, I determined to press on away from it, and taking **Louis'** hand I set out. On ordinary nights it would have been dark, but there was a nameless glare, a terrible—a horrible reflection which came down from the **sky,** mingled with the smoke. Hardly had I risen from the ground when, in **the** direction of the woods **on** the other side of the clearing, I heard a clashing noise, a mingled gnashing and hoarse barking, which I instantly recognized as that of wolves, and I scarely had time to snatch up Louis and run behind a magnificent pine tree, whose trunk was at least six feet in diameter, before I heard them scrambling up the side of the hill, and felt them rush by me.

They did not stop for an instant, and when they passed, there came in their tracks a herd of deer, uttering cries that seemed almost human in their intense agony. They ran blindly, for something more terrible than wolves was behind them; they struck the tree and were hurled back by the shock, some of them falling back upon those below. The stampede seemed to last for full ten minutes, and when it was over, and I, trembling with fear, dared once more to emerge from my refuge and look across the clearing, I saw the woods at its edge already burning—saw it lurid through the smoke, and felt its terrible heat upon my face. I turned and fled in the wake of the deer and wolves. My shoes were stripped from my feet, and my ankles were torn and bloody. Fallen trees lay in my way, but I clambered over and crawled under them in my desperate flight. I was agonized with terror and despair, and finally sank to the ground with my boy in my arms.

I must have fainted, for I knew nothing of what passed till I was rudely shaken by the shoulder and heard a wild gibbering laugh. I opened my eyes, and above me stood my mother with a drawn knife in her hand. The woods seemed all ablaze, although the air was not so intolerably hot as it had been. My mother looked down upon me with eyes blazing with that hated light of insanity.

"Ho, ho!" said she, "fine time of night for a mother and child to be running through the woods! Fine night this! Night—it is day! Look at the red light—'tis the light of dawn. And the rocks are burning! Call on them to fall upon you! The clouds of thunder and the day of doom! The Lord is coming, and the wheels of his chariot burn with his mighty driving! Let us go up to meet him in mid-air! Let us ride on the smoke and thunder and sweep the stars from the heavens! Come, you shall go with me!" and she seized Louis who had thrown himself upon me and was clinging in terror to my breast.

I sprang to my feet and cried, "Mother, mother! what would you do—would you kill me and Louis?"

"Kill you? Yes! Why wait? The Lord calls and the devil drives. He has let loose his imps against the world. The trees fall crashing in the forest; for all hell's demons pull them down with hooks of fire. I have seen them as I followed you. I have seen you all the way. I rode over on a wolf: 'twas a loup garou, an old friend of mine, brought me over safely, and kept me from the deer. I will kill you! Would you burn to death? You shall go up—up, higher than the moon, and beyond the fire. Come, let us go!" and again she seized Louis, while a knife gleamed in the air.

I sprang at her, and with all the strength of a mother in my arms, I struggled with her. Torn, worn, and bleeding, as I was, the thought of my child and husband gave me the strength of a giant. I overpowered the mad woman, and forgetting that she was my mother—that she was anything but the would-be murderess of my boy—I seized her by the throat when she was down rolling on the ground, and I could have strangled her. Her insanity had almost made me mad, and I felt then what a murderous maniac feels.

But then I thought that my mother was lying almost dead and powerless, and the fire would soon advance and overwhelm us all. My hand was stayed, and when my mother rose to her feet all her wildness was gone, and in its place that calmness—almost imbecility—which had characterized her for the last few years. She was ready and willing to do everything that I told her, but I kept the knife fast in my hand.

The wind was falling, and a slight rain was dropping among the leaves overhead, as we went on for an hour or two longer, and then, overpowered with exhaustion, and no longer greatly dreading the fire, we lay down in a hollow and fell asleep. When we awoke it was morning. I was sick and completely exhausted, and hardly knew that there were men around us. Yet there were, and good, kind men, too, who gave us food, and drove us to a place of shelter, whence, as soon as we were able, we went to Green Bay, where I soon recovered from my sickness and terror of that dreadful night. My mother continues in that same state of imbecility, which the doctor says will soon become complete dementia. Louis was not long in recovering, but as yet I have heard nothing from my husband.

AN OLD VETERAN WHO "STAYED TO SEE IT OUT."

A man named Allison Weaver, who reached Detroit from Port Huron, had a curious and narrow escape from being roasted alive in the North Woods.

Weaver is a single man, about fifty years old, and served all through the war in an Ohio Regiment of infantry. Up to two weeks before the fire he was at work for a man named Bright, ten miles from Forrestville, as a fireman of a shingle mill. Two or three days before the approach of the flames, which eventually destroyed that section, Bright and his family left for Forrestville, and the next day all the men employed about the place either followed his example or made haste to reach their homes. On leaving, Bright informed his men that the fire would sweep that way, and warned them to lose no time in making their escape. Having no property to lose or family to take care of, Weaver determined, as he says, "to stay and see the circus out," meaning that he intended saving the mill if possible. He has a stubborn sort of a spirit and the fact that everybody else went induced him to stay.

As soon as the men left he set to work and buried all the provisions left in the house, and during the day buried the knives, belts and other light machinery of the mill, as well as a stove and a quantity of crockery ware. There was plenty of water in the vicinity of the mill, and he filled several barrels full, besides wetting down the house, mill, stock, and everything which would burn, scattering several hundred pailfuls of water on the ground around the buildings. When night came and the fire had not appeared, he began to jeer his absent comrades. About ten o'clock the heavens were so light that he could distinguish the smallest objects around him, and there was a roaring in the forest which sounded like waves beating against rocks on the shore. He began to suspect that he was soon to receive the visit predicted, and accordingly made preparations for it. In leveling up the ground around the shingle mill, earth had been obtained here and there, and Weaver went to work and dug one of these pits deep enough for him to stand up in.

He then filled it nearly full of water, and took care to saturate the ground around it for a distance of several rods. Going to the mill he dragged out a four inch plank, sawed it in two, and saw that the parts tightly covered the mouth of the little well. "I kalkerlated it would tech and go," said he, "but it was the best I could do." At midnight he had everything arranged, and the roaring then was awful to hear. The clearing was ten or twelve acres, and Weaver says, that for two hours before the fire reached him there was a constant flight across the grounds of small animals. As he rested a moment from giving the house another wetting down, a horse dashed into the opening at full speed and made for the house where he stopped and turned toward the fire. Weaver could see him tremble and shake in his excitement and terror, and felt a pity for him. After a moment the animal gave utterance to a snort of dismay, ran two or three times around the house, and then shot off into the woods.

Not long after this the fire came. Weaver stood by his well, ready for the emergency, yet curious to see the breaking in of the flames. The roaring increased in volume, the air became oppressive, a cloud of dust and cinders came showering down, and he could see the flames through the trees. It did not run along the ground, nor leap from tree to tree, but it came on like a tornado, a sheet of flame reaching from the earth to the top of the trees. As it struck the clearing he jumped into his well and closed over the planks. He could no longer see, but he could hear. He says that the flames made no halt, whatever, nor ceased their roaring for an instant, but he had hardly got the opening closed before the house and mill were burning like tinder, and both were down in five minutes. The smoke came down to him powerfully, and his den was so hot that he could hardly breathe.

He knew that the planks above him were on fire, but remembering their thickness, he waited until the roaring of the flames had died away, and then with his head and hands turned them over, and put out the fire by dashing up water with his hands. Although it was a cold night, and the water had at first chilled him, the heat gradually warmed it up until he says that he felt quite comfortable. He remained in his den until daylight, frequently turning over the planks and putting out the fire, and then the worst had passed. The earth around was on fire in spots, house and mill were gone, leaves, brush and logs were swept clean away, as if shaved off and swept with a broom, and nothing but soot and ashes were to be seen.

After the fire had somewhat cooled off, Weaver made an investigation of his caches, and found that considerable of the property buried had been saved, although he lost all his provisions except a piece of dried beef, which the fire had cooked as in an oven without spoiling it. He had no other resource than to remain around the place that day, during the night, and the greater part of next day, when the ground had cooled enough so that he could pick his way to the site of the burned village. He was nearly twelve hours going the twelve miles, as trees were falling, logs were burning, and the fallen timber had in some places heaped up a breastwork which no one could climb.

An Affecting Incident.

HOW A MOTHER AND HER CHILDREN ESCAPED FROM FIRE—FIVE CHILDREN IN AN OARLESS BOAT THREE DAYS AND NIGHTS.

A thrilling incident, and miraculous escape from death was in the case of the family of five children of Mr. William Mann, of Rock Creek. When the mother saw that they must leave their home, after fighting the fire all day, she told the children (five in number) to go to the lake and she would follow as soon as she had gathered up a few articles to take with her. They reached the lake just in time to be taken into a fishing boat, which three neighbors were about to shove off. The mother in the meantime had gathered up what she could carry, and started for the lake, but found the road which her children had taken so full or smoke, and fire, and falling trees, that she took another course through the woods, coming out some distance above where the children were. She knew not whether her pets had passed through the fiery ordeal safely or not. She naturally feared the worst, but finally heard they had been taken off by the boat.

Here commences the romantic and thrilling part of the story. There was not an oar or sweep on board; a piece of board was all they had to control the boat with. For some time the boat rode gently on the water, all the time working a little out from the shore, although they did not realize, on account of the density of the smoke, how far they were getting from the shore. They presumed they could easily return at their pleasure. It soon became apparent, on account of the roughness of the lake, that they were rapidly drifting into the lake, and they made all the efforts they possibly could to guide their unwieldy craft toward the shore. Hour after hour they labored, but all in vain. They knew if they continued to drift, death was almost sure. All were in the greatest despair.

The oldest of the children, a girl of eleven summers, was the bravest of the lot. She held the baby almost constantly during that terrible trip. On they went, the waves frequently breaking over them—of course all were wet and cold. Night came on with Egyptian darkness. After weary, and long, long hours of suffering, daybreak was joyously hailed. They were then beyond the smoke of the burning forests. They were sure they would hail some vessel. All day long they looked, until darkness again set in, without seeing a sail. At about two o'clock in the morning of the third day out, one of Mr. Mann's children, a boy of three summers, died from hunger and exposure; when it died it was lying in the bottom of the boat, with water half over its little body. The little eleven years old girl said she wanted the men in the boat to put it on the bedding, but they would not, and she was too weak and was holding the baby, and could not do it. The children did not cry much on the last day, as all were nearly exhausted. Finally, after three days and nights, they were drifted on shore at Kincardine, Ontario, where their wants were speedily attended to, and from there sent to Port Huron.

During these three days the reader can imagine the mother's feelings. Everybody that knew of the circumstances supposed, of course, they had gone to the bottom of the lake. The mother arriving at Port Huron, at once went to the relief rooms. After making herself known, and bewailing the fate of her children in piteous sobs and moans (she had supposed them all dead till this moment), Mrs. Fred. Wells, the secretary of the Relief Association, told her her children were there, well and apparently happy. I cannot picture the scene. "Oh! is it so? is it so?" "God bless their little hearts!" "Where are they?" "Take me to them at once!" Mrs. Wells informed her they were near by, and she would take her there at once. Another and more painful part of the story was yet to be told Mrs. Mann. How to do this was a query, all the ladies in the room dreading to break the dreadful tidings to her. At last Mrs. Mann began to ask her how Emma was, and then the next one. Finally she asked how little Charlie was. No one answered for a moment. She looked up and saw at once all was not right. "Is he dead? is he dead?" and commenced weeping as only a fond and loving mother can, for the loss of her boy.

THIRTY-TWO PEOPLE PERISH IN A WELL.

An eye-witness of the recent devastating fires near Uniontown, Wisconsin, relates an incident occurring during the conflagration, which is absolutely unparalleled in the history of all similar horrors. He writes:

"The most horrible of all was at Boorman's well. Mr. Boorman's house was the largest in the village, and in the center of the yard, midway between the house and barn, was a large but shallow well. Several of the neighbors were supplied with water from this fountain, and it is likely that in the conflagration, when all hope was cut off, the neighborhood, insane with terror, thronged with one purpose to this well. The ordinary chain and wheel pump used in that place had been removed, and the wretched people had leaped into the well as the last refuge. Boards had been thrown down to prevent them being drowned; but, evidently, the relentless fury of the fire drove them pell-mell into the pit, to struggle with each other and die, some by drowning and others by fire and suffocation. None escaped. Thirty-two bodies were found there; they were in every imaginable position, but the contortions of their limbs, and the agonizing expression of their faces, told the awful tale.

REMARKABLE PHENOMENA.

A citizen of Green Bay who passed through the fire at Peshtigo, and saved himself and a woman and children he met, by getting on a low spot of ground or in a ditch, and covering them over with wet blankets, tells the story; They had got well-covered up in this burrow, when a half-frantic woman rushed along with a great bundle in her arms. She had been well dressed, but her clothes were half off. She stopped and deposited her bundle, which consisted of a child and a lot of clothing, and then shrieked, "Great God, where is my baby?" At this the narrator sprang up, and saw, a few rods off, a baby in its night-clothes lying on the road and kicking up his heels in great glee, while a billow of flame rolled over it, striking the ground beyond, and leaving the baby in the center of a great arch of fire. The baby had slid out of the bundle, unperceived by the mother in her haste. He immediately sprang for the child, and with difficulty rescued it. It is no wonder that the mother fainted when she secured the child.

Walter Heath was one of the proprietors of the Peshtigo House. When the fire occurred, his family, with the girls employed in the house, escaped from the hotel by a team, and were saved on the low land below Ellis' House. Heath got into the river on the west side of the bridge and clung to the center pier of the bridge. The wind blew the fire from the hotel to where he was. The hotel was near the south end of the bridge and on the west side of the street. At the north end of the bridge and east of the street was the Peshtigo Company's water mill, and the flames from that also blew directly to his position. Thus it seems that the wind on two sides of the river blew in exactly opposite directions. Heath was saved from the fact that, being on the west side of the pier, the flames from the water mill divided at the pier and passed him on both sides. The bridge being on fire he dare not swim through with the current, but when the fire on the bridge had got uncomfortably close he took off his coat, pulled off his boots, and swam up stream to a place of safety. He had a very narrow escape from death, and has not yet recovered from breathing the hot air and smoke.

He tells us that the most vivid imagination can not picture the scene of the calamity as bad as it actually was. In his opinion as many as 1,000 people lost their lives on the Peshtigo; that 752 bodies have been buried, and that many were entirely burned up. The names of half the dead will never be known. They are buried all over Peshtigo, and the boards that mark their graves are marked "2 unknown," "3 unknown," etc.

Much has been said of the intense heat of the fires which destroyed Peshtigo, Menekaunee, Williamsonville, etc., but all that has been said can not give the stranger even a faint conception of the realities. The heat has been compared with that engendered by a flame concentrated on an object by a blow-pipe, but even that would not account for some of the phenomena. For instance, we have in our possession a copper cent, taken from the pocket of a dead man in the Peshtigo Sugar Bush, which will illustrate our point. This cent has been partially fused, but still retains its round form, and the inscription upon it is legible. Others in the same pocket were partially melted off, and yet *the clothing and the body of the man were not even singed*. We do not know how to account for this, unless, as is asserted by some, the tornado and fire were accompanied by electrical phenomena.

The house, barn, and fences, of Mr. Hill, of the upper Sugar Bush, were burned, and Mr. Hill and his family all lost. By the side of the family was a narrow alley, just wide enough to drive through. In this alley stood a wagon, and while the barn and fence were entirely destroyed, the wagon box was not even singed.

Alfred Phillip's house, in the upper Sugar Bush, was destroyed, but the family escaped. They state that two opposite currents of air apparently struck the house, which was 16 by 24 feet, and carried it bodily into the air, about 100 feet. It then burst into flames, and in a few minutes was entirely destroyed. The house was not on fire when it left the ground.

We do not believe that any other explanation of the great calamity can be made than that it was caused by fire, wind and electricity.

More than a hundred villages and hamlets were destroyed, besides about six hundred farms with all their stock and utensils, numerous saw mills, flouring mills, and lumber men's camps. The loss of life is said to have been not less than 1,400, and the loss of property in Michigan, Wisconsin, and Minnesota, is estimated at $11,000,000. It will require a quarter of a century to recover from the terrible disaster.

We might fill a book much larger than this with interesting incidents of these fires, many of them unutterably tragic, but all partaking of the general character of those contained in the preceeding pages; and it is therefore proper to state that we have selected those possessing the most interest for readers at large, giving the best and most comprehensive idea of the great events they describe.

The relief of the sufferers throughout the northwest was prompt and adequate. Contributions of money and clothing were made by the people everywhere in the same spirit that prompted them to respond to the appeal of Chicago, and the hungry and naked were fed and clothed with a celerity almost magical. God bless all the noble hearts that so generously responded to the cry for succor.

REFUGEES FROM WHITE ROCK, HURON CO., MICH. SEEKING SAFETY IN THE WATER.

The Great Fires of the Past.

ROME.

In Ancient History we find an account of a terrible fire in Rome, A. D. 64, said to have been kindled at the instigation of the famous Nero, whose ambition was to destroy the city, that he might rebuild it and call it by his own name.

In the words of the historian.

"Of all calamities which ever befell this city from the rage of fire, this was the most terrible and severe.

It broke out in that part of the circus, which is contiguous to Mount Palatine and Calius, and being accelerated by the wind, it acquired strength and spread at once through the whole extent of the circus. It invaded first the lower portion of the city, then mounted to the highest, then again ravaging the lower it baffled every effort to extinguish it, and raged for five days with unabated violence.

At length on the sixth day the conflagration was stayed at the foot of Esquil, by pulling down an immense number of buildings so that an open space might check the raging element by breaking the continuity.

Two days later the fire broke out afresh with no little violence, and still greater havoc was made among the temples and porticos dedicated to amusement.

*　　　　*　　　　*　　　　*　　　　*　　　　*

Of the fourteen sections into which Rome was divided, four only were standing entire; three were levelled with the ground and in the seven others there remained only here and there a few remnants of houses, shattered and half consumed.

MOSCOW.

On the 16th of September, 1812, at midnight, Napoleon, in utter exhaustion of body and mind, retired to rest. Suddenly the cry of "fire" resounded through the streets. Far off in the East immense volumes of billowy smoke, pierced with flames, were rolling up into the stormy sky. Loud explosions of bursting shells and upheaving mines scattered death and dismay around. Suddenly the thunders as of an earthquake were heard in other directions. A score of buildings were thrown into the air. Flaming projectiles of the most combustible and unquenchable material were scattered in all directions, and a new volcano of smoke and flame commenced its ravages. Earthquake succeeded earthquake, and volcano succeeded volcano. The demon of the storm seemed to exult in his high carnival of destruction. The flames were swept in all directions. The shower of fire descended upon all the dwellings and all the streets. Mines were sprung, shells burst, cannons were discharged, wagons of powder and magazines blew up, and in a few hours of indescribable confusion and dismay, the whole vast city was wrapped in one wild ocean of flame. The French soldiers shot the incendiaries, bayoneted them, tossed them into the flames, but still, like demons, they plied their work. Napoleon awoke early in the morning and looked out upon the flames, which were sweeping through all parts of the city. For the first time in his life he appeared excessively agitated. His far-reaching mind apprehended at a glance the measurelessness of the calamity which was impending. He hurriedly paced his apartment; dictated hasty orders, and from his window anxiously watched the progress of the fire. The Kremlin was surrounded with gardens and shrubbery, and seemed for a time to afford shelter from the flames; but mines of powder were in its vaults, with various combustibles arranged to communicate the fire. As Napoleon gazed upon the conflagration he exclaimed, "What a frightful spectacle! Such a number of palaces! The people are genuine Scythians." "Not even the fiction of the burning of Troy," said Napoleon afterward, "though hightened by all the powers of poetry, could have equalled the reality of the destruction of Moscow."

During the whole of the 17th, and of the ensuing night, the gale increased in severity, and the fire raged with unabated violence. The city now seemed but the almost boundless crater of an indistinguishable volcano. Various colored flames shot up to an immense height into the air; incessant explosions of gunpowder, saltpetre out of iron and stone, and burning rafters were hurled far off into the surrounding plain, crushing many in their fall. Multitudes encircled by the flames in the narrow streets were miserably burned to death. The scene of confusion and dismay has probably never been equalled. The soldiers, stifled with smoke, singed with flames and lost in the streets of the burning city, fled hither and thither, before a foe whom they were unable even to attack. They were often seen staggering beneath immense packages of treasure, which they were frequently compelled to abandon to effect their escape. Miserable women were seen carrying one or two children on their shoulders and dragging others by the hand, attempting, often in vain, to flee from these accumulating horrors. Old men, with beards singed by the fire, crept slowly and feebly along, and in many cases were overtaken and destroyed by the coils of flames that pursued them. Napoleon was indefatigable in his exertions for the rescue of his soldiers and the remaining inhabitants.

At length it was announced that the Kremlin was on fire. The flames so encircled it that escape seemed almost impossible. The fire was already consuming the gates of the Citadel. It was not until after a long search that a postern could be found through which the imperial escort could pass. Blinded by cinders and smothered with heat and smoke, they pressed along on foot, till they came to a roaring sea of fire, which presented apparently an impassable barrier. At last a narrow, crooked, diverging street was found blazing in various parts, and often overreached with flame. It was an outlet which despair alone could enter. Yet into this formidable pass Napoleon and his companions were necessarily impelled. With burning fragments falling around, and blazing cinders showered upon them, they toiled along, almost blinded and suffocated with heat and smoke.

At length the guide lost his way, and stopped in utter bewilderment. All now gave themselves up for lost. It was remarked that, in this terrible hour, Napoleon was perfectly calm and self-possessed. Just then they caught a glimpse of Marshal Davoust, who, with a company of soldiers, was in search of the Emperor. The marshal had signified his determination to rescue the hope of France or perish in the attempt. Napoleon affectionately embraced the devoted Prince. They soon encountered, in the blazing streets, a convoy of gunpowder, along which they were compelled to pass, while flaming cinders were falling around. The energies of Napoleon's mind were so disciplined for the occasion that not the slightest indication of alarm escaped him. They soon emerged from the walls of the city, and Napoleon retired to the castle of Petrowshoi, about three miles from the burning metropolis. The Emperor, as he looked back upon the city, gloomily remarked: "This forbodes no common calamity." "It was," said he, years afterward, "the spectacle of a sea and billows of fire, a sky and clouds of flame, mountains of red, rolling flames like immense waves of the sea, alternately bursting forth and elevating themselves to skies of fire, and then sinking into the ocean of flame below. Ah, it was the most grand, the most sublime, the most terrific sight the world ever beheld."

The fire began to decrease on the 9th **for want** of fuel. "Palaces, and temples." says Karmanzin, "monuments of art and miracles of luxury, remains of ages long since past and the creations of yesterday, the tombs of remotest ancestry and the cradles of children of the rising generation, were indiscriminately destroyed. Nothing was left of Moscow save the remembrance of its former grandeur. The French army was now encamped in the open fields around the smouldering city. Their bivouacs presented the strangest spectacle which had ever been witnessed.

Immense fires were blazing, fed by the fragments of the most costly furniture of satin wood and mahogany. The soldiers were sheltered from the piercing winds by the tents **reared from the** drapery **of the regal** palaces. Superb armchairs and sofas, in the richest upholstery of imperial purple and **crimson velvet** afforded seats and lounges for all. Cashmere shawls, Siberian fans, pearls and gems of Persia and India, were strewed over the ground in wild confusion. In the midst of all these wrecks of boundless opulence the soldiers were famishing.

LONDON.

Among the great conflagrations of the past, that of London, in September 1666, will always stand pre-eminent for its terrible destructiveness. It followed upon the great plague, which had carried off one-third of the population in the previous year, and swept over nearly five-sixths of the space included within the city walls at that date. It lasted four days, and the ruins covered four hundred and thirty-six acres. It destroyed eighty-nine churches (including St. Paul's), the Royal Exchange, the Custom-House, Guildhall, Zion College, and many other public buildings, besides 13,200 private houses. Four hundred streets were entirely laid waste, and about 200,000 of the inhabitants of the city were obliged to encamp **for some time** in the open fields of Islington and Highgate. The most disastrous **fire since that** date occurred on the 25th of March, 1748, when 200 houses in the Cornhill Ward were destroyed. Many destructive fires have occurred in the British metropolis at later dates, the most recent worthy of special note being the burning **of the** cotton and **other** wharves of Tooley street in June and July, **1861.** The fire continued raging with greater or less fury for nearly a month. Several persons were killed, and property was destroyed to the value of £2,000,000.

HAMBURG.

On the 5th of May, 1842, a fire broke out in the City of Hamburg, Germany, **which** raged with great fury for four days, destroying about one-third of the city. Sixty-one streets containing 1,747 houses, were utterly laid waste, and thousands of people were rendered homeless. There were few public buildings of value destroyed, and that portion of the city was quickly rebuilt in a much more substantial manner than before.

NEW YORK.

In this country great fires, especially before the day of improved fire-engines, have been comparatively frequent, and New York has had her full share. In September, 1776, soon after the city came into the hands of the British, 500 houses were destroyed, forming at that time a large part of the town. The buildings were rather huddled together at the lower end of the island, and were mostly of wood, and **the** district west of Broadway and below Cortland street, was swept bare.

New York was visited by another great conflagration, the greatest in its history, on the 18th of December, 1835. Six hundred warehouses, and property to the extent of $20,000,000, were consumed. Our oldest inhabitants still remember the horrors of that terrible disaster. On the 6th of September, 1839, the city had another severe visitation, when forty-six buildings, and property valued at $10,000,000 were destroyed. The next conflagration of large extent in this city took place on the 19th of July, 1845, when 302 stores and dwellings in the lower part of the city were destroyed. These, however, were of comparatively inferior value, the whole loss amounting to $6,000,000. Four lives were lost on this occasion. Since that time, owing to the increased efficiency of the means employed to prevent and extinguish fires, they have generally been confined to a single building or a small group.

QUEBEC.

In the same year of the last great fire in New York, Quebec suffered terribly from the same destroying element. On the 28th of May a fire broke out in the Faubourgh St. Roch which destroyed 1,500 buildings before it could be quelled. Several lives were also lost. Exactly one month later 1,300 buildings were burned, and by these two conflagrations nearly two-thirds of the city was laid in ruins. The pecuniary loss has been stated at $8,000,000.

ST. JOHN'S.

In the same year, on the 12th of June, nearly the whole town of St. John's, Newfoundland, was destroyed, and 6,000 people were rendered homeless.

ALBANY.

Albany suffered from a great conflagration on the 9th of September, 1841. Six hundred buildings, besides steamboats, piers, and other property, valued altogether at $3,000,000 were burned. Twenty-four acres of land within the city limits were covered with ruins.

ST. LOUIS.

St. Louis had a great fire in May, 1849, when fifteen blocks of houses and twenty-three steamboats were consumed, causing a loss of over $3,000,000.

PHILADELPHIA.

Philadelphia has been fortunate in having few great fires, but one occurred in that city on the 9th of July, 1850, which destroyed 350 buildings. These were of inferior value, and the whole loss was but $1,500,000, though twenty-five persons were burned to death, nine drowned, and one hundred and twenty injured.

SAN FRANCISCO.

A large portion of San Francisco was destroyed in 1851. On the 3d of May a fire broke out which consumed nearly 2,500 buildings, causing a loss of $3,500,000 and several lives. A little over a month later, on the 22d of June, 500 more buildings were burned, valued at $3,000,000 or more.

SYRACUSE.

Twelve acres of land in Syracuse were burned over on the 8th of November, 1866. About 100 buildings were destroyed, and the loss of property amounted to $1,000,000.

PORTLAND.

The scene most naturally recalled by this fearful disaster in Chicago, is the terrible celebration of the Fourth of July in Portland, Me., in 1866. The leading facts in that great event are still fresh in the public mind. The fire, beginning in a boot shop on High street, swept North, and destroyed in its course nearly one-half of the city. The pecuniary loss was about $15,000,000, and one-fourth of the population were rendered houseless.

SKETCH OF THE BURNED CITY OF GENEVA.

The smoke from the smouldering embers of Chicago has hardly been dissipated when there comes from beyond the water intelligence that another "City of the Lake" has all but suffered the fate of its American sister, to which it bears so close a resemblance. Geneva, if not as complete a waste as Chicago, has so narrowly escaped it as to afford almost a parallel to our unparalleled calamity. The full extent of the calamity has not yet been ascertained, and can not be estimated for some days.

Fortunately Geneva offered natural barriers to the progress of the flames which very greatly lessened the extent of the disaster. It is situated upon the slopes of two hills which are divided by the Rhone, which in its course from the lake forms two islands, on one of which a portion of the town is built. On the other of these islands there is a handsome promenade. The islands and the two principal parts of the city are connected by a fine suspension bridge. The streets are wide and spacious. The public buildings include the Catholic Cathedral (Mgr. Mermillods), the Hotel de Ville, the University, (founded by Calvin and Beza), the Hotel de la Couronne (which was burnt), the Hotel de l'Ecu, the museums of art and natural history, the public library, containing 30,000 volumes, and many valuable manuscripts. The largest section of the city is on the left bank of the river. The Quartier de St. Gervais, on the right bank, is the seat of the manufactures and the residences of the humbler classes. The Quartier des Bergnes is the fashionable section. The manufactures of the town are world-famous. The population of the Canton, of which it is the capital, is about 64,000, including 34,000 Protestants, 29,000 Catholics, and a few hundred Jews.

If it were admissible to trace a historical or social contrast between a city which has a history older than the Christian era, as well as social surroundings long established and widely connected, and a mushroom city of yesterday, with its society in a metamorphic if not a wholly chaotic condition, it would not be difficult to discover many points of resemblance between the centre of Swiss commercial and mental activity and the great commercial centre of the West, besides the facts that both are cities of the lakes and that both have suffered from that enemy which both, of all other cities existing, should have been best prepared to fight.

Few towns of Europe have a more interesting or varied history than this city, which, having passed through so many trials, now undergoes the ordeal of fire. A hundred names rise to the lips when Geneva is mentioned; names famous in letters, in arms, in criticism, diplomacy, politics, and theology, saints and sinners, heresiarchs and martyrs, pedestrians and latitudinarians, orthodox believers and incorrigible skeptics, reformers and believers in Rome, infallibilists, and haters of the Scarlet Lady, friends of Imperialism and admirers of the universal republic, members of the Peace Society and come-outers of all kinds, by no means forgetting the arbitrators of the little trouble between these States and Great Britain. Geneva is not a town of last week, or of the month of October. In the second century before Christ it was of sufficient importance to attract the attention of Rome—the legions of which made it their own—and even since, Rome, pagan and papal, has had its eyes on this important center—political, commercial, social and religious. Of the stormy history of this capital during all the period from the days of Charlemagne down to the Reformation, and thence to-day, almost every one knows something. In war it has become the object of attack of the German, the Italian, and the Gaul, and with varying fortune it has generally returned to its old love—a republican form of government and political association with Switzerland. In religion it has been a central point of the fight between Calvinism and Catholicism, and at the present day this fight is carried on with as great bitterness as in the days of the Prince Bishops and Calvin and William Farel. Marie d'Aubigne on one side, and Mgr. Mermillod on the other, are fair types of the contest in which they are so eminent leaders. It is a curious incident of this quarrel that the most accurate and the earliest news of Rome and of Catholicism is now to be obtained through the agencies of this capital of Calvinism and free thought.

Of the great names whom business or leisure have associated with this city and the delightful region that surrounds it, mention may be made of Francis of Sales, Calvin, Jean Jacques Rousseau, Beza, Madame de Stael, Voltaire, Gibbon, Marie d'Aubigne, Mermanod, Byron, Shelly, John Knox—who was enrolled a citizen of Geneva—Necker, our own statesman, Gallatin, Beranger, Cassaubon, Marie Louise, Josephine, Sir Humphrey Davy, Sismondi, and Dumont, and the eminent scientific scholars, De Luc, De Sauserre, Bonnet, Huber and De Candolle.

CHICAGO.

The terrible fire in Chicago has no parallel in modern history, unless in the conflagrations kindled by war. Even the great fire of London, though relatively more destructive, did not equal it in absolute extent. The London of that day was little more than two-thirds the size of the Chicago of to-day, having less than 250,000 inhabitants; and if two-thirds of Chicago is in ruins, the desolate territory is far greater than the five-sixths of London said to have been laid waste in 1666.

IMPROVISED SHANTIES AFTER THE FIRE.

J. N. JANES AND WIFE TRYING TO SAVE A FAVORITE DOG AND THEIR CANARY BIRDS.

RESCUE OF LADIES FROM THE FLAMES.

Index.

	PAGE.
DEDICATION.	4
LIST OF ILLUSTRATIONS.	11
INTRODUCTION.	17
PIONEER HISTORY.	29
Chicago as it was in Earlier Days.	29
Facts and Incidents.	29
GENERAL HISTORY.	41
Improvements.	41
Town and City Organizations.	41
Price of Real Estate.	41
Instances of Sudden Fortunes.	41
Cession to the United States by the Pottawatamie Tribe of Indians.	42
Commencement of Progress.	44
Granting of the City Charter.	45
Rapid advance in Valuation of Property	45
PRESENT HISTORY.	55
Chicago's Pre-eminence.	55
A GENERAL ACCOUNT.	
Of what the Author saw and heard, including his personal view of the Fire and many Thrilling Incidents,	61
THE GREAT CONFLAGRATION HISTORICALLY TREATED.	83
THE GREAT FIRE OF OCTOBER EIGHTH.	89
The Elevators.	107
Public Buildings.	107
Breweries Destroyed.	108
Field, Leiter & Co.	108
Banks, &c.	109

INDEX.

	PAGE
Lawyers.	109
Distilleries.	109
Coal Yards.	109
Newspaper Offices.	109
City Property.	110
Additional Losses.	111
THE BURNING CITY, (Poem.)	117
INCIDENTS, ACCIDENTS, TRAGEDIES, and WONDERFUL ESCAPES.	119
Record of Facts.	119
Sufferings of Women.	119
Heart Rending Mistake.	122
Unexampled Bereavement.	122
George Howard.	123
A Happy Occasion.	124
A Surprise.	125
Fuel to the Flames.	126
Horrors.	126
Bereavement.	127
Miraculous Escape.	128
The Last Scene.	128
The Morgue.	131
A Retrospect.	133
Taken by Surprise.	136
Adventure of a young Englishman and his Roommate.	141
A Timely Rescue.	141
Romantic Incident.	149
Running the Gauntlet of Flame.	153
Incidents of Personal Experience.	153
FIRE MARSHAL'S STORY.	171
Graphic account of the Great Fire.	171
Startling Incidents forcibly detailed.	171
Blowing up.	173

INDEX. 313

	PAGE.
HOW VALUABLE RECORDS WERE SAVED.	179
What a Woman Relates.	181
A Touching Home Picture.	182
ORIGIN OF THE FIRE.	183
Another Theory.	184
Still Another Theory.	185
Confession of a Member of a Secret Organization.	186
Burning of the Business Portion of the City.	190
CALL FOR HELP, (Poem.)	199
STARTING OF THE FIRST TRAIN OF SUPPLIES, (Poem.)	204
RELIEF,	207
The Great Heart of the People Aroused.	207
Firemen from Abroad.	208
Unexampled Liberality of City Governments and Corporations.	209
Illinois Legislature.	211
Railroads.	212
Magnificent Liberality.	212
Munificence of New Yorkers.	217
Donations of the Press.	218
Generosity of Cincinnati.	223
St. Louis to the Rescue.	224
Sisters of Mercy.	225
Louisville.	225
Houses of Worship.	226
Bible Society.	231
Washington, D. C.	231
Typographical Union.	232
Juvenile Generosity	232
Relief Societies.	237
Honor to the Ladies.	238
Mr. E. Hudson's Generosity.	238

	PAGE
EFFECT OF THE NEWS IN ENGLAND	239
Active Measures Taken for Relief of Sufferers.	239
LIBERAL CONTRIBUTIONS FROM THE CAPITAL OF THE GERMAN EMPIRE.	241
Interesting Correspondence between U. S. Consul Kreismann and Mayor Mason.	241
Empress Augusta.	242
Chinamen's Contributions.	242
Chicago Aid Society.	242
Charity of the Right Sort.	246
Woman's Industrial Aid Society.	246
Miss Barton.	249
Robert Collyer.	250
Touching Words of Thanks.	253
Gen. P. H. Sheridan.	253
Insurance Companies.	254
FIRES OF THE GREAT NORTH-WEST.	260
Full Description.	260
Thrilling Incidents.	260
THE PESHTIGO FIRE.	260
A Vivid Picture.	260
In the Flames.	262
Schwartz the Hermit.	262
Down in a Well.	267
Burned in a Wagon.	267
Suddenly Extinguished Prospect of Safety.	267
Fire Balloons.	268
Path Through the Fire.	268
The only Trace.	268
Only House Left.	268
How Articles were Saved.	269
Honeymoon Tragedy.	269
Suicide.	269

INDEX. 315

	PAGE
Fatal Mistake.	270
Minor Incidents.	270
THE MANISTEE FIRE.	277
A Thousand People Homeless.	278
After Scenes.	278
The Future.	279
AHNAPPE.	280
The Terrible Story of the Last Wisconsin Hamlet that Fought the Hurricane of Fire.	280
ST. CHARLES.	284
An Eventful Experience.	284
THRILLING NARRATIVE.	286
A Fight for Life through a Flaming Forest.	286
Struggle with a Maniac.	286
Rain of Fire.	286
The Rescue.	286
Story of Mrs. Mechand.	286
An Old Veteran who Stayed to See it Out.	290
An Affecting Incident.	291
How a Mother and her Children escaped.	291
Five Children in an Oarless Boat for three days and nights.	291
Thirty-two People Perish in a Well.	292
Remarkable Phenomena.	293
GREAT FIRES OF THE PAST.	299
Rome.	299
Moscow.	299
London.	301
Hamburg.	301
New York.	301
Quebec.	302
St. John.	302
Albany.	302

	PAGE.
St. Louis.	302
Philadelphia.	302
San Francisco.	302
Syracuse.	302
Portland.	302
Geneva.	303
Chicago.	304

PANIC STRICKEN CITIZENS CARRYING THE AGED, SICK AND HELPLESS

WELLS & COMPANY,

SUBSCRIPTION BOOK PUBLISHERS,

No. 432 BROOME ST., NEW YORK.

LIST OF POPULAR WORKS
Specially Suited to Sales Through Agents.

PLAIN HOME TALK,
AND
MEDICAL COMMON SENSE,
By E. B. FOOTE, M. D.

12MO.   912 PAGES.   200 ILLUSTRATIONS.   FOUR PARTS IN ONE VOLUME.

"Every chapter, paragraph and sentence is crammed full of matter-of-fact information of the most vital importance to every member of the human family. It is a curious and remarkable work not simply a guide to health, comfort and happiness, but furnishing just that kind of information with regard to the human system, our sexual relations and social natures, most essential for all to understand, and yet possessed by so few. * * * * *
There never has been a work of a similar nature published. It is too valuable to be for a moment compared to dollars and cents."—*New York Democrat.*

Price, in Cabinet Library Binding..$3 75
  " Extra Cloth.. 3 25
German Edition.. 3 50

WELLS'
EVERY MAN HIS OWN LAWYER,
AND
Business Form Book,
A Complete Guide in all Matters of Law and Business Negotiations
FOR EVERY STATE IN THE UNION.

With full Instructions for Proceeding without legal assistance in Suits and Business Transactions of every description.

"Wells' 'Every Man His Own Lawyer and Business Form Book,' New York, John G. Wells & Co. As a legal adviser always at hand to instruct the reader how to proceed in suits and business transactions of all kinds; as a form book to enable the least learned to draw up deeds, mortgages, leases, orders, wills, &c.; a guide in regard to the laws of the various States, concerning exemptions, liens, limitations of actions, and so on, the volume in question is certainly invaluable to men of business; and it is not surprising that a hundred thousand copies soon found their way into the homes and counting-houses of the multitude. Here we have not only all the various changes in the laws of the different States; but a full digest of the action of the General Bankrupt Law, the Patent Laws, the Pension Laws, the Homestead Laws, the Internal Revenue Laws, etc., with full instructions to all who may be interested in them. The publisher has been determined to make this work complete, and, to our thinking, he has succeeded. No businessman or woman can with safety be without a copy of it."—*New York Times.*

The Work embraces 650 large 12 mo. pages, and is printed on fine paper, handsomely bound.

PRICE:

Leather Binding........................$2 50 | Half Library........................$2 00
Cabinet Library Binding................ 2 25 | German Edition...................... 2 50

The Book for the People at the Present Time, and for all Time.

WELLS'
Illustrated National Hand-Book.

A TEXT BOOK FOR ALL,
AND SHOULD BE IN THE POSSESSION OF EVERY MAN AND YOUTH IN THE LAND.

THE WORK IS A COMPLETE COMPENDIUM
OF THE
Political History of the Country from the Original Formation of the Government to the Present Time.

TOGETHER WITH

Fugitive Slave Law.—Kansas and Nebraska Act.—Population of the United States at Decennial Periods.—Electoral Vote for President and Vice-President, from Washington to Grant, with the Important Incidents of each Administration.—Great Seal of the United States, and Seals of all the States, with History and Description.—Mottoes of the United States and of Individual States.—Population of the Principal Cities and Towns.—Supreme Court of the United States.—Population, Debt, and Military Force of the United States. Debt, and Military Force of the Principal Nations of Europe.—Immigration—Table showing the Total number of Passengers that have arrived at Castle Garden under Emigration Regulation.

A Complete Chronological Record of Events, and other invaluable Information of Universal Interest connected with the Political History of the Country. One of the Best Selling Books of the Season, as it just *the* work for the Times—suited to all parties, and the only complete and comprehensive Book of the kind ever published.

As a Text Book for Reference alone, this Work is worth many times its cost.

Price, in Morocco Cloth, $1.50. In Cabinet Library Binding, $2.00.

YOUTHS' PICTORIAL HISTORY
OF
INDIAN WARS & CAPTIVITIES,

BY JOHN FROST, L. L. D.
AND
PROF. SAMUEL C. DRAKE.

The most popular writers on this subject of this or any other age, and so well known that comment is unnecessary.

A truthful, instructive, and intensely interesting History of all the important Indian Wars and Captivites of the American Continent.

A work full of thrilling interest; portraying, in detail, all of value in History connected with a War full of startling incidents—bloody encounters—atrocities—individual daring—hair-breadth escapes—and astounding revelations of captivities &c.

The Work, consisting of about 700 pages Royal Octavo, will be embellished with 200 Illustrations, representing every feature of special interest connected with the subject.
Price, handsomely bound in Morocco Cloth, $3.50.
Price, elegantly bound in Library Binding, $4.50.

Agents Wanted Everywhere.

To sell the most popular works ever before introduced to the American Public. Works that an Agent can engage in the sale of with a certainty of success and a knowledge of the fact that by every book he has sold he has contributed a certain benefit to mankind—that he has added to human happiness, and contributed to elevate the standard of social, physical and mental enjoyment.

We want good live agents—men who can fully appreciate the merits of our works, and the fact that they meet a universal want—agents who desire to do good as well as make money,

WELLS & COMPANY,
432 Broome Street, N. Y.